MW00781570

Celebrating the Wounde Psychotherapist

Why would someone decide to become a psychotherapist? It is well known within the field that psychoanalysts and psychotherapists are often drawn to their future professions as a result of early traumatic experiences and being helped by their own psychoanalytic treatment. While dedicating their lives to relieving emotional suffering without being judgmental, they fear compromising their reputations if they publicly acknowledge such suffering in themselves. This phenomenon is nearly universal among those in the helping professions, yet there are few books dedicated to the issue.

In this innovative book, Farber and a distinguished range of contributors examine how the role of the "wounded healer" was instrumental in the formulation of psychoanalysis, and how using their own woundedness can help clinicians work more effectively with their patients, and advance theory in a more informed manner.

Celebrating the Wounded Healer Psychotherapist will be of interest to psychoanalysts and psychoanalytic psychotherapists, graduate students in clinical disciplines including psychology, social work, ministry/chaplaincy and nursing, as well as the general public.

Sharon Klayman Farber, Ph.D., is a psychotherapist and psychoanalyst, clinical social worker, author, teacher, and independent scholar. She maintains a private practice in Hastings-on-Hudson, New York, treating children, adolescents, and adults.

"Dr. Sharon Farber's new book condenses a great deal of information that is vital to all of us who practice psychotherapy and psychoanalysis. Her unique focus is on the way so many of us are 'wounded healers,' the way we utilize our own history of wounds — abuse, abandonment, mis-attunement, violence, narrative distortions — to recognize and heal the wounds of our patients. She also shows how some become "wounding healers," how what we do with patients can become a repetition of what was done to us. Jung was one of the first to describe the wounded healer and Freud a major example of someone who, in avoiding his own history of loss and neglect, became a wounding healer. One of Farber's central points is that one's own therapy or analysis is crucial in using one's history in effective ways.

The book is filled with case examples that illustrate these themes, including ten chapters written by other therapists, each with a specific focus that enriches and expands the major points. Overall, the book is scholarly and well researched, clearly and compellingly written, with evocative imagery that brings the material alive." **Louis Breger**, Ph.D., Professor Emeritus, California Institute of Technology; author of *Freud: Darkness in the Midst of Vision*

"When asked what makes a great psychologist, Jung responded, 'Someone who has to spend his life in a mental hospital, the only question whether as a patient or doctor.' Sharon Farber's work explores how wounds we undergo can make us more sensitive to others. Her focus is on people who became therapists, partly as a way of healing themselves by helping others. The idea that a psychotherapist suffers injuries shared by many is neither idealized nor debunked. What matters is the creative response to what one must go through and the value this has for therapeutic work." **Michael Eigen**, Ph.D., Author of *Faith* and *Contact With the Depths*

"In this comprehensive and insightful book, Sharon Farber succeeds in humanizing therapists, outing them as 'wounded healers' in a way that opens an otherwise intimidating door for both clients and the professionals themselves. From therapists to shamani to religious gurus, she asks the question: Is the wound an eye that sees? Does it cultivate compassion or a badge that feeds the therapists' narcissism? Anyone considering psychotherapy either as a client or as a profession would do well to read this cautionary book so that they may be better equipped to tell the difference." **Andrea Celenza**, Ph.D., Training and Supervising Analyst, Boston Psychoanalytic Society and Institute; author of *Sexual Boundary Violations: Therapeutic, Supervisory and Academic Contexts* and *Erotic Revelations: Clinical Applications and Perverse Scenarios* (www.andreacelenza.com)

"Finally, a book that explores—even celebrates—the psychotherapist's humanity, sensitivity and imperfections, in all their vibrant forms. By challenging the myth of the fully healed healer, Sharon K. Farber pulls away the protective veil behind which psychotherapists have often felt forced to hide their wounds. In doing so, she reveals the vulnerability that all human beings share and that often compels one to become a psychotherapist. Farber and the other authors in this vital collection show us how the wounds that bind are often the very same ones that heal." **Steven Kuchuck**, LCSW, Editor, *Clinical Implications of the Psychoanalyst's Life Experience: When the Personal Becomes Professional*

"*Celebrating the Wounded Healer Psychotherapist* is a great example of how scholarly work can be blended with personal experience to make text more readable for larger and more diverse audiences. I found the personal accounts of the wounded healers—who might also be called 'wounded heroes' for the ways in which they survived their struggles and helped others—especially interesting and evocative." **Lee Gutkind**, Editor, *Creative Nonfiction Magazine*

Celebrating the Wounded Healer Psychotherapist

Pain, post-traumatic growth and self-disclosure

Edited by
Sharon Klayman Farber

Routledge
Taylor & Francis Group

LONDON AND NEW YORK

First published 2017
by Routledge
2 Park Square, Milton Park, Abingdon, Oxon OX14 4RN

and by Routledge
711 Third Avenue, New York, NY 10017

Routledge is an imprint of the Taylor & Francis Group, an informa business

British Library Cataloguing in Publication Data
A catalogue record for this book is available from the British Library

Library of Congress Cataloging in Publication Data
Names: Farber, Sharon Klayman, editor.
Title: Celebrating the wounded healer psychotherapist : pain,
    post-traumatic growth and self-disclosure / edited by
    Sharon Klayman Farber.
Description: Milton Park, Abingdon, Oxon ; New York, NY : Routledge,
    2017.
Identifiers: LCCN 2016011485| ISBN 9781138926721 (hbk) |
    ISBN 9781138926738 (pbk.) | ISBN 9781315683058 (ebk)
Subjects: LCSH: Psychotherapy—Practice—Psychological aspects. |
    Psychotherapist and patient.
Classification: LCC RC480.5 .C415 2017 | DDC 616.89/14—dc23
LC record available at https://lccn.loc.gov/2016011485

ISBN: 978-1-138-92672-1 (hbk)
ISBN: 978-1-138-92673-8 (pbk)
ISBN: 978-1-315-68305-8 (ebk)

Typeset in Times New Roman
by Swales & Willis Ltd, Exeter, Devon, UK

I dedicate this book to the many patients who challenged me to expand my capacity for tending to their wounds. Although you came to me for healing, working with you has helped me heal in so many ways. I also dedicate this book to the brave wounded healers who contributed their stories of how they became wounded healers, and to wounded healers everywhere.

Contents

Preface

This is my third book and the same thing happened this time as occurred before. I discover books that I've had for years in my library that now have far more meaning for me. As I do my research, I want to know more and more. I am like a dog on a bone, borrowing more and more books from the public library and acquiring more and more.

Compiling this book has been an extraordinary adventure, taking me to so many places where I learned so much. In addition to learning about Carl Jung's concept of the wounded healer archetype, I've learned a bit more about Jung and have become intrigued by what I've learned, especially that it was his conception of treatment that anticipated the development of the relational school of treatment even before Ferenczi and Harry Stack Sullivan. Learning about his and Freud's painful relationship and the development of his own analytical psychology was fascinating, as was learning more about Freud's history and his determination to become a hero.

The experience of reading chapters submitted by contributors was very moving, at times overwhelming. I am proud to be associated with these brave, gutsy people who became my brothers and sisters under the skin.

Acknowledgements

I want to thank Kate Hawes for the wonderful opportunity to publish with Routledge. The late Professor Martin Bergmann has helped me acknowledge what I know, regardless of psychoanalytic politics. I received substantial help from Dr. Andrea Celenza in attempting to stop a psychopathic therapist from continuing to prey upon vulnerable patients and I want her to know how grateful I am. As always, Mike McCoy, research librarian at the Hastings-on-Hudson Public Library, came through for me: thank you, Mike. I am always grateful to my husband Stuart who good-naturedly accepts my writing life and the inconveniences it brings, and for my son, daughter-in-law and three lovable grandchildren for being the best diversions from it.

Contributors

Sharon K. Farber has a Ph.D. in clinical social work and is a board-certified Diplomate in Clinical Social Work in practice in Hastings-on-Hudson, New York. She is an independent scholar and public speaker, and has taught at several universities and the Cape Cod Institute. She has been an invited speaker in North America and abroad. She is the author of several papers and two books: *When the Body Is the Target: Self-Harm, Pain, and Traumatic Attachments* (2000, 2002) and *Hungry for Ecstasy: Trauma, the Brain, and the Influence of the Sixties* (2012). She was formerly on the editorial board of the *Clinical Social Work Journal* and consultant to the writing program "New Directions in Psychoanalytic Thinking." She won the Phyllis Meadow Award for Excellence in Psychoanalytic Writing, 2007.

She leads a group for clinicians who want to learn to write about their work and/or lives in a lively, accessible way. Her blog for *Psychology Today*, "The Mind-Body Connection," can be found at https://www.psychologytoday.com/blog/the-mind-body-connection. She may be contacted at sharonkfarber@gmail.com and her website is at drsharonfarber.com

Elisabeth Hanscombe has a Ph.D. in psychology and is a writer in Australia who completed her doctorate in 2011 on the topic "Life Writing and the Desire for Revenge." She has published a number of short stories and essays in the areas of autobiography, psychoanalysis, testimony, trauma, and creative non-fiction in *Meanjin, Island, Tirra Lirra, Quadrant* and *Griffith Review* as well as in the journals *Life Writing* and *Life Writing Annual: Biographical and Autobiographical Studies* and also in psychotherapy journals and magazines throughout Australia and in the United States. She is winner of the 2014 Lane Cove Literary Award for her short memoir *A Trip to the Beach*, which was shortlisted for the *Australian Book Review*'s 2009 Calibre Essay Prize, and long-listed in 2011 and 2014. She contributed chapters to *Stories of Complicated Grief: A Critical Anthology* (2015), edited by Dr. Eric Miller, and to *Eavesdropping: The Psychotherapist in Film and Television* (2015), edited by Lucy Husskinson and Terrie Waddell. She is an adjunct research associate at the Swinburne Institute for Social Research and blogs at http://sixthinline.com. She may be contacted at hanscombe@netspace.net.au

Gretchen Heyer is a Jungian psychoanalyst in Houston, Texas with a Ph.D. in literature and creative writing, and a master's in divinity. She is a Texas licensed professional counselor. Her website is at www.gretchenheyer.com and she may be contacted at lexington1835@sbcglobal.net

Susan Kavaler-Adler has a Ph.D. in clinical psychology, is a Diplomate in Psychoanalysis, holds an honorary doctorate in literature, and is a fellow of the American Board and Academy of Psychoanalysis. She is co-founder of the Object Relations Institute for Psychotherapy and Psychoanalysis (O.R.I.) in New York City. She is a training analyst and a senior psychoanalytic supervisor. She has forty years' experience in object relations psychoanalytic practice, specializing in psychotrauma, grief and mourning of losses, blocks to creativity and intimacy, erotic transference, self-sabotage, fears of success, love addiction, inhibitions, compulsions, demon lover addictions, haunting regrets, repetitive issues, betrayal in love, etc. Dr. Kavaler-Adler is a prolific author, with five books and sixty peer-reviewed articles and book chapters in the fields of complex psychoanalytic object relations cases and thinking, developmental mourning, finding the creative voice, integrating creativity and love, erotic desire and all the transferences, compulsion versus desire, fear of success, self-sabotage, etc. She has received fifteen awards for her writing in the field of psychoanalysis, including the Gradiva Award from N.A.A.P. in 2004, and four competitive Arlene Wohlberg Memorial Awards. She may be contacted at drkavaleradler@gmail.com and her website is at www.kavaleradler.com

Ruth M. Lijtmaer, Ph.D., is a senior supervisor, training analyst, and faculty member at the Center for Psychotherapy and Psychoanalysis of New Jersey, and is in private practice in Ridgewood, New Jersey. She frequently presents lectures and papers at both national and international levels. She is the author of several scholarly publications and book chapters concerning multicultural and religious issues, ethnicity, social trauma, and transference-countertransference. She is a board member of the International Forum for Psychoanalytic Education. She may be contacted at ruth.lijtmaer@verizon.net

Annita Perez Sawyer, Ph.D., has treated children, adolescents, adults, couples, and families in a full-time practice for over thirty years. She supervises pre-doctoral psychology fellows in child and family therapy at Yale. Her prize-winning essays have appeared in both literary and professional journals and creative nonfiction anthologies. *Smoking Cigarettes, Eating Glass: A Psychologist's Memoir* (2015), the book from which this contribution was taken, won the 2013 Santa Fe Writers' Project Nonfiction Grand Prize (judged by Lee Gutkind). Using herself as a case study, Annita speaks to clinical audiences around the country. Her talks, essays, and stories illuminate lifetime consequences of childhood trauma, the harmful effects of fads in psychiatric diagnosis and treatment, the high cost of stigma and shame, and the power of human connection to heal. She can be

contacted at annitas@sbcglobal.net and her website is at www.smokingcigaret
teseatingglass.com

Colleen Russell is a licensed marriage and family therapist and certified group
psychotherapist who has maintained a general psychotherapy practice for over
twenty-two years in Kentfield, Marin County, San Francisco Bay Area. She specializes in loss, trauma, motherless daughters (women who have lost their mothers
through death, illness, separation, or estrangement), and cult or high-demand
group education and recovery (former members, including those born and raised
in them, families of someone currently involved, and mental health professionals). She works collaboratively with individuals, couples, families, and groups, in
office settings and via Skype or phone. Since 1997 she has facilitated motherless
daughters groups and, since 2003, a group for former members of high-demand
groups. Colleen presents on cults and high-demand groups at venues nationwide.
Periodically, Colleen offers workshops for former cult members, and for family members of a loved one currently in a cult. Her journal article "Touched:
Disconfirming Pathogenic Beliefs of Thought Reform through the Process of
Acting" was published in the *Cultic Studies Review* (volume 9, no. 1, 2010).
She also facilitates groups for survivors of domestic violence with the Center
for Domestic Peace in San Rafael, California. Her website is at www.colleen-
russellmft.com and she may be contacted at crussellmft@earthlink.net; phone:
415-785-3513.

Emily Samuelson is a psychologist in private practice in Towson, Maryland
who specializes in treating trauma. She has been on the faculties of several
universities, a guest on radio programs, and a lecturer on child sexual abuse.
Dr. Samuelson traveled around the United States, interviewing a diverse group
of men and women who were sexually abused in childhood about what happened
to them, how they were affected, and what they have done to heal. She also took
black and white portraits of each of the survivors. The edited interviews and photographs are in her forthcoming book, *Soaring above the Ashes: The Stories and
Portraits of Thriving Survivors of Childhood Sexual Abuse*. She may be contacted
at Samuelson01@comcast.net

Eric Sherman is a licensed clinical social worker in private practice in New York
City and Montclair, New Jersey. He is also a faculty member and supervisor at
the National Institute for the Psychotherapies in New York and the Center for
Psychotherapy and Psychoanalysis of New Jersey. He is the author of two books,
including *Notes from the Margins: The Gay Analyst's Subjectivity in the Treatment
Setting*, and is a contributor to *When the Personal Becomes Professional: Clinical
Implications of the Analyst's Life Experiences*. He is on the editorial board of
the *Journal of Gay and Lesbian Psychotherapy*. He is in private practice in New
York City and Montclair, New Jersey. He can be contacted at eric.sherman.lcsw@
gmail.com

John A. Sloane, M.D., is a psychiatrist (trained at the Institute of Living in Hartford, Connecticut) and a psychoanalyst (trained at the Toronto Institute of Psychoanalysis) presently in private practice of psychoanalysis and psychotherapy in Toronto. He is an assistant professor in the Department of Psychiatry at the University of Toronto where he supervises residents in psychotherapy. He teaches and supervises candidates in the Institute for the Advancement of Self Psychology (I.A.S.P.) and at the Toronto Institute for Contemporary Psychoanalysis (T.I.C.P.) where he has also participated in its Relational Study Group for many years. He has also been an active participant in the Anglican Center for Theological Dialogue and its successor, a small discussion group called Challenging Christianity. He has been lucky enough to be the husband of a wonderful person who has taught him a lot about "good-enough mothering" over the years, and is the proud father of five lively daughters and twelve grandchildren who continue to teach him about good-enough fathering. He can be contacted at john.sloane@rogers.com

Anthony Rankin Wilson, M.S.W., is in private practice in Toronto and is a father of two adult daughters. Through his sixty-five years, Anthony has become passionate about songwriting, the dip of paddle and glide of canoe, loon call, his garden, his dog, and his bicycle, synthesizing and reconciling his environmental concern with psychoanalytic psychotherapy and his intimate relationship with his wife as spiritual path. His clinical social work history includes inpatient and outpatient psychiatry. Following graduate school, he was first trained as a bioenergetic psychotherapist and has had a long-standing interest in Jungian analysis, archetypal psychology, and ecopsychology. He has written and presented papers on the interface of clinical theory and practice and the environmental crisis at several international psychoanalytic conferences, and is a recording artist with two CDs of original songs. His music and writing can be found at www.anthonyrankin wilson.com and he may be contacted at anthwilson@sympatico.ca

Part I

The wounded and wounding healer

Introduction

Nothing to hide, plenty to celebrate

Sharon K. Farber

Some people who have been hurt by experiences in their life have learned something valuable, and in turn want to help others as they have been helped, often through their own psychotherapy. They become wounded healer psychotherapists. This is indeed something to celebrate.

Some wounded healers, however, hurt those they are meant to help and bring shame to this profession. All psychotherapists, even the most outstanding ones, can damage a patent severely when circumstances in their own lives and in the treatment of a particular patient are such that the damaging acts seem at that moment to be the solution to a major problem in the treatment. This can happen to any psychotherapist.

This became painfully clear to me when I discovered that an analyst whom I had greatly admired, respected, and with whom I had done collaborative work, lost his professional license after having a sexual relationship with a patient. He had formerly been president of his area's psychoanalytic society, clinical professor of medicine, a training and supervising analyst. He was also author of many journal articles and several books. He and I reviewed each other's writing. I looked up to him and in some ways he was a mentor to me. This news left me feeling confused, disillusioned, angry, and betrayed. Who was this man anyway? What was wrong with me for trusting him? But after some time, I came to feel as sad for him as for the patient whose trust he had betrayed. The practice of psychoanalysis, as you will read, is indeed a perilous calling (Sussman 1995).

The wound in the psychotherapist

Long before I began thinking of the concept of the wounded healer, I was well aware that colleagues whom I had gotten to know fairly well had been deeply hurt in their lives. Then when I did my doctoral dissertation (Farber 2015), I discovered that a number of therapists hurt and wounded themselves quite literally.

When I decided on the topic of my doctoral dissertation study, I had also begun specialized training in the treatment of patients with eating disorders. When I discovered that there was a very strong comorbidity between eating disorders and self-mutilation, I become intrigued. Further exploration revealed that there was virtually nothing in the literature to explain it and so I did a study exploring the factors I suspected might be involved (Farber 1995, 1997, 2000). The severity of the self-harm behavior these subjects presented was staggering, potentially life-threatening, and I was shocked when a surprising number of subjects identified themselves as professional social workers, psychologists and psychiatric aides. I certainly knew that many therapists had considerable problems but I never would have imagined that they suffered such life-threatening psychopathology.

More recently, a candidate in a psychoanalytic training program consulted with me about her self-mutilating behavior getting worse. Apparently, those who interviewed her for the training program knew nothing about this or that she had been diagnosed with dissociative identity disorder and had been treated several times in an inpatient unit for trauma-related disorders. She cut herself the evening before seeing me. To assess the severity, I asked to see it. I was shocked to see on her midriff a jagged network of bright red bloody cuts, very different from the "delicate self-cutting" (Pao 1969) seen in those who cut themselves less severely. I was appalled that someone so much in danger of killing herself had been admitted to a psychoanalytic training program undetected. I wondered how many others there were like her, wounded healers who wounded themselves severely. When I collected chapters for this book, Annita Perez Sawyer described how she cut and burned herself, banged her head against the wall, and swallowed broken glass in her memoir *Smoking Cigarettes, Eating Glass* (Perez Sawyer 2015). She submitted a chapter, and so did Gretchen Heyer who came close to death from anorexia nervosa. Both are included.

Who becomes a psychotherapist and why

We ask patients to disclose painful personal experiences so that they can begin to recover. At a time when people are more candidly coming out about their own struggles in life, we in the mental health field have been conspicuously silent for fear of being stigmatized. Therapists are often expected to be immune to the kind of problems that they help clients through (Adams 2014) and often try to project that persona. In linking therapists' personal histories to their choice of career, Adams challenges psychotherapists to take a step back and consider their own well-being as a vital first step to promoting change in their patients.

Recovering from these painful experiences is an ongoing process. Even though our own psychotherapy or psychoanalysis helped us heal, disclosing this experience continues the healing process. There is a myth, which contains some truth, that psychotherapists are emotionally disturbed people, which is what attracts them to do the work they do. Thomas Maeder (1989), son of two psychiatrists, interviewed many psychotherapists, children of therapists, and former patients, and found that many therapists' children spoke of their parents' horrendous early life and difficulties in coping with their families, something they believed was the critical factor in their parents' choice of profession. Maeder concluded there is something amiss with those who proclaim that they want to help others.

They may be attracted to the position of authority, the dependence of others, the image of benevolence, the promise of being idolized, and, last but not least, the hope of vicariously healing themselves.

Other research reveals a connection between choosing psychotherapy as a profession and one's own woundedness. When Gertrud Mander examined candidates who wanted to train as psychotherapists or counselors, a main theme was that they felt "summoned by an internal voice, a call from the super-ego which forms the basis of any vocation" (Mander 2004, p. 161). When Marilyn Barnett (2007) interviewed experienced psychoanalytic and psychodynamic therapists about their personal and professional histories, two major themes were early object loss and narcissistic needs.

The psychoanalytic mystique

All modern methods of psychotherapy started with psychoanalysis and so psychotherapy continues to be associated with Freud and psychoanalysis, a process depicted in *New Yorker* cartoons showing the patient lying on a couch. The patient may be a man, woman, cat, dog or rooster lying on the couch, literally at the feet of a man, often bearded, who sits behind the patient. This is the wise, omniscient analyst, silent, and impassive, as Freud was thought to be.

In fact, Freud was not a silent analyst until late in life when many oral surgeries for cancer of the jaw made talking painful for him (Gay 1988). Previously, he had been a rather talkative analyst. The truth is that Freud asked patients to lie on the couch simply because it made him anxious to be looked at all day. (Many things made him anxious, which you will read about later.) For the patient to go more deeply into himself, he should not be distracted by the analyst's facial expression or objects in the room, and so, ever since Freud, psychoanalysts have continued to use the couch, which has become an icon, along with the notion that the patient lies on the couch four to five times a week. In fact, purchasing the couch has become something of a rite of passage for a psychoanalyst (Gordon 1992). A photograph of the late Martin Bergmann, one of my favorite teachers, shows him sitting on his psychoanalytic couch, covered with colorful Oriental rugs much like Freud's, which can be seen at the Freud Museum in London.

Psychoanalysis has evolved considerably since Freud's day. It is rare for the patient to have sessions four or five times a week; one or twice a week is usual; if U.S.-managed care insurance has its way, it will be less than once a week. It is also rare for the patient to lie on a couch as most treatment is done sitting up, face to face. The couch in my office is simply a piece of furniture. Some patients sit on it, others use the chair directly across from mine. When a patient is distracted by my face or office, he can lie down or look away.[1] One patient simply sits up and closes her eyes when she needs to.

Psychotherapists do not use any mysterious means to help those who are suffering from emotional distress. As Adam Phillips simply put it: "a psychoanalyst is anyone who uses what were originally Freud's concepts of transference, the unconscious, and the dream-work in paid conversations with people about how they want to live" (Phillips 1994, p. xiv). When psychoanalysis works the way it should, there is nothing esoteric about it; it is a form of conversation that helps some people feel better. It differs from ordinary conversation in being a kind of reciprocal free association, with the patient saying what comes to his mind without censoring it while the analyst listens with free-floating attention and then may share his thoughts with the patient, facilitating the emergence, understanding, and interpretation of what the patient is saying (Isakower 1992). This is really an altered state of consciousness for both patient and therapist.

Interest in the personal lives of psychotherapists

Ever since the mid-1980s, there has been a growing interest in the personal lives of psychotherapists, as shown by the publications of Jeffrey Kottler (2010), Carl Goldberg (1991), James Guy (1987), Michael Sussman (1992, 1995), Lee Kassan (1996), Steven Kuchuck (2013), and Marie Adams (2014). Despite the bashing psychoanalysis has taken in the media, *The New York Times* recently began publishing postings about psychoanalysis which have generally been quite favorable (opinionator.blogs.nytimes.com).

Because Carl Jung was one of the first to articulate the concept of the wounded healer, most publications on the wounded healer are from a Jungian perspective (Hockley & Gardner 2010; Merchant 2011; Sedgwick 1994). This book is a pioneering contribution by a non-Jungian psychotherapist, combining theory and clinical practice with personal contributions written by wounded healers.

Psychotherapy is a two-way process in which both people are changed. The intimate connections formed in long-term psychotherapeutic relationships can result in changes in the therapist that last a lifetime:

> We find ourselves talking in sessions, preaching lessons to our clients, and then realize, suddenly, that we are really talking to ourselves. We end up taking the advice that we offer to others when we tell them such things as the importance of living more in the present moment or spending more quality time with loved ones.
>
> (Kottler & Carlson 2005, p. 4)

One therapist, Laura Brown, said "Anyone who meets us, changes us. Every encounter we have, transforms us. How could we be therapists and not be transformed personally in all kinds of ways?" (Kottler & Carlson 2005, p. 214). She said that one patient opened a sense of the divine in her that was healing. In Martin Buber's (1970) concept of the I–Thou relationship, in which the sacred is potentially present in any relationship, our relationship lives in the space between us—not between me or you or even in the dialogue between us—it lives in the space we live together and that is a sacred space. Irvin Yalom describes the patient and therapist as "fellow travelers, both on a journey of discovery together" (Yalom 2002, p. 8).

Although there are many theoretical schools of psychotherapy, I write from a psychoanalytic orientation. Despite my training having been in the one-person psychology of classical psychoanalysis and ego psychology, I knew that the two-person or relational psychology was the most important factor in successful therapy. I knew the therapist should *not* "be opaque to his patients and, like a mirror, should show them nothing but what is shown to him" (Freud 1912, p. 118). It is the patient–therapist attachment relationship that is transformative for the patient (Wallin 2007).

The rationale for all this secrecy about the analyst derives from traditional thinking that much of the psychoanalyst's healing power comes from observing and analyzing the transference, those interpersonal attitudes and expectations learned early in life that the patient unconsciously transfers to the therapist. The transference may be positive, as in assuming the therapist will be interested and caring, or negative, as in assuming the therapist will be uncaring, competitive, or shaming, and is quite revealing about how the patient sees others. When the analyst interprets the transference, thus making these unconscious assumptions conscious, it frees the patient to relate to himself and others more realistically. This is the origin of Freud's *tabula rasa* or blank screen concept, meaning the less the patient knows about the therapist leaves the room there is for the patient to form a transference.

My own experience over the years has told me, however, that transference forms with or without the therapist's intentional self-disclosure. Many believe that the judicious use of self-disclosure, when done to meet the needs of the patient, adds a most human and needed dimension in therapy and can enhance the attachment bond.

Common sense tells us it is impossible for the therapist to be a blank screen. Our demeanor, gender, appearance, accent, race, ethnicity, location, and decoration of the office all provide patients with personal information that allows them to infer the therapist's socioeconomic status, his formality or lack of it, his warmth, frustration, tolerance and many other qualities. Simply by our look of recognition or lack of it, we show whether we are familiar with the movie, restaurant, book, music or slang the patient brings to the dialogue. And of course, when he wants to know more about his therapist, there is always the Internet and Googling.

In my training the notion that the analysts' own transferences and countertransferences might be used to impact the treatment positively was never considered. Today, relational theory believes all feelings, thoughts and actions of both patient and analyst are embedded in an intersubjective field. For example, in projective identification, when the patient, unable to contain an unacceptable affect or thought, projects it into the therapist (Klein 1964), it is described by Bromberg (1998) as a process of communication by which the patient could dissociate and project his own unacceptable emotions into the analyst, who could then know experientially what the patient was feeling. The analyst might disclose what was felt to the patient, which might help the patient disclose more.

Relational self-disclosure

The headline on the front page of *The New York Times* was "A Down-to-Earth Defense Lawyer with Felonies on His Resume."

> A well-worn felon with more than a decade spent in places like Sing Sing and Rikers Island stood before the judge. But as Allan P. Haber appealed for mercy, he did so not for himself, but for a client. Mr. Haber, 75, is one of the more unlikely criminal defense lawyers in New York. For the last three decades, first as a public defender and then in private practice, Mr. Haber has long represented the kind of hardened criminals who might seem beyond redemption. As ethical lawyers must, he has always kept his clients' secrets. But throughout his career, Mr. Haber has also kept tight guard of a secret of his own. Mr. Haber was once a drug dealer, selling heroin in Midtown Manhattan, carrying a gun, running a stash house and earning thousands of dollars a day selling bundles of heroin . . . through a network of distributors. He had 10 convictions in his 20s and early 30s, including three drug-related felonies. It was not until he was in his 40s that Mr. Haber, fully disclosing his past during the application process, obtained college and law degrees from New York University and admission to the bar . . . .
>
> And when Mr. Haber asks a judge for leniency for a client, he does so with the certainty that some people do benefit from a second chance . . . John Sexton, the president of N.Y.U., said that Mr. Haber's "story should inspire all who care about our society to reflect on the power of mercy and the human capacity for growth." Mr. Sexton is qualified to judge: in 1981, he taught Mr. Haber civil procedure in his first semester at law school . . . Clients whom Mr. Haber has told about his prior life reacted positively, he said. "It made me feel like I could trust you," wrote an imprisoned former gang member who agreed to answer questions, on condition of anonymity, that Mr. Haber emailed at the request of *The New York Times*. "I felt like you would fight for me even harder because you understood what it felt like to be in my position."
>
> (Weiser 2015)

As patients discover more about the real lives of their psychotherapists, I imagine many will have a similar positive reaction.

Self-disclosure in psychotherapy evolved from the concept of a two-person psychology in which the mind of both patient and therapist are constantly engaged in a cross-fertilization of mutual influence (Farber 2006; Kuchuck 2009; Mitchell 1993; Stolorow & Atwood 2002). Like all human beings, we psychotherapists need self-respect and have a healthy narcissistic need to tell our story. We need to feel connected to others, appreciated and respected. As James McLaughlin said, what each of us needs from the other . . . is at depth pretty much the same. We need to find in the other an affirming witness to the best that we hope we are, as well as an accepting and durable respondent to those worst aspects of ourselves that we fear we are.

(McLaughlin 1995, p. 461)

We need to know that we matter. Robert Akeret wrote of

[the] awful frustration built in to being a psychotherapist: I never know how the story ends. When the patient walks out of my office after our final session, that is it. The rest of his or her life remains a mystery to me.

(Akeret 1995, p. 15)

Although occasionally a therapist hears from a former patient, it is not usual and we are left to wonder if the positive changes lasted. "Did I actually provide lasting help for my patients? . . . Was life sweeter, fuller than it might have been if we had never encountered one another?" (op. cit., p. 225). This question burned so much in Akeret's mind that he began tracking down former patients all across the U.S. and Europe.

Although the general rule of psychotherapy is that the therapist should never intrude uninvited into a patient's life, I decided that enough time had passed to render this rule moot. Further, I promised myself that if any of the voices on the other end of the line sounded remotely hesitant, I would not pursue any further.

(op. cit., p. 18)

Similarly, psychoanalytic historian and psychoanalyst Louis Breger (2012) did a long-term follow-up that showed the effectiveness of modern analytic psychotherapy. He surveyed over thirty former patients to see if their progress, begun in therapy, had continued, expanded or regressed, asking them to highlight what they remembered as being most helpful.

We sometimes feel a need to reveal more of ourselves than has been customary:

As we emerge from hiding and therapeutically reveal more of our true, sometimes less than idealizable selves, we learn—as patients do—that imperfection and mistakes are part of our humanity and in many cases even enhance the work, or at least can be tolerated and survived. Learning through experience that we do not have to live up to theoretically antiquated and stifling ego-ideals, that we can have a bias, judgment, unresolved issues, and imperfections—some of which might need to be or invariably get communicated through self-disclosure—and still be good-enough, even excellent, analysts, can be relieving and healing for all parties.

(Kuchuck 2009, p. 1022)

I believe we do this work because we want very deep connections with other human beings, even greater than that what is possible in our personal lives. As therapists become increasingly aware that remaining a blank screen is impossible, "we have been finding ourselves in exciting but often frightening and strange new territory" (Kuchuck 2009, p. 1008). This book is part of this frightening and strange new territory. Gays are not the only ones to come out of the closet.

It has been somewhat anxiety-provoking to try to anticipate the responses of some patients who might come across the book. They will certainly know a lot more about me than what they have learned about me in their treatment. Some will probably be shocked that their therapist has not led such a charmed life, and may want to speak with me about it, while some others may have already figured that it goes with the territory of being drawn to this work. I also anticipated that because my son has some friends who are psychotherapists or are married to one, he might hear about how I came to do this work, so I decided to share with him what I have written so that he can hear it from me first.

Relational self-disclosure through writing

Contributors to this book have made courageous personal disclosures. Each one has been on a hero's journey (Campbell 1972), a universal motif of adventure and transformation that runs through most of the world's mythic traditions

Upon hearing about this book, some therapists were very excited and wanted to contribute while even more were excited but anxious about contributing. One therapist with an academic position was warned by colleagues that if she had any hopes of obtaining tenure, she would not contribute a chapter. There were a few people who initially planned to submit a chapter but either submitted but then rescinded it or never submitted it, but wrote to me of how helpful an experience it was to write about themselves in this way. They felt better after writing and learned some things about themselves along the way. When Jung agreed to write his autobiography, *Memories, Dreams, Reflections*, Aniela Jaffe, his editor, wrote "his distaste for exposing his personal life to the public eye was well known. Indeed, he gave his consent only after a long period of doubt and hesitation" (Jung 1961, p. v). Jung remarked:

> A book of mine is always a matter of fate. There is something unpredictable about the process of writing, and I cannot prescribe for myself any predetermined course. Thus this "autobiography" is now taking a direction quite different from what I imagined at the beginning. It has become a necessity for me to write down my early memories. If I neglect to do so for a single day, unpleasant physical symptoms immediately follow. As soon as I set to work they vanish and my head feels perfectly clear.
>
> (Jung 1961, p. vi)

Anthony Rankin Wilson, whose chapter is included in this book, wrote:

> It has been a powerful experience to write this piece—a deeper diving into the pool of an old wound . . . yielding new angles, understandings, and softening pain. I appreciate this opportunity you have offered, and regardless of the rightness for your book, it has been more than worth the blood, sweat, and tears!
>
> (Wilson, private communication)

Reading these chapters has been a very powerful experience for me, as I felt their courage and vulnerability, making me feel quite connected to people I have never met and giving me more courage to contribute my own chapters. I know personally the therapeutic benefits of writing and have more than a wish to write; I have a need to write (Farber 2005, 2013). I usually have several writing projects going on simultaneously. Like Freud, I am happiest when writing.

In *Narrative Means to Therapeutic Ends*, White and Epston (1990) said that we experience problems when the stories of our lives, as they or others have invented them, do not sufficiently represent our actual lived experience. Therapy then becomes a process of telling and retelling the story of our lives and experiences, and in this way narrative comes to play a central role in therapy. Expressive writing, in which the narrative approach is used to help individuals to rewrite their own life stories, has made its way into the therapeutic community (Bolton et al. 2004; Krueger 2002). I use it a good deal in my work, often finding that many patients can more readily write about what they are feeling than speak about it. My paper on the subject is called "Free Association Reconsidered: The Talking Cure, the Writing Cure" (Farber 2005).

Expressive writing has been found to boost one's mood and provide health benefits (Brand 1989; Pennebaker 1991). It has been found that holding back our feelings is very hard work for the body and that writing expressively about these experiences for as little as twenty minutes a day for four days in the week reduced physician visits for illness, improved serum immune function and enhanced work performance.

> Over time, the work of inhibition undermines the body's defenses. Like other stressors, inhibition can affect immune function, the action of the heart and vascular systems, and even the biochemical workings of the brain and nervous systems. In short, excessive holding back of thoughts, feelings, and behaviors can place people at risk for both major and minor diseases.
>
> Whereas inhibition is potentially harmful, confronting our deepest thoughts and feelings can have remarkable short- and long-term health benefits. Confession, whether by writing or talking, can neutralize many of the problems of inhibition.
>
> (Pennebaker 1991, p. 2)

Wounded healers speak out

The archetype of the wounded healer was created by Carl Jung who believed the wounded healer's suffering is both a burden and a compelling force in his need to heal the problems of others (Farber 2013; Jung 1951). You will read how psychotherapists' earlier difficulties played a part in their decision to become a psychotherapist.

At times I have been honored to hear colleagues' stories of their own healing process, something which is not openly discussed. The therapists in this book have revealed themselves as wounded healers, as real and human as the patients they see, and have developed a great deal of resilience. This book grew out of my own clinical experience and writing about my work. The more I write about my work, the more I tend to disclose the personal information I think will help the reader to understand the concept or emotion I am trying to convey, just as I do in treatment.

Inevitably, every therapist will hurt some patient in some way, at some time. When he can acknowledge this and make a genuine apology to the patient, sometimes the wound can be healed. But some psychotherapists may succumb to the worst aspects of themselves and hurt a patient severely. You will read about them and how it can happen to any one of us. You will read about how Jung himself was a wounding healer. And so was Freud, who made rampant boundary violations, thus setting a template for the development of subsequent wounding healers.

For several years I ran a monthly group for therapists who wanted to learn to write about their work and their lives in a lively, engaging way. One woman wrote about how having a mentally ill brother shaped her life and was a major factor in a number of significant decisions she has made, including the decision not to have children and the decision to become a psychotherapist. She has written about how this experience affects her work, for better and worse, and how she continues to struggle with it. We have cried and laughed with her. Although not a psychotherapy group, coming out about her experiences was therapeutic for her. Listening to her contributed to my decision to create this book.

I owe the concept of celebrating the wounded healer to Peter Martin (2011), a psychologist who had a depressive breakdown, and stopped seeing clients for six months. When he published his story, it produced responses from therapists who wanted to write about their lives. He interviewed seventeen of them in his paper "Celebrating the Wounded Healer." Martin thought that although woundedness is just another metaphor for our humanness, for many psychotherapists it is a hidden secret, a deceit often masked as "professionalism."

> Why would we want . . . to admit to any kind of weakness? Why, above all, would we want to *celebrate* such a self-description? We could indeed consider the concept of the wounded healer a deficit model . . . Perhaps woundedness is just another metaphor for our humanness? Yet it is a very potent metaphor . . . Yet for most of us, most of the time, this awareness is

a secret, something to be apologised for and quickly forgotten in favor of a quick return to so-called "normal life."

(Martin 2011, pp. 10–12)

I am a wounded healer and had thought tentatively about sharing more of my experience but feared being stigmatized and shamed. But not identifying myself made it seem that I had something shameful to hide. Then I thought about some well-known people in the mental health field who disclosed their woundedness and went on to heal others. They include Kay Redfield Jamison, Lauren Slater and Marsha Linehan (Farber 2013), about whom you will read more in this book.

We have all been wounded in some way, some more severely than others. When we can learn from our woundedness and develop empathy for ourselves, and can use our empathy to help others, this is something to feel good about. We all have a story to tell.

In imagining this book, I knew I would need to include my own story but did not know if I could allow myself to do it. Thinking about it made me anxious. But how could I ask other therapists to be courageous enough to write about theirs if I would not write about my own? It did not seem right. I knew I needed to. So I decided to write about it privately, just for myself, not for publication, just to see if I *could* do it—a private experiment. Once I got started, it was surprisingly easy to disclose material that even some very close friends do not know. The words just flowed. This should not have surprised me because I am so committed to how disclosure, written or spoken, is so good for our health (Farber 2005; Pennebaker 1991). I had given a course at the Hudson Valley Writers' Center on writing for emotional and physical health and addressed a group of former cult members at a conference about how expressive writing could help them understand and integrate this experience into their lives. If it can be good for others, why shouldn't it be good for me too? So I decided to put my money where my mouth is and write my own chapter and ask other psychotherapists to contribute. Reading the contributions of others made me feel less alone and gave me more courage to do it. I no longer feel that I have something shameful to hide.

We have something valuable to share not only with our colleagues but with others who have been wounded by life. I read a quote in the aluminum foil covering of a square of Dove dark chocolate: "The more you praise and celebrate your life, the more there is in life to celebrate." Wanting to know who said that, I discovered that it was attributed to Oprah Winfrey, who was born into poverty to a teenage single mother, and raped at nine. Oprah has certainly been on a hero's journey herself. It is time for us to celebrate our triumphs. I hope you will join us in the celebration.

Note

1 In this book, examples are quoted of both male and female therapists and patients (and other participants). When referring to generalities, terms such as "he" or "she" are used for the sake of simplicity and are not intended to imply gender-specific roles.

References

Adams, M. (2014). *The Myth of the Untroubled Therapist: Private Life, Professional Practice*. London and New York: Routledge.

Akeret, R. (1995). *Tales from a Traveling Couch: A Psychotherapist Revisits His Most Memorable Patients*. New York: Norton.

Barnett, M. (2007). What Brings You Here? An Exploration of the Unconscious Motivations of Those who Choose to Train and Work as Psychotherapists and Counselors. *Psychodynamic Practice: Individuals, Groups and Organizations, 13*: 257–274.

Bolton, G., Howlett, S., Lago, C., & Wright, J. (2004). *Writing Cures: An Introductory Handbook of Writing in Counseling and Psychotherapy*. New York and Hove (U.K.): Brunner-Routledge.

Brand, A. G. (1989). *The Psychology of Writing: The Affective Experience* (Contributions in Psychology series). New York: Greenwood Press.

Breger, L. (2012). *Psychotherapy: Lives Intersecting*. Piscataway, NJ: Transaction.

Bromberg, P. (1998). *Standing in the Spaces: Essays on Clinical Process, Trauma, and Dissociation*. Hillsdale, NJ and London: Analytic Press.

Buber, M. (1970). *I and Thou*. Trans. and notes by Walter Kaufmann. New York: Charles Scribner's Sons.

Campbell, J. (1972). *The Hero with a Thousand Faces*. Princeton, NJ: Princeton University Press.

Elkins, D. (1998). *Beyond Religion: Eight Alternative Paths to the Sacred: A Personal Program for Building a Spiritual Life outside the Walls of Traditional Religion*. Wheaton, IL: Quest Books/Theosophical Publishing House.

Farber, B. (2006). *Self-Disclosure in Psychotherapy*. New York: Guilford Press.

Farber, S. (1995). A Psychoanalytically Informed Understanding of the Association between Binge-Purge Behavior and Self-Mutilating Behavior: A Study Comparing Binge-Purgers who Self-Mutilate Severely with Binge-Purgers who Self-Mutilate Mildly or Not at All. Ph.D. dissertation, New York University School of Social Work, AAT 9603317.

Farber, S. (1997). Self-Medication, Traumatic Reenactment, and Somatic Expression in Bulimic and Self-Mutilating Behavior. *Clinical Social Work Journal, 25* (1): 87–106.

Farber, S. (2000). *When the Body Is the Target: Self-Harm, Pain, and Traumatic Attachments*. Northvale, NJ: Jason Aronson.

Farber, S. (2005). Free Association Reconsidered: The Talking Cure, the Writing Cure. *Journal of the American Academy of Psychoanalysis and Dynamic Psychiatry, 33* (2): 249–273.

Farber, S. (2013). *Hungry for Ecstasy: Trauma, the Brain, and the Influence of the Sixties*. Lanham, MD: Jason Aronson/Rowman & Littlefield.

Farber, S. (2015). "Tell Them it Is Not Too Late for Someone Like Me." A "Failure-to-Thrive Child" Grows Old and Begins an Attachment-Based Psychotherapy at Sixty-Seven. *Attachment: New Directions in Psychotherapy and Relational Psychoanalysis, 9*: 57–81.

Freud, S. (1912). Recommendations to Physicians Practising Psycho-Analysis. In: *The Standard Edition of the Complete Psychological Works of Sigmund Freud*, vol. 12 (pp. 109–120). London: Hogarth Press.

Gay, P. (1988). *Freud: A Life for Our Time*. New York: Norton.

Goldberg, C. (1991). *On Being a Psychotherapist*. Northvale, NJ: Jason Aronson.

Gordon, M. (1992). Analyzing the Analyst's Couch. *The New York Times*, March 19. Retrieved from http://www.nytimes.com/1992/03/19/style/analyzing-the-analyst-s-couch. html

Guy, J. (1987). *The Personal Life of the Psychotherapist: The Impact of Clinical Practice on the Therapist's Intimate Relationships and Emotional Well-Being*. New York: Wiley.

Hockley, L., & Gardner, L. (2010). *House: The Wounded Healer on Television: Jungian and Post-Jungian Reflections*. New York and London: Routledge.

Isakower, O. (1992). The Analyzing Instrument: Further Thoughts. *Journal of Clinical Psychoanalysis, 1*: 200–203.

Jung, C. (1951). *Fundamental Questions of Psychotherapy*. Princeton, NJ: Princeton University Press.

Jung, C. (1961). *Memories, Dreams, Reflections*. New York: Vintage.

Kassan, L. E. (1996). *Shrink Rap: Sixty Psychotherapists Discuss Their Work, Their Lives, and the State of Their Field*. New York: Jason Aronson.

Klein, M. (1964). *Contributions to Psychoanalysis*. New York: McGraw-Hill.

Kottler, J. (2010). *On Being a Therapist*. San Francisco: Jossey-Bass.

Kottler, J., & Carlson, J. (2005). *The Client who Changed Me: Stories of Therapist Personal Transformation*. New York and Hove (U.K.): Routledge.

Krueger, D. (2002). *Integrating Body Self and Psychological Self: Creating a New Story in Psychoanalysis and Psychotherapy*. New York and London: Brunner-Routledge.

Kuchuck, S. (2009). Do Ask, Do Tell? Narcissistic Need as a Determinant of Analyst Self-Disclosure. *Psychoanalytic Review, 96*: 1007–1024.

Kuchuck, S. (2013). *Clinical Implications of the Psychoanalyst's Life Experience: When the Personal Becomes Professional*. New York: Routledge.

Maeder, T. (1989). Wounded Healers. *The Atlantic Monthly* (January): 37–39.

Mander, G. (2004). The Selection of Candidates for Training in Psychotherapy and Counseling. *Psychodynamic Practice: Individuals, Groups and Organizations, 10*: 161–172.

Martin, P. (2011). Celebrating the Wounded Healer (original research paper). *Counseling Psychology Review, 26* (1): 10–19.

McLaughlin, J. (1995). Touching Limits in the Psychoanalytic Dyad. *Psychoanalytic Quarterly, 64*: 433–465.

Merchant, J. (2011). *Shamans and Analysts: New Insights on the Wounded Healer*. London: Routledge.

Mitchell, S. (1993). *Hope and Dread in Psychoanalysis*. New York: Basic Books.

Pao, P. (1969). The Syndrome of Delicate Self-Cutting. *British Journal of Medical Psychology, 42*: 195–206.

Pennebaker, J. (1991). *Opening Up: The Healing Power of Confiding in Others*. New York: Avon.

Perez Sawyer, A. (2015). *Smoking Cigarettes, Eating Glass: A Psychologist's Memoir*. Santa Fe: Santa Fe Writer's Project.

Phillips, A. (1994). *On Kissing, Tickling and Being Bored: Psychoanalytic Essays on the Unexamined Life*. Cambridge, MA: Harvard University Press.

Sedgwick, D. (1994). *The Wounded Healer: Counter-Transference from a Jungian Perspective*. New York: Routledge.

Stolorow, R., & Atwood, G. (2002). *Contexts of Being: The Intersubjective Foundations of Psychological Life*. New York: Routledge.

Sussman, M. (1992). *A Curious Calling*. Northvale, NJ: Jason Aronson.

Sussman, M. (1995). *A Perilous Calling: The Hazards of Psychotherapy Practice*. New York: Wiley.

Wallin, D. (2007). *Attachment in Psychotherapy*. New York: Guilford Press.

Weiser, B. (2015). A Down-to-Earth Defense Lawyer with Felonies on His Resume. *The New York Times*, September 12.

White, M., & Epston, D. (1990). *Narrative Means to Therapeutic Ends*. New York: Norton.

Yalom, I. (2002). *The Gift of Therapy: An Open Letter to a New Generation of Therapists and Their Patients*. New York: HarperCollins.

Chapter 1

The mystique of the psychotherapist

Sharon K. Farber

Several years ago I saw the play *Freud's Last Session*. Upon leaving the theater, I was given a button to pin to my coat, saying "I Had a Session with Freud." The mystique of the psychoanalyst remains with us.

There has been an increasing and dramatic shift in the past two decades in recognizing the importance of the therapist's contribution to the therapeutic process. The increased focus on the relational and intersubjective places the emphasis not on the analyst's authority as the expert, but on the relationship between two vulnerable human beings who are constantly influencing and affecting each other.

Nonetheless, there is an imbalance of power that makes the patient uniquely vulnerable and so selecting a therapist should be made from an informed vantage point. Both credentialed persons as well as quacks can be harmful therapists (Singer & Lalich 1996), as you will read later.

Potential patients must be aware of their rights and choices and not be afraid of being inquisitive. Do not assume that a therapist has been trained in one of the mental health disciplines, will know what kind of treatment you need, and can refer you to someone who specializes in it, if necessary. Do not assume that the therapist has had his own personal experience of the psychoanalysis or psychoanalytic psychotherapy that is essential for the therapist to be aware of his own wounds and blind spots.

The truth is that many so-called therapists are not trained in a mental health discipline, an unfortunate state of affairs because there has been inadequate monitoring of the profession in general. In the U.S., licensing requirements vary from state to state. For example, in New York, there is no license to practice psychotherapy so anyone who wants can hang out a shingle stating that he or she is a psychotherapist. The phone repairer can; so can the butcher, the baker, and candlestick maker. There are, however, licenses in clinical psychology, clinical social work, psychiatry, creative arts therapy, marriage and family therapy, psychoanalysis, and mental health counseling. What the public does not know is that an individual can be licensed in these professions and listed on insurance panels, but that this is no guarantee that the clinician has actually had the specialized training, consistent supervision, and his own personal psychotherapy that is needed to become a competent psychotherapist. Patients risk being harmed by some of the therapies in vogue, being exploited by unscrupulous psychotherapists. Any potential patient should ask about these matters.

The public is presented with many bewildering choices that proclaim to address a variety of symptoms and disorders. A sampling of just a few of the more recent therapist offerings includes guided visualization, hypnotherapy, past-life regression, thought-field therapy, eye movement desensitizaton and reprocessing, somatic experiencing, psychoanalysis, rebirthing, psychoanalytically oriented psychotherapy, alien abduction therapy, inner child healing, breathwork, cognitive-behavioral therapy, dialectical behavioral therapy (DBT), and more. Some are legitimate treatments, while some may be what have been called crazy therapies (Singer & Lalich 1996).

Often fad therapies are promoted by practitioners imposing an agenda that may not fit the patient's needs and that has nothing to do with research and science. The therapist may present himself as the expert, the authority on mental disorders to the needy vulnerable patient who is in pain and wants relief—a clear imbalance of power. It is the therapist's ethical duty not to exploit this imbalance but unfortunately, as in all professions, there are those who are ethical and others who are not. A therapist may be clever and charismatic enough to disguise the unethical and sometimes illegal nature of what is occurring. Women in particular have been victims of "crazy therapies" at the hands of male therapists. Good therapy should help one to become more independent, autonomous, and responsible.

Unfortunately, however, only a small proportion of professional training programs in the mental health field require their candidates to be in their own personal psychotherapy. I think that most therapists go into this field because it resonates with personal difficulties they have grown up with themselves; they can be regarded as wounded healers. Their own experience of confronting their own difficulties in their own psychotherapy can give them a special kind of empathy in understanding their patients. But there are therapists whose understanding of their own difficulties is inadequate, leading them to use the patient's treatment for their own self-serving needs

Why should anyone seeking a psychotherapist look for someone trained in the use of transference, the unconscious, and dreams when there are so many other different kinds of therapy to select? In general, finding a good psychoanalytic psychotherapist is a good way to start. A good therapist is flexible enough to integrate techniques from other schools of treatment when needed, such as cognitive-behavioral, family systems or dialectical behavioral therapy. In the course of treatment, the therapist may find that another kind of treatment may be needed as an adjunct to psychoanalytic treatment. For example, he may recommend EMDR (eye movement desensitization and reprocessing) to a patient who has experienced severe trauma that remains unresolved. Some therapists may be trained in EMDR as well as psychoanalytic psychotherapy; if not, the patient may have a few EMDR sessions with an EMDR therapist while continuing his usual psychotherapy. A good therapist must be flexible enough to know that there is no one-size-fits-all treatment, and must be able to integrate other modalities into the basic therapy. That is, your therapist may find that there are times when it is necessary to integrate non-analytic techniques into the treatment, either doing it himself or referring out to another clinician.

The therapist as enlightened witness

An enlightened witness is someone who has found the courage to face up to his own woundedness, who has achieved autonomy without having to compensate by exercising power over others (Miller 2007). People need the help of an enlightened witness to cope with their present life and at the same time stay in touch with the knowing and suffering children they once were.

> The body remembers everything done to it but cannot express itself in words . . . Unlike the body, the adult cognitive system knows little about events of long ago. Conscious memories are fragmentary and unreliable. But the cognitive system has extensive knowledge, a well-developed intellect, and a trove of experience that children cannot have. As adults are no longer helpless, they can give the inner child (the body) protection by listening to it, by enabling it to tell the stories in whatever way it can. In the light of these stories, the adult's mysterious and incomprehensible fears and emotions will begin to make sense. At last they are situated in a context and are no longer so menacing. In the company of someone ready to take the distress of children seriously, one is no longer alone with one's stories. This is where the therapist comes in.
>
> (op. cit., p. 122)

It is possible to find the right therapist if you know what you want and need. You need an honest, empathic person who can help you take the knowledge stored in your body seriously because that person has successfully done it himself. To find out if a therapist is that kind of person, you need to ask many questions about whatever you need to know. You can ask the therapist if she had difficult experiences in her own childhood. Was she abused or otherwise humiliated? You can ask about her experiences during her training. What helped? What did not? Many therapists will probably be surprised by such questions because most patients do not know or are too afraid to ask them, but nonetheless should have the courage and self-confidence to respond candidly. It is not necessary for the therapist to reveal details of her private experience, but should tell you enough to let you feel that this person just might be an empathic witness to your life story.

The importance of the therapist's personal psychotherapy and advanced training

Some psychotherapists go into treatment initially because of personal problems and then realize, through their treatment, that they want to go on to use what they have learned about themselves to help others, and so enroll for advanced training at a psychoanalytic institute, an out-of-pocket expense that is considerable and is not covered by scholarships or fellowships. After training, some therapists choose to have private psychotherapy, which is generally more intensive than the training analysis he may have as part of his training. Even after his personal analysis has ended, he may return periodically as needed. If he runs into some difficulty with a patient, he may return to his analyst for help in dealing with it or may pay for private consultation or supervision. Any or all of this is completely voluntary and not legally necessary. The therapist does this because he wants to be able to use himself optimally in order to help others resolve their own pain and struggles.

The psychoanalytic relationship

The psychoanalytic relationship is unlike any other, lacking the niceties and refinements of ordinary social relationships. When we as therapists ask how a patient is, we really want to know. When the patient asks "How are you?"—a social nicety—a good therapist generally will not disclose that he is really in a lousy mood or is bloated with gas unless there is a good reason for the patient to know this.

The therapist has to study himself at least as carefully as the patient, without taking the focus off the patient, and evaluate the relational process occurring between the two. It is the joint participation of patient and psychotherapist that becomes a unique *analyzing instrument* (Isakower 1992). The patient's free association and the analyst's free-floating attention comprise the two halves of the analyzing instrument, a kind of reciprocal free association, where both may say what pops into their minds without censoring it. The analyst "must turn his own unconscious like a receptive organ towards the transmitting unconscious of his patient. He must adjust himself to the patient as a telephone receiver is adjusted to the transmitting microphone" (Freud 1912, pp. 115–116). Once the session starts, each goes into an altered state of consciousness in which they communicate effectively with each other (Farber 2013; Farber in press). They become

> both artist and medium for each other. For the analyst as artist his medium is the patient . . .; for the patient as artist the analyst becomes his medium . . . as living human media they have their own creative capabilities, so that they are both creators themselves.
>
> (Loewald 1988, p. 75)

Psychoanalytic treatment at its best permits the patient to tell his own story in his own way, in his own words, revealing that which he may have hidden out of shame, embarrassment, guilt, or the feeling that no one would be really interested. A good therapist will join the patient in a mutual exploration of how the problem began and what the patient can do to free himself of it. Through examining the story of his life with a therapist who can listen empathically and help him develop a new perspective on it, they can together find ways to change the life story for the better.

Success in therapy is correlated with the "fit" between patient and therapist, usually apparent within the first few sessions. The successful therapist does what a good parent does. He creates a safe and secure attachment relationship (Wallin 2007), which is the best predictor of success in treatment.

The whole self of the therapist must be attuned to the patient, understanding his feelings conceptually as well as feeling his feelings. A good therapist uses himself like a microtonal tuning fork that resonates with multiple emotional pitches and the nuanced quiver of emotional tone of the patient (Farber in press; Hopenwasser 2008; Wylie & Turner 2011). It must be

> a hands-on, body-on, mind-on therapy, in which the therapist's whole self vibrated like a tuning fork to every quiver in the client's being without, however, losing the basic emotional stability that the client needed to regulate his or her runaway emotions.
>
> (Wylie & Turner 2011, p. 25)

Long-term psychoanalytic psychotherapy, sometimes called psychodynamic treatment, has been found to be an effective treatment for complex mental disorders, at least as effective as cognitive-behavioral therapy (CBT) (Leichsenring & Rabung 2008; Shedler 2010). Those advocating "evidence-based therapy" tend to denigrate psychodynamic treatments or, as Shedler's research has shown, their own stereotyped caricatures of psychodynamic treatment. Psychodynamic therapies aim at enhancing self-knowledge in the context of a deeply personal relationship between therapist and patient. Learning to do it effectively is a never-ending process. I am often amazed by how much I continue to learn.

The best practitioners choose to obtain their own personal psychoanalytic treatment and consistently continue to seek help throughout their careers from respected colleagues or return for another stint at treatment (Bellows 2007). They have the flexibility to go from the role of therapist to that of patient quite easily without feeling any stigma or weakness of character.

> They practice what they preach . . . Their attitude is the same as for friends and neighbors who ask what to do about crises or neurotic problems; they suggest that they commence therapy. They believe in what they are doing and they perceive therapy as a constructive measure that not only relieves symptoms but also leads to personal growth.
>
> (Greenberg & Kaslow 1984, p. 20)

You can gauge what kind of therapist a clinician is when you meet with him and find that he listens and asks questions in a way that lets you feel understood. Not all therapists have this special talent. Sometimes it means traveling a bit further than you would like rather than settling for one of several names included on your insurance plan or for someone who is conveniently located.

The initial consultation

There is no "one-size-fits-all" therapist and there is no "one-size-fits-all" treatment. The initial consultation is just that, a consultation that can give you the opportunity to see if the therapist has something of value to offer you, such as a shift in perspective on your problem or a sense of hope, or perhaps he may think that you might do better to consult with a different kind of therapist and may make such a referral. The therapist should consider whether he has the knowledge or expertise to be particularly helpful to you or whether it might be better to refer you to a colleague who does. For example, many patients suffer the effects of childhood trauma and would be wise to seek a therapist who specializes in trauma or trauma-related conditions.

When making that initial phone call or online inquiry, you should feel free to ask the therapist about his training and experience. The relationship between patient and therapist is a unique one, in very important ways comparable to the relationships between clients and lawyers, physicians, dentists, and accountants. It is important that the patient be told that largely what will happen is that they will talk; the therapist will listen carefully, ask questions when needed to clarify certain matters, and provide feedback to the patient or ask further questions. The therapist should tell you what to expect. You should expect to hear how the therapist understands the problem and what the treatment should be.

Boundary crossings and boundary violations

There are common boundary crossings that are minor departures in everyday technique which may be harmless, done by the therapist who thinks the patient may benefit, such as accepting a gift or hugging when it seems called for. Then there are the boundary crossings which may be a harbinger of a downward slide on a slippery slope toward frank boundary violations (Celenza 2007). For example, many of the steps on the slippery slope, if taken separately or in certain contexts, may be part of the therapist's natural style and may not be problematic and must be examined from both the therapist's and patient's point of view. It is not the behaviors *per se* that are problematic; it is when they are engaged in for the therapist's self-serving reasons that they become problematic.

Oddly enough, although psychoanalytic psychotherapy seems to present the greater risk because of the more intense and intimate nature of the patient–therapist relationship, compared to family therapy or cognitive-behavioral treatment, those who practice it have the lowest rate of boundary violations (Celenza 2007).

If at any time you are in psychotherapy you find yourself having doubts about the treatment or your therapist, the best thing you can do is to talk with your therapist about it. If this is not helpful, you should consider consulting with another therapist about it. You need a professional opinion other than your therapist's, from someone who has no vested interest in the outcome. Sometimes it is necessary to end your therapy and find another therapist.

References

Bellows, K. (2007). Psychotherapists' Personal Psychotherapy and Its Perceived Influence on Clinical Practice. *Bulletin of the Menninger Clinic, 71*: 204–226.

Celenza, A. (2007). *Sexual Boundary Violations: Therapeutic, Supervisory, and Academic Contexts.* Lanham, MD: Jason Aronson.

Farber, S. (2013). *Hungry for Ecstasy: Trauma, the Brain, and the Influence of the Sixties.* Lanham, MD: Jason Aronson/Rowman & Littlefield.

Farber, S. (in press). Becoming a Telepathic Tuning Fork: Anomalous Experience and the Relational Mind. *Psychoanalytic Dialogues.*

Freud, S. (1912). Recommendations to Physicians Practising Psycho-Analysis. In: *The Standard Edition of the Complete Psychological Works of Sigmund Freud*, vol. 12 (pp. 109–120). London: Hogarth Press.

Greenberg, S., & Kaslow, F. (1984). Psychoanalytic Treatment for Therapists, Residents, and Other Trainees. In: *Psychotherapy with Psychotherapists* (pp. 19–32). New York: Psychology Press.

Hopenwasser, K. (2008). Being in Rhythm: Dissociative Attunement in Therapeutic Process. *Journal of Trauma and Dissociation, 9* (3): 349–367.

Isakower, O. (1992). The Analyzing Instrument in the Teaching and Conduct of the Analytic Process. *Journal of Clinical Psychoanalysis, 1*: 182–222.

Leichsenring, A., & Rabung, S. (2008). Effectiveness of Long-Term Psychodynamic Psychotherapy: A Meta-Analysis. *Journal of the American Medical Association, 3* (13): 1551–1565.

Loewald, H. (1988). *Sublimation: Inquiries into Theoretical Psychoanalysis.* New Haven, CT: Yale University Press.

Miller, A. (2007). *Free from Lies: Discovering Your True Needs.* New York: Norton.

Shedler, J. (2010). The Efficacy of Psychodynamic Psychotherapy. *American Psychologist, 65* (2): 98–109.

Singer, M., & Lalich, J. (1996). *Crazy Therapies: What Are They? Do They Work?* New York: Jossey-Bass.

Wallin, D. (2007). *Attachment in Psychotherapy.* New York: Guilford Press.

Wylie, M., & Turner, L. (2011). The Attuned Therapist: Does Attachment Theory Really Matter? *Psychotherapy Networker, 35* (2): 18–49.

Chapter 2

The concept of the wounded healer

Sharon K. Farber

Carl Jung (1951) believed we have a collective unconscious in which exists the archetype of the wounded healer, whose wounds are both a burden and a driving force in his need to heal the problems of others (Farber 2013). He adopted the term *wounded healer* from the ancient legend of the physician Asclepius, who, because he was able to identify his own wounds, could create a sanctuary in order to treat others. Jung thought that an illness of the soul could be the best possible form of training for a healer and wrote that only a wounded healer who had healed his own wounds could heal effectively.

> We could say, without too much exaggeration, that a good half of every treatment that probes at all deeply consists in the doctor's examining himself, for only what he can put right in himself can he hope to put right in the patient. It is no loss, either, if he feels that gives the measure of his power to heal. This, and nothing else, is the meaning of the Greek myth of the wounded physician.
>
> (Jung 1951, p. 116)

The wounded healer's awareness of his own wounds can equip him with a special advantage in working with the wounded activating his own healing power and empathy (Adler 1956). Martin Lipp said, "My wounds become my spectacles, helping me to see what I encounter with empathy, and with a grateful sense of privilege" (1980, p. 107).

All theories of psychotherapy include a theory of how change takes place in the patient but there has been little said about how the therapist is changed by the encounter (Kottler & Carlson 2005). However, Jung said, anticipating the relational approach, that psychotherapy worked best when the patient brought the perfect balm for the therapist's wound, when both are changed or healed by this process.

> A client brings up an issue and we realize, as we are responding, that it is one we have not yet fully resolved. We talk about finding new meaning in life and discover new meaning for ourselves. We confront a client about some actions

taken and realize that we were talking as much to ourselves as to the client. A particular conversation comes back to haunt us, gripping us in a way that we can't let go of unless we face the underlying issue. New decisions in our lives are based, in part, on dialogue we have had with clients. On and on the parallel process continues, every week, day, and hour . . . .

All the while I was confronting my client with the extent he was exaggerating reality and engaging in self-pity, a part of me soon recognized that I was talking as much to myself as I was to him . . . the more I confronted my clients about the ways they were inflicting misery on themselves, the more I had to look at the ways I was doing the same thing.

(Kottler & Carlson 2005, pp. 6–11)

There is a kind of reciprocal influence and mutual growth that occurs in therapeutic relationships. As Jung said, "The meeting of two personalities is like the contact of two chemical substances; if there is any reaction, both are transformed" (Jung 1955, p. 49).

Irvin Yalom, who considers treatment as an individual, dialectical process, in which the therapist, as a person, participates just as much as the patient, said, "I prefer to think of my patients and myself as fellow travelers, a term that abolishes distinctions between 'them' and 'us' (the healers)" (Yalom 2009, p. 8).

Jung (1961) thought the wounded healer never fully overcomes the major problems of his life but by struggling with and subduing them, he can continue developing his sensitivity toward and empathy for others. "In a word, the traveler who has suffered deeply and recovered can boldly face other sufferers' deepest feelings . . ." (Goldberg 1991, p. 13). In doing psychoanalytic work, we cannot really hide our wounds or weaknesses. We must confront them and make them conscious.

One analyst recently told the author that he would never quit practicing and seeing patients because if he did he would get sick again. In substance he is saying that it is only through his own exposure in analytical work with patients that he is able to stay in touch with himself and find the roots and sources of wholeness to the degree that he can stay in some kind of balance.

(Groesbeck 1975, p. 144)

Perhaps this is why Martin Bergmann maintained a 30-hour-a-week practice until his death at the age of almost 101.

The psychotherapist

"looks for patients, as that is his vocation . . . Because of his illness, the patient activates his inner . . . healer" (Groesbeck 1975, pp. 127–128). This inner healer, however, is not integrated into consciousness, but is projected onto and constellated in the outer person of the healer. So too, the healer's own vulnerability . . . is activated by his contact with the sick person.

This largely unconscious, opposite pole of the archetypal image is projected onto the patient, rather than being integrated. Groesbeck continues:
"If the relationship remains like this, no movement to a real cure occurs
though outward remedies, physical and psychological, are applied. Real cure
can only take place if the patient gets in touch with and receives help from his
inner healer. And this can only happen if the projections . . . are withdrawn.
Hence, the healer must be in touch with and be aware of his own wounded
side, if these projections are to be withdrawn. If the projections remain, both
healer and patient attempt to manipulate the other to conform to inner need."
(Miller & Baldwin 1987, pp. 141–142)

The patient as therapist to the analyst

The research of Henry (1971) and Burton (1972) found that most therapists came
from families in which a serious problem existed, occasionally a devastating physical illness but more often a serious mental disorder (O'Connor 2001). A child in
such a family may be selected be a healer for the ill person, as Alice Miller (1979)
described. Many psychotherapists grew up with an unusual ability for empathy
that grew out of their parent's narcissistic need for the child to repair his defective
sense of self. This ability became a gift, as they became wounded healers.

Searles (1979) believed the child has an inherent need to rescue his parents that
later becomes transformed into an inherent need to rescue the analyst (Flarsheim
1975).The patient is ill, says Searles, because his therapeutic strivings have been
warped by his family environment. It is the analyst's failure to recognize that
the patient's long-repressed striving accounts more than any other interpersonal
element in the treatment, for the patient's unconscious resistance to the therapeutic
process. The patient wants to be a therapist to his analyst. Erich Fromm said:

> The analyst analyzes the patient but the patient also analyzes the analyst,
> because the analyst, by sharing the unconscious of the patient, cannot help
> clarifying his own unconscious. Hence, we have the relational concept that
> the analyst not only cures the patient but is also cured by him.
> (Fromm 1960, p. 112)

I met with a professional woman in her mid-seventies, whose concerns turned
to retiring from her full-time academic position and starting a new part-time
position, a partial retirement, which led to voicing her fears and anxiety about
death. I shared these existential concerns too and told her that and how helpful
I too found it to talk with her about this.

Author Susan Sontag wrote, "One can't look steadily at death any more than
one can stare at the sun" (Roiphe 2016, p. 23). Having read Yalom's (2009)
Staring at the Sun: Overcoming the Terror of Death, I told her how helpful I had
found it. She read it too. At the end of one session she remarked with surprise
that our time had gone by so quickly, to which I blurted out, "Time really flies

when you're talking about death," and we both dissolved in laughter. Norman Cousins (1981) knew what he was talking about when he said that laughter is the best medicine.

Well-known wounded healers who have come out of the closet

The helping professions—medicine, nursing, the ministry and psychotherapy—attract more than their share of those with psychological problems (Gilroy et al. 2002). Oliver Sacks wrote numerous best-selling books, mostly collections of case studies of fascinating neurological oddities, or *fascinomas* as they are called in medical slang (Farber 2013). In her review of one of his books Wendy Lesser said, "Everybody is peculiar. Oliver Sacks wants us to know that we are all links in the great chain of weirdness" (Lesser 1995, p. 1).

Born to orthodox Jewish parents, both physicians, he was the youngest of four children. A number of traumatic experiences in childhood took their toll on him. His brother Michael was schizophrenic, erupting at times in floridly psychotic and delusional states that made him and his two other brothers ashamed and embarrassed. When Oliver was six, he and Michael were evacuated together to a boarding school to escape the wartime blitz. Unbeknownst to his parents, they lived on meager rations of vegetables and suffered punitive treatment by a sadistic headmaster.

He did not publicly disclose his homosexuality until he wrote about it in his memoir (Sacks 2015), published shortly before he died at age eighty-two. When he was eighteen and his father, concerned that he seemed to have little interest in girls, inquired about it, he confessed that he was attracted to boys but had not acted on his feelings. He knew his mother could not tolerate knowing about this and told his father not to tell her. He told her anyway.

> "You are an abomination," she said. "I wish you had never been born." Then she left and did not speak to me for several days. When she did speak there was no reference to what she had said (nor did she ever refer to the matter again), but something had come between us. My mother. so open and supportive in most ways, was harsh and inflexible in this area. A Bible reader like my father, she loved the Psalms and the Song of Solomon but was haunted by the terrible verses in Leviticus: "Thou shall not lie with mankind, as with womankind. It is an abomination."
>
> (op. cit., pp. 9–10)

He lived alone for most of his life, revealing that his extreme shyness was a life-long impediment in his personal life. He remained celibate for about thirty-five years, beginning a relationship with writer Bill Hayes when he was seventy-seven.

Oddly enough, Sacks knew five surgeons with Tourette's syndrome, characterized by convulsive tics, involuntary mimicry of others' words or actions, and occasional involuntary obscenities (Sacks 1996). The thought of someone with Tourette's practicing surgery is the stuff of nightmares. Mort Duran has Tourette's syndrome, obsessive-compulsive disorder and attention deficit hyperactivity disorder. Not only is he a surgeon, he, believe it or not, also flies a plane. He can harness the power of his mind to focus on what he needs to do, whether in the operating room or the cockpit.

Duran began having tics at seven, soon followed by movements that were either involuntary or compulsive, strange hoots and utterances, and sudden rages during which he could not help throwing things. He was thirty-seven years old by the time he was diagnosed with Tourette's. Over the years he learned to compensate for his twitching habits. "Every time I felt one of my tics coming on, I would back off my surgery, do my twitch, and then resume again," he said. Now, his tics remit almost completely while he is performing surgery. Duran's hospital colleagues were accustomed to his Tourette's and he felt at ease with them, feeling free to touch or tap them with his fingertips. When sharing a sofa with a colleague, Sacks observed him twisting suddenly on his side and tapping his colleague's shoulder with his toes. He told Sacks that when he first began working at the hospital, he allowed himself to skip in the hallways only after checking to be sure no one was looking but now when he skips or hops, no one pays attention. Sometimes the staff prepared his patients by telling them that Doran is a wonderful surgeon and although he sometimes makes strange movements and sounds because he has Tourette's, they should not worry, because it never affects his surgery. Sacks observed him in the operating room. Although Duran's surgical assistants have worked with him for years, they are still amazed to see his Tourette's disappear and say it is like a miracle. Duran himself is amazed that he can become so focused, confident, and absorbed in what he is doing.

Alice Flaherty is another neurologist who is a wounded healer (Farber 2013; Flaherty 2004). She had to take medication to get her overwhelming need to write under control. Although she had always written more than most people, she had no intention of writing a book when she was a neurology resident, working up to 110 hours a week. She took notes so compulsively that it took over her life. The notes were transformed into her first book, *The Massachusetts General Hospital Handbook of Neurology* (Flaherty & Post 2000), described as the most widely used neurology text in its class. Then she became pregnant and gave birth to stillborn twin boys. She sank into a deep depression for ten days when she suddenly became wildly agitated and full of ideas, scribbling them on her arm while driving or on toilet paper while in the bathroom. Her writing had spiraled out of control, becoming hypermanic ecstasies of writing, a manic defense against her terrible sense of loss. She ricocheted daily between euphoria and terror.

> The world was flooded with meaning, I believed I had unique access to the Kingdom of Sorrow, about which I had an obligation to enlighten my very tolerant friends and colleagues through essays and letters. While postpartum major depression occurs after one in ten deliveries, postpartum mania occurs

after one in a thousand. Mania and depression can come in complicated mixtures. As I found out, one manic feature is hypergraphia . . . Its principal effect on me was to make me hole up in my office and write. Why pathologize this and call it a disease? I could still do my normal job. But my writing *felt* like a disease: I could not stop, and it sucked me away from family and friends. Sensations outside of language dried up: music became irritating discord, the visual world grew faint . . . While my hypergraphia felt like a disease, it also felt like one of the best things that has ever happened to me. It still does.

(Flaherty 2004, p. 11)

What does Flaherty's personal experience have to do with the writing of so-called normal people? "The answer is that although my brain has a screw loose, everyone has the same screw" (Farber 2013, p. 308; Flaherty 2004, p. 13). Diagnosed with bipolar illness, her wildly shifting moods were stabilized with the help of medication and her hypermanic writing calmed down (Flaherty 2004). She seemed to have rapid-cycling bipolar disorder, in which a period of depression or mania can, in some cases, last only a few minutes before the patient retreats back into the opposite mode. This is the most dangerous type of bipolar illness because the person is more likely to attempt suicide (Garcia-Amador et al. 2009; Tillman 2014) or kill himself unintentionally when acting on hypermanic grandiose beliefs. The psychiatric unit where Alice Flaherty was hospitalized is the same one where she later became a neurological consultant.

Her woundedness taught Flaherty a great deal about the drive to write and she published *The Midnight Disease: The Drive to Write, Writer's Block, and the Creative Brain* (Farber 2013; Flaherty 2004). Through her illness, Flaherty learned that it is emotion, the powerful wish to communicate, that drives language. When the drive to communicate is hindered, powerful neural changes result. Flaherty found that people who are suffering comprise the largest group of amateur writers. "Suffering triggers limbic system and temporal lobe activity through their roles in emotion, and . . . increases the desire to write and communicate" (Flaherty 2004, p. 42).

Clinical psychologist Marsha Linehan developed dialectical behavior therapy, a treatment modality designed for patients with borderline personality disorder, but also used to treat other kinds of mental health disorders. She was brave enough to disclose that she has suffered from what she thinks is borderline personality disorder all her adult life. She was hospitalized for twenty-six months, during which she cut and burned herself and banged her head against the floor and walls. Much of the time, she had to be physically restrained. With the help of outpatient psychotherapy, she was able to turn her life around, earned a Ph.D. in clinical psychology, obtained further training and became a prominent clinician and researcher.

"Are you one of us?"

The patient wanted to know, and her therapist, Marsha M. Linehan, . . . had a ready answer. It was the one she always used to cut the question short, whether a patient asked it hopefully, accusingly or knowingly, having glimpsed the macramé of faded burns, cuts and welts on Dr. Linehan's arms: "You mean, have I suffered?"

"No, Marsha," the patient replied, in an encounter last spring. "I mean one of us. Like us. Because if you were, it would give all of us so much hope."

"That did it," said Dr. Linehan, 68, who told her story in public for the first time last week before an audience of friends, family and doctors at the Institute of Living, the Hartford clinic where she was first treated for extreme social withdrawal at age 17. "So many people have begged me to come forward, and I just thought—well, I have to do this. I owe it to them. I cannot die a coward."

(Carey 2011, pp. A1–A17)

Kay Redfield Jamison also wrote about the intriguing relationship between mood disorders and creativity. As an adolescent, she knew there was something very wrong with her when she became transformed from an exuberant person into a psychotically depressed and delusional person who wanted to end her life (Jamison 1995). Raised in a very White, Anglo-Saxon, Protestant, military world, where order and appearances were paramount, she had no idea that she was ill or that there was treatment for it. Even if she had known that she had a treatable illness, it would not have been acceptable to be treated for it. Years later, after marrying and obtaining her doctorate in clinical psychology, she joined the faculty in the Department of Psychiatry at the University of California in Los Angeles.

I was hired as an assistant professor . . . got good parking for the first time in my life, joined the faculty club posthaste, and began to work my way up the academic food chain. I had a glorious—as it turns out, too glorious—summer, and within three months of becoming a professor, I was ravingly psychotic.

(op. cit., p. 63)

Her full-blown mania started out with feeling wonderful, enthusiastic, and having boundless energy. She went on shopping sprees, bringing home expensive jewelry, sexy clothing, even a dozen snakebite kits (cheaper by the dozen), because God had told her that an infestation of rattlesnakes was about to happen. She pounced upon twenty books published by Penguin; how wonderful to have her own personal penguin colony. She stayed up all night working round the clock; she could not follow the course of her own thinking. Her marriage was falling apart, and she separated from her husband. She dated a colleague who thought she was manic-depressive and confronted her with the need to take lithium. It became terrifying to find that she did not have a mind to rely on any more. She was a psychologist and although she wanted help, was deeply embarrassed about having to seek it. She found herself doing what had previously been unthinkable because she realized she had no choice; if she did not get professional help she was likely to lose her job, her already rocky marriage, and her life (Jamison 1995). Lithium had only recently been approved for use in mania when it was prescribed for her, and she was given a much higher dose than is usual today. She had terrible side effects but even worse was her self-denial (Jamison 1995). Although she knew very well that if manic-depressive illness remains untreated, it returns with a vengeance—more severely and more frequently, she was convinced that she was the exception that proves the rule. What was more to the point was that she clung ferociously to her manic ecstasies, like many other manic-depressives. Life seemed boring when she was "normal."

And so she went on and off lithium for years. Having been raised in a world where she was expected to be totally self-reliant and not need anything resembling a crutch, it simply was not done. When she was twenty-eight, she took a huge overdose of lithium to kill herself. Fortuitously, her phone rang and she picked it up. It was her brother calling to check on her. Each time she stopped taking her lithium, she became suicidally depressed. It took several such episodes before she could accept the reality that she needed both medication and psychotherapy.

> At this point in my existence, I cannot imagine leading a normal life without both taking lithium and having the benefits of psychotherapy. Lithium prevents my seductive but disastrous highs, diminishes my depressions, clears out the wool and webbing from my disordered thinking, slows me down, gentles me out, keeps me from ruining my career and relationships, keeps me out of a hospital, alive, and makes psychotherapy possible. But ineffably, psychotherapy heals. It makes some sense of the confusion, reins in the terrifying thoughts and feelings, returns some control and hope and possibility of learning from it all. Pills cannot, do not, ease one back into reality; they only bring one back headlong, careening, and faster than can be endured at times. Psychotherapy is a sanctuary; it is a battleground; it is a place I have been psychotic, neurotic, elated, confused, and despairing beyond belief. But, always, it is where I have believed—or learned to believe—that I might someday be able to contend with all of this. No pill can help me deal with the problem of not wanting to take pills; likewise, no amount of psychotherapy alone can prevent my manias and depressions. I need both. It is an odd thing, owing life to pills, one's own quirks and tenacities, and this unique, strange, and ultimately profound relationship called psychotherapy.
>
> (Farber 2012, pp. 303–304; Jamison 1995, pp. 88–89)

Lauren Slater, another clinical psychologist, practiced for eleven years before embarking on a full-time writing career. She takes anticonvulsant medication daily, has had auras all her life and symptoms that have been diagnosed as being consistent with temporal lobe epilepsy. She also suffered from severe depression, anorexia, and self-injury, and was one of the first people to take Prozac. In *Three Spheres* (Slater 2005), she wrote of visiting her new patient in the same hospital where she herself had been hospitalized (Farber 2013).

Mental health doesn't mean making the pains go away. I don't believe they ever go away. I do believe that nearly every person . . . has the same warped impulses, the same scarlet id as the wobbliest of borderlines, the most florid of psychotics. Only the muscles to hold things in check—to channel and funnel—are stronger. I have not healed so much as learned to sit still and wait while the pain does its dancing work, trying not to panic or twist in ways that make the blades tear deeper, finally infecting the wounds.

(Slater 2005, p. 17)

Trauma expert Bessel van der Kolk (2014) grew up in postwar Holland, playing in bombed-out buildings. His father was such an outspoken opponent of the Nazis that he was sent to an internment camp. Although he never spoke of his war experiences, he was given to outbursts of explosive rage that stunned Bessel. He was also frightened by his mother, who at times alluded to her own childhood trauma. "She had the unnerving habit of fainting when I asked her what her life was like as a little girl and then blaming me for making her so upset" (op. cit., p. 9).

Wounded healer, shaman, medicine man, witch doctor

The native professional who alleviates distress and anxiety is known as the medicine man, witch doctor, native healer, voodoo sorcerer, or shaman (Kakar 1982; Merchant 2011). Many in Western culture construct their suffering as signs to explore a shamanic path. Years ago I was startled to hear a patient say her boyfriend was studying to become a shaman. I laughed when I spotted a book titled *So You Want to Become a Shaman*, not then realizing that the path of the psychotherapist is similar to the shaman's.

Many physicians, nurses, psychotherapists, and clergy embody Jung's (1951) archetype, having experienced severe trauma and/or mental illness. In the 1960s, Allen Ginsburg told us that life should be ecstasy and went to India in pursuit of it. "And so began his quest for beatitude that sent him to India and Japan, changing his life and generating several generations of beatniks, hipsters, artists and writers, gurus, shamans, cult leaders, and the mentally ill" (Farber 2013, p. 105). Eastern religions, with their emphasis on the cultivation of trance states, became appealing, and the shaman, who could self-induce a trance in order to heal people of "spirit illness," acquired a romanticized image as a very wise man with knowledge of another separate reality (Kakar 1982).

Just as the talented psychoanalyst comes to his clinical wisdom through knowing his own suffering, the shaman's wisdom is thought to come to him through his suffering, particularly the voluntary mutilation and starvation of his body (Farber 2013; Jung 1954; Kakar 1982). Jung said:

the shamanistic techniques in themselves often cause the medicine-man a good deal of discomfort, if not actual pain. At all events, the "making of a medicine man" involves, in many parts of the world, so much agony of body and soul that permanent psychic injuries may result. His "approximation of the saviour" is an obvious consequence of this, in confirmation of the mythological truth that the wounded healer is the agent of healing, and that the sufferer takes away suffering.

(Jung 1954, p. 256)

The shaman is not specially groomed or trained; he is an ordinary person who has suffered a great emotional crisis in his life which has resulted in his falling ill. Through his illness he is thought to have gained a special wisdom that enables him to become a native healer. The illness really is an initiation rite to be survived so that he can emerge reborn, with the wisdom to heal. Claude Levi-Strauss (1964) pointed out that the shaman provides the sick member of his society with a language by which unexpressed and otherwise unexpressible psychic states can be immediately expressed. Both the shaman and the psychoanalytic psychotherapist establish a direct relationship with the patient's conscious mind and an indirect one with his unconscious, the analyst through listening, the shaman through speaking. Both must enter a trance or dissociated state in order to communicate most effectively with the patient (Bromberg 1998; Farber 2013; Kakar 1982).When Freud said, "The analyst must turn his own unconscious like a receptive organ towards the transmitting unconscious of his patient. He must adjust himself to the patient as a telephone receiver is adjusted to the transmitting microphone" (Freud 1912, pp. 115–116), he was referring to the analyst's state of absorption, a dissociated or trance-like telepathic process (Farber in press; Hesse & Van IJzendoorn 1998). I have noticed that with many patients, although we greet each other in the waiting room, upon entering the treatment room they say hello again, a subtle recognition of anticipating a shift into an altered state of conscious,

Both the shaman and the psychotherapist become transferential objects for the patient and, through the representations induced in the patient's mind, the protagonists of his conflict.

When the transference is established, the patient puts words into the mouth of the analyst by attributing to him alleged feelings and intentions; in the shaman's incarnation, on the other hand, the shaman speaks for the patient, putting into his mouth answers to questions that correspond to the interpretation of the patient's condition and with which he must become imbued.

(Kakar 1982, p. 91)

Rachel Naomi Remen, pioneer in integrative medicine, said:

The healing of our present woundedness may lie in recognizing and reclaiming the capacity we have to heal each other, the enormous power in the simplest of human relationships: the strength of a touch, the blessing of forgiveness, the grace of someone else taking you just as you are and finding in you an unsuspected goodness. Everyone alive has suffered. It is the wisdom gained from our wounds and from our own experiences of suffering that makes us able to heal. Becoming expert has turned out to be less important than remembering and trusting the wholeness in myself and everyone else. Expertise cures, but wounded people can best be healed by other wounded people. Only other wounded people can understand what is needed, for the healing of suffering is compassion, not expertise.

(Remen 1997, p. 221)

Christians consider Jesus a wounded healer, who knows how to heal our wounds because he experienced them himself. He is the Healer, the Wounded Healer. Henri Nouwen, a Catholic priest who struggled with depression, emphasized that

Loneliness is the minister's wound not only because he shares in the human condition, But also because of the unique human predicament of his profession. It is this wound which he is called to bind with more care and attention than others usually do. For a deep understanding of his own pain makes it possible for him to convert his weakness into strength and to offer his own experience as a source of healing to those who are often lost in the darkness of their own misunderstood sufferings.

(Nouwen 1979, p. 87)

Nouwen cited a Talmudic legend:

Rabbi Yoshua ben Levi came upon Elijah the prophet while he was standing at the entrance of Rabbi Simeron ben Yohai's cave . . . He asked Elijah, "When will the Messiah come?"
    Elijah replied, "Go and ask him yourself."
    "Where is he?"
    "Sitting at the gates of the city."
    "How shall I know him?"
    "He is sitting among the poor covered with wounds. The others unbind all their wounds at the same time and then bind them up again. But he unbinds one at a time and binds it up again, saying to himself. 'Perhaps I shall be needed: if so I must always be ready so as not to delay for a moment.'"
    The Messiah . . . is sitting among the poor, binding his wounds one at a time, waiting for the moment when he will be needed. He is called to be the wounded healer, the one who must look after his own wounds but at the same time be prepared to heal the wounds of others.

(op. cit., p. 81)

Nouwen tells the clergyperson that he needs to be at home in his own house, that he has to discover the center of his own life in his own heart. This is done by withdrawing into himself. James Hillman, director of studies at the C. G. Jung Institute in Zurich said:

> For the other person to open and talk requires a withdrawal of the counselor. I must withdraw to make room for the other . . . This withdrawal, rather than going-out-to-meet the other, is an intense act of concentration, a model for which can be found in the Jewish mystical doctrine of Tsimtsum . . . God had to create by withdrawal; He created the not-Him, the other, by self-concentration . . . On the human level, withdrawal of myself aids the other to come into being.
>
> (Hillman 1975, p. 31)

I have treated three wounded healer clergy, all women. One was an Episcopal priest; another became an Episcopal priest; and the third was a cantor in a synagogue. Interestingly, all three had eating disorders. The one who became a priest was a compulsive eater, in business initially. As I heard her spiritual concerns, I suggested that she read Episcopal priest Margaret Bullitt-Jonas' (1999) *Holy Hunger*, in which she wrote of her binge eating as a thwarted spiritual desire. The book spoke profoundly to her and she realized that it was a spiritual life she hungered for, not food. She enrolled in divinity school and became an Episcopal priest. The compulsive eating stopped with little conscious effort.

For many, the decision to become a psychotherapist is experienced as a calling in much the same way that some are called to the religious life, a sacred relationship. Theologian Martin Buber (1970) characterized the common form of human interaction as an "I–It" relationship, where subject deals with object, a superficial and meaningless relationship. In the I–Thou relationship, each person is both subject and object, and can recognize the wholeness of the other. Buber believed the greatest thing one person can do for another is to confirm the deepest thing within him. And so when a psychotherapist relates openly with a patient, he is creating an I–Thou relationship, which contributes to the wholeness and healing of each (Miller & Baldwin 1987). For psychologist and former minister David Elkins, "I–Thou comes by grace, a shaft of sunlight that penetrates our normal world . . . the sacred suddenly manifesting in what was only moments before an ordinary relationship" (Elkins 1998, p. 71).

Like those called to the religious life, we certainly do not do this work for the money. Compare psychotherapists' incomes to those in the financial industry and it is a joke. Many teachers do better financially. The rates for managed care insurance payments are insulting, even decreasing over time. This work is a labor of love, a calling.

Jung's archetype may have been derived from another Greek myth, that of the centaur Chiron, who was known as the Wounded Healer after he had been poisoned by one of Hercules' arrows. Because he was not able to heal himself, he suffered from an incurable wound and unending pain (Smith 1997). Shortly before he died, Jung wrote about Chiron. Perhaps Jung really knew on some level that like Chiron, he too had not healed his woundedness sufficiently, and had become a healer who hurts others, a wounding healer, a story told by John Kerr (1993) in *A Dangerous Method: The Story of Jung, Freud, and Sabina Spielrein*. Jung was the son of a chronically mentally ill mother. No wonder that he became a psychiatrist. When completing his psychiatric residency at the Burgholzli psychiatric clinic in Zurich, he was married and a father when he met his first patient, the psychotic, bizarre, and beautiful Sabina Spielrein. She improved dramatically and quickly due to his warmth and understanding. He was more than her doctor; he became her friend. As she continued to improve, their relationship became increasingly more romantic and he allowed her to seduce him. Their affair lasted a number of years before Jung ended it. This occurred in the early days of psychoanalysis, when Jung became Freud's closest colleague. When Freud discovered the affair, this was the beginning of the end of their collaboration and the start of Jung's deterioration (Jung 2012). He was never hospitalized, nor treated for his apparently psychotic breakdown, including hallucinations, gross disorientation, and suicidal thinking. It was ten years before he recovered, becoming a more complete, conscious, and compassionate person and psychiatrist.

The best-known wounding healer in popular culture is Hannibal Lecter, the serial killer and cannibal psychiatrist in the film *The Silence of the Lambs*. Another is Gregory House, M.D., from the television series *House*, a globally successful long-running television series (Hockley & Gardner 2011). House limps through the hospital with his walking stick, the concrete sign of his woundedness. Underlying the concept of the wounded healer is the notion that the experience of having been wounded will somehow increase his empathy for others, but House's empathy does not increase. He walks around as if he is God; his narcissism is infuriating. He embodies the best and worst aspects of being a physician. Brilliant at diagnosing the most complex illness, he arrogantly flaunts his acumen, delivering a diagnosis or prognosis with brutality. He exemplifies the four different types of wounded healer (Cotter 2010): the healer who both wounds and heals, the healer who has walked close to death and recovered, the healer who bears a permanent wound, and the healer who heals through his wounds.

> At home with the mechanics of modern medical health care, and undoubtedly functioning brilliantly as a diagnostician within this framework, House remains curiously unschooled, indeed almost inept, in the world of emotions . . . Indeed his boss, Cuddy, tells him in this episode that people who get close to him get emotionally battered . . . The primary patient in this episode appears at first sight to have a split between right- and left-brain functioning. This dysfunction allows House the opportunity to decry the right brain in a most unmitigated way. House insists that he is a man of the left brain, i.e. valuing cognition, thinking and intellect, those very qualities privileged in current Western society. By his and society's insisting on the advantages of these qualities, the right brain is inevitably cast into shadow. The right-brain

world concerns basic survival by means of emotion and intuition; it is primarily non-verbal. Indeed in this episode, House finds the right brain to be pure encumbrance . . . In an ironic twist at the end of series five, we see the doors of a psychiatric hospital . . . close in on House. He has committed himself as a voluntary patient after realizing the depth of his hallucinations and his need for help in freeing himself of them. The viewer is left to wonder how he will manage in this uncanny role of being a patient after so many years.

Whatever the future holds at this point, it could be said that House has pushed his left-brain world too far—that he has always been on the edge of sanity but now has moved beyond that edge.

(Cotter 2010, p. 101)

Like so many people who have had difficult lives, House feels special and entitled to break hospital rules and treat people badly. In one episode he said, "Humanity is overrated." Irritable with colleagues and patients alike, he is addicted to the pain-killer Vicodin, which is self-medication for his leg pain as well as his rage and aggression (Khantzian 1985). His father had been quite punitive and abusive. The pain of past experience has greatly wounded him in a way he cannot understand, so he repeats the trauma by wounding others. He both heals and wounds others. He entered a psychiatric hospital voluntarily and was discharged when he allowed himself to feel vulnerable. He went to his psychiatrist to talk about his pain rather than rejecting everyone, a real breakthrough.

A perilous calling

When the calling to become a psychoanalyst grows out of the narcissistic needs of one's parents, this disconnects the person from his own needs for self-care—for recreation, fun, and intimate relationships with people who are not their patients (Miller 1979), making this a potentially perilous calling, with an inclination toward depression and grandiosity. Clinical psychologist Michael Sussman (1995) interviewed psychotherapists about what motivated them to choose this profession and found that practicing psychotherapy can impede one's ability to form healthy, fulfilling personal relationships when the relationships with one's own patients becomes the sole source of fulfilling relationships. When this occurs, the therapist becomes more prone to mental illness, substance abuse, sexual acting out, and suicide.

We must contend with our rescue fantasies and must keep in mind that although we can help some to heal, inevitably there will be those who we cannot help. We must contend with our sexual and murderous wishes and anxieties. The practice of psychotherapy can exert tremendous stress on the therapist's intimate relationships, on his role as a parent, and can create a deep sense of isolation. It can exacerbate the therapist's own psychological vulnerability and the risk in dealing with suicidal patients is great. Some therapists struggle through these difficult times, finding them to be opportunities for further personal growth and development, while others do not and remain less effective than they could be or even harmful to their patients. In his foreword to *A Perilous Calling* Herbert Strean wrote:

> The final lesson we learn . . . is that to do therapy well we have to strive to become more loving and less hateful human beings, accepting that our patients have strengths that we may not have, and that we have limitations that they may not have.
>
> (Sussman 1995, pp. xii–xiii)

Sussman recaptured in Freud's writing his "fantasy of a sublime, transcendent vocation that would satisfy both my dreams of greatness and my wish to possess a secret knowledge of things unseen" (Sussman 1995, p. 15). He recalled sitting in the waiting room of an office suite at nineteen, watching one therapist after another greet their anxious, needy, depleted patients, while the therapists seemed to have it all together. They were calm, composed, and self-contained. He knew then that that was what he wanted to be, free of his own aggression and destructiveness.

But the therapeutic relationship is no refuge from aggression; far from it, it stimulates the therapist's aggression. Often this occurs when patients reenact painful scenarios from the past, casting the therapist in the role of the aggressor or abuser. I recall something that the late Martin Bergmann said in his heavy Viennese accent with his great sense of humor, "We are required to absorb more aggression than is usually available on the open market." I remember thinking that several patients I treated were capable of inducing their own murder and, rereading several times what Winnicott (1958) said about hating one's patients, that the analyst must be able to hate his patient without doing anything about it.

When Sussman asked a clinical social worker what she finds most difficult about her work, she replied:

> Being used as an instrument who is smashed against the wall . . . kicked, reviled . . . Just the enormous range of emotions I get subjected to on a daily basis in my body, mind, soul. And the cumulative effect over the years of being the container for all that intense emotion . . . I can't think of a more masochistic profession. To deny one's own needs, to contain the other person's. *Especially* when, most likely, one's been used like that one's whole life in some way, or you wouldn't be doing it in the first place . . . .
>
> (Sussman 1992, pp. 183–184)

Another way that doing this work can be masochistic is when we become involved with psychoanalytic training institutes, which have the potential to become cultic and plagued by authoritarian practices such as intolerance of disagreement with the "party-line" thinking of the leaders, instilling fear and inducing blind obedience to the institute's high priests (Farber 2012). In a paper, "Thirty Methods to Destroy the Creativity of Psychoanalytic Candidates," Kernberg (1996) said this long list includes systematic slowing down of institutional progression of candidates, repetitive and unquestioning teaching of key papers by Freud, mono-lithic tendencies regarding theoretical approaches, isolation of candidates from the professional and scientific activities of the psychoanalytic society, accentua-tion of the hierarchical relations among the psychoanalytic faculty, graduation rituals, discouragement of original contributions by candidates, intellectual iso-lation of institutes, lack of full presentation of clinical work by senior members of the faculty, neglect of studies of controversies regarding psychoanalytic tech-nique, 'paranoiagenic' features of the relationship among faculty and regarding requirements for candidates, the 'convoy' system, neglect of exploration of the scientific and cultural boundaries and applications of psychoanalysis and the effects of institutional conflicts around the appointment of training analysts. Martin Bergmann had much to say about this. Steven Reisner said:

> Martin organized non-institutional psychoanalytic study groups and private supervision. He remained critical of institutional psychoanalysis through-out his life . . . I remember one day, early in my analysis, bringing up the possibility of finding an institute. His response was: "Haven't you been infantilized enough?" He was a one-man non-institutional institution.
>
> (Reisner, email correspondence)

A great deal of self-denial is needed to do this work—the physical inactivity, refraining from responding to the patient in kind, the delay needed to formulate interpretations, and the social isolation can all lead to related countertransference difficulties. To this add the fact that most social workers are women. Social work is low in the status hierarchy of mental health profession and low in the amount of payment. When I worked in hospitals, it was galling to be regarded as "the handmaiden to the physician." Male social workers were treated this way as well.

Sussman was motivated partly by the wish for high status.

> I wished for magical powers . . . I hoped to be admired and idolized . . . I hoped to make up for the damage I believe I had inflicted on my fam-ily as a child . . . I hoped to transcend my own aggression and destructive-ness . . . I hoped to escape my own problems by focusing on those of other people . . . I hoped to internalize my own therapist better by doing what he did . . . I hoped to achieve a deep level of intimacy within a safe context . . . I hoped to meet my own dependency needs vicariously by attending to those of my patients . . . I believed that I might become free of limitations . . . .
>
> (Sussman 1992, pp. 16–22)

He became more and more disillusioned with these aims and became humbled by facing his painful truths. He discovered what Harry Stack Sullivan said: "All of us are much more human than otherwise" (Sullivan 1953, p. 4). In his extensive research Sussman found "behind the wish to practice psychotherapy lies the need to cure one's inner wounds and unresolved conflicts" (Sussman 1992, p. 19).

And inner wounds we have, to be sure. The suicide rate in psychotherapists exceeds that of the general population, with female psychiatrists committing suicide at a rate forty-seven times that of the general population. Psychiatric residents committed suicide at a rate far higher than any other medical specialty (Sussman 1992). In one study it was found that more than ninety percent of psychotherapists experienced a wide variety of serious mental disturbances (Strean 1993). In a study of over 100 graduates of the Columbia University Psychoanalytic Center for Training and Research, Daniel Shapiro said:

> Considering the special considerations of persons attracted to psychoanalysis as a life work, the relatively high percentage of personal pathology acknowledged by this group reflects the degree to which pain, suffering, conflict, and the wish to understand and master them can prompt a sustained, even life-long interest in introspection, understanding, and resolution of conflict.
>
> (Cited by Strean 1993, p. 20)

The analyst must struggle with narcissistic conflicts around voyeurism and exhibitionism (Aron 1996; Strean 1993).

> Why else . . . would we choose a profession where we listen so intently to others while sitting silently and hidden? The fact that analysts are never really invisible—even if they try—and that patients often want desperately to know us, raises tremendous anxiety for those struggling with our own longing to be known and defensive temptation to hide.
>
> (Kuchuck 2013, p. xix)

Kenneth Frank (2013) was among the first who saw our personal openness and transparency and the dialogue about it in our work as essential. How much should we disclose about ourselves and to whom and why are questions we struggle with, along with concerns about protecting our privacy. He wrote that he had had an intensifying certainty that most of the field's theoretical and technical papers failed to address the therapist's personal experience, attitudes, and involvement, which may well comprise the genuine core of psychotherapy. I have had the same growing conviction ever since I began my psychoanalytic training. Frank also raised the question of what effect his openness in writing about this matter might have on a patient who happens to discover his intimately written memoir. Or what effect would reading it have on readers he does not know? He questioned, as I did, how open he could, would, or ought to be. In *Out From Hiding*, he said:

> I came to realize that this chapter is itself an enactment of its title and theme, embodying my personal struggle between concealment and a willingness to be known. I realized, too, that it's time for those of us who endorse openness to "walk the walk."
>
> (Frank 2013, p. 66)

Like Frank, for many of us writing about it has helped us to come out from hiding (Kuchuck 2013).

In his book *Shrink Rap*, Lee Kassan (1996) interviewed psychotherapists. In answer to the question "What was your experience as a patient?" a female social worker said:

> After my marriage broke up, I was miserable, and I went to a very good therapist, and was in individual and group with her, and that was a very good experience. She was very smart and interactive, and there as a person. She was a very good role model for me. I was looking for a different kind of mother and found one with her.
>
> (Kassan 1996, p. 415)

Kassan found that many had negative experiences in their treatment, some with someone who was actively harmful, some with a therapist who was not helpful. A male psychiatrist/psychoanalyst said:

> It could have been a hell of a lot better. What was wrong with it was that it was a training analysis, which means that I don't think there was enough interpretation of the negative transference . . . This was in contrast to a super-visor who was very big on negative transference, and who had a profound influence on the way I work.
>
> (op. cit., p. 425)

Several people highlighted some of the problems with training analyses. A female social worker said:

> In my analytic training I had one of the poorest treatments I ever had. I felt that my analyst . . . had not worked out some of the same issues she was try-ing to work on with me and wasn't able to keep it to herself. Therefore it made the treatment feel very muddy. Also, I believe there was a lot of judg-mental stuff going on at my institute. She was also one of my supervisors. Boundaries were not kept carefully and well, and it really did interfere with the treatment process a lot.
>
> (op. cit., p. 429)

Several people spoke of real boundary violations. Another female social worker said:

> I had a negative experience in college. She was an Adlerian and a very stereotypically social worker type, Jewish, a mother who nagged me, and there wasn't any sense of psychological understanding, just follow the rule . . . Then she thought it would be very good for me to be in a group, which was also a disaster, with another Adlerian. There were no boundaries.

He was friends with the patients and encouraged everyone to be friends, to have them at your house and at parties.

(op. cit., p. 430)

Another female social worker said, "My very first therapist, when I was twenty-four, kissed me on the mouth before a vacation, and I never went back to him" (op. cit., p. 430).

This work requires us to look below the surface and learn about many "forbidden" issues. Patients' disclosure of their sexual life and wishes can be very stimulating (Sussman 1995).The therapist may be tempted to let himself be seduced by the patient or to seduce the patient. Kassan asked, "Have you ever been sexually attracted to a patient? How did you handle that?" A male psychologist said:

One of my first patients was a beautiful Eurasian woman, and much to my dismay, I realized I was sexually attracted to her, and I talked about it with colleagues and supervisors, and once I understood that she really was objectively attractive, then it really was okay to feel attracted.

(op. cit., pp. 454–455)

With more clinical experience, therapists seem to feel more comfortable accepting their sexual feelings toward patients. Some spoke of times when it is an indication of countertransference. Some said it was important not to let the patient know about it. A woman with an M.S. degree said in response to the question, "Haven't we all? I was more troubled by it in the first years than now. I acknowledge them to myself, own them, and don't act on them" (op. cit., p. 454). A male psychologist said:

I try to stay conscious. There's a very clear example of analyzing the countertransference . . . You have to keep reminding yourself what a disaster it would be if you allowed yourself to act out on desire. You can easily make the mistake of thinking that outcome is really the desired outcome, when nothing could be further from the truth.

(op. cit., p. 456)

A female psychiatrist said, "It changes one's attentiveness. It's distracting. I'll often think about it in terms of what I know about whom I'm sexually attracted to, and see what it tells me about this patient" (op. cit., p. 456). A male social worker said, "I tell myself it's okay to feel that way, but I must make sure that I don't let the patient know that, and not let that interfere. It hasn't happened that often" (op. cit., p. 457).

Kassan asked psychotherapists if they had ever had a patient make threats toward others or to them. A female therapist said:

I was working with a couple, and he was just furious about what was going on, not so much with me as with his spouse, and he turned around and said he was going to get me. And I said I don't work in a climate like that and they would both have to leave. And they did.

(op. cit., p. 452)

A female therapist diffused a dangerous situation with her confident response, which seemed to be reassuring to the patient. "I once had someone pull a knife out. I got very motherly, and said 'Put that thing away!' and he did. I chose not to see him and terminated the treatment" (op. cit., p. 452). A male psychologist said:

I've had a guy who stalked his ex-girlfriend. He verbalized that he could see killing her, killing her boyfriend. This was a guy I don't think would do it. But I was apprehensive. Am I supposed to do something? Is this the case I'm supposed to report?

(op. cit., p. 448)

Yes, he *is* supposed to do something. He is legally obligated to warn his patient's ex-girlfriend and her boyfriend, a legal decision resulting from the Tarasoff case, a landmark case even before anti-stalking laws were established, that gave rise to the Tarasoff decision in 1974. A University of California psychologist treating a male student was so anxious about his patient's potential aggressiveness that he tried unsuccessfully, to have him committed involuntarily. In compliance with the ethic of therapist–patient confidentiality, he did not warn Tatiana Tarasoff, a student who took a vacation to get away from his unwanted advances. She was murdered the day she returned. Her parents filed a suit against the therapist for contributing to her wrongful death, giving rise to the Tarasoff decision that mental health professionals have a duty to protect individuals who are in danger of being harmed by a patient. A 1976 rehearing of the case called for a legal duty to protect the intended victim even if the patient is not verbally threatening to harm her. That is, stalking behavior itself is threatening enough. Since then, the Tarasoff ruling has become a national standard of care for psychotherapists. "The protective privilege ends where the public peril begins" (Farber 2015; Galeazzi et al. 2005; Kaplan 2006; Meloy 1999; Meloy & Boyd 2003; Meloy & Fisher 2005; Truman & Mustaine 2011; Walcott et al. 2001, p. 329).

Extremes of emotion are commonly felt in psychotherapy. Sometimes a therapist may find himself feeling love for his patient, something Freud wrote to Jung about on December 12, 1906, letting him know that he could say what he was going to say only to a few select colleagues.

It is not possible to say anything to a hostile public; accordingly I have kept certain things that might be said concerning the limits of the therapy and its mechanisms to myself, or spoken of them in a way that is intelligible only to the initiate . . . Essentially, one might say, the cure is effected by love.

(McGuire 1994, p. 10)

Lawrence Friedman thought there was something we might call psychoanalytic love.

> It is especially impressive that some analysts have been willing to even contemplate general loving feelings toward patients, given that the possibility of affective responses toward patients made them squirm for years, for obvious reasons. The technical model of psychoanalysis is a paradox: the analyst is supposed to be an objective observer, but one whose inner responses are in important ways uncontrolled and freely *moved* by the patient's impact. Theory seems to forbid and require detachment.
>
> (Friedman 2005a, p. 350)

If the analyst were to have a real love relationship with the patient, it would not be the idealized love for which the patient yearns, a love which does not want or demand anything (Friedman 2005b). The love which does not want or demand anything is as close to a selfless love that anyone will ever have or give (Farber 2013). Having treated a woman who had been molested by her mother and had been cutting and burning herself since she was ten, it was a most successful treatment. Once, after presenting this case to a group of colleagues, one of those present said, in a tone of wonder or astonishment, "You loved her; you really loved her!" I could only plead that I was "guilty as charged" (Farber 2013, p. 367).

When so many patients have managed care benefits that they wish to use, dealing with managed care can be unduly time-consuming and frustrating. With some companies, over time, instead of reimbursement rates increasing, they are decreasing. The aim of managed care is to make a profit for the company, which is effectively done by denying necessary mental health benefits. In response to Kassan's question "When are you disappointed in your work?" several therapists said the business aspect is the most draining. A colleague of mine retired from practice because she could tolerate it no longer.

Another occupational hazard is the therapist's vulnerability to depression or anxiety, either through heredity or projective identification (Heath 1991). Through the process of projective identification, a dissociative process of communication, the patient can get the therapist to feel what he is feeling. If the patient is depressed he can induce a depressed state in the therapist through the process of projective identification. The same is true for anxiety (Bromberg 1998; Klein 1946).

The power of the relationship

The question "How do you think psychotherapy works?" is the primary issue. How important is the technique used, the insight gained by the patient, the therapist's personality, the patient–therapist relationship? A female social worker said, "It works mostly because of the relationship. Something gets changed inside because of something happening outside, and it's in the relationship. All the techniques, and all the things that you say, are all in the service of the relationship" (Kassan 1996, p. 295). Another female social worker said:

> I think it's the relationship and the attachment. The sense of comfort, and being understood by someone, and being able to share things that are old and painful or disturbing. Or current things that are troubling, or even exciting, good things. I know there's two hundred or three hundred different approaches to therapy, and what it comes down to is the relationship. If you go to a person and you feel comfortable talking to them, and if something felt off or wrong you could say that, then you'd be okay.
>
> (Kassan 1996, p. 296)

Several spoke of the relationship as being a corrective emotional experience (Alexander 1958). The therapy consists of learning new ways to regulate anxiety, in part through a corrective emotional experience to repair the traumatic influence of previous experiences. A male psychologist said, "Love is not enough, but without it nothing cures. The only thing that cures is love. It's ultimately a corrective emotional experience. It's the process that cures" (Kassan 1996, p. 298). A female psychologist said:

> Therapy provides a corrective emotional experience. There are several steps. First you have to be able to have your feelings, then your behavior changes, and then your feelings change after that. There has to be an atmosphere in which you can talk and not be judged.
>
> (op. cit., p. 298)

Others emphasized the insight gained. A male psychologist said:

> My feeling is that therapy works by shifting emphasis from the external to the internal, and then the patient develops some kind of awareness of their own internal process, how they function. They become curious about themselves, and in that process . . . there is a liberation, because rather than being critical of themselves, they start asking questions: Why do I do this? Why do I prefer that? Why do I have this fantasy? There develops a respect for oneself, one's impulses. one's opinions, one's thoughts, one's body.
>
> (op. cit., p. 300)

Why we do this work

It can be very frustrating to psychotherapists that they often do not get enough positive feedback for their good work but are deeply affected by their failures which "come back to haunt them, often under conditions that do not give another crack at the job—yet, if the patients succeed they may more often than not are never heard from again" (Marston 1984, p. 457). How, then, can we know that we matter? So many wounded healers grew up feeling that they did not matter to their parents, the most important people in their lives, and so became psychotherapists to feel that they matter a great deal to their patients. Given that there is much that is difficult about the practice of psychotherapy, it seems to provide a great deal of satisfaction and the feeling that we matter.

> I love being a therapist. It's the only job I ever had that didn't get boring and repetitive after a year. It's constantly fresh and new, each new hour and each new patient. I consistently feel challenged and engaged by what I'm doing. The work is intrinsically meaningful, unlike many other jobs that seem to consist mainly of moving papers around an office.
>
> (Kassan 1996, p. 582)

In answer to the questions "Do you like being a psychotherapist? What do you like best?" a male psychologist said, "I love it, I'd do it even if I wasn't being paid. Don't tell anyone" (op. cit., p. 579). I suspect the managed care companies know this and know they can get away with such poor reimbursement rates. A woman psychologist said:

> I like that it's something that changes, that it's a new story all the time. It's like a new chapter every hour in a different book . . . I find it fascinating, and sometimes I sit here and think, "Wow, I'm getting paid for this." You have to take very good care of yourself but I love it.
>
> (op. cit., p. 579)

A female social worker said, "I love it. I'll never retire, they'll have to drag me out by my heels. I get better as I get older" (op. cit., p. 579). Another female social worker said, "I love my career. I go to work every day and I can't believe I roll out of bed and love what I do" (op. cit., p. 579). Another woman said:

> I love it. Philosophically, given that we're born and we die, what happens in between is the only thing we can control. If you think that you've had impact on people's lives, and they feel better about themselves and have benefitted from knowing you, that's a marvelous thing.
>
> (op. cit., p. 579)

Some of them pointed out more specific aspects of the work. A male psychologist said, "I like working with people, being intimate" (op. cit., p. 579). Another male psychologist said, "I like being part of a process that has deep meaning, the sharing of that deep sense of meaning" (op. cit., p. 579).

Michael Eigen (1999) tells us that many psychotherapists and psychoanalysts, religious or not, may be touched by the sense of something sacred in the work. For Eigen and for me too, this work is sacred (Farber 2013).

I need these experiences. They reset, deepen, redirect, renew me . . . I read psychoanalytic texts the same way. I need texts that add to my life, that open experiencing, that speak to my condition. I am not in psychoanalysis merely as a business or intellectual exercise. It is a life and death matter. It is my life I am spending in it, my time. Either I get the most I can from . . . I say this because I think there are many of us who do, but are afraid to own this double tendency. Either we are put down for being psychoanalytic, or put down for being mystical . . . It is awful to think one must stay on one or the other side of a permeable membrane and try to stop the flow.

(Eigen 1999, p. 39)

For a patient who is a cantor, she sings the Hebrew liturgy so that her congregants have the sense of the sacred. For her, however, that is work. She experiences my office as sacred space.

Stages in the development of the wounded healer

The wounded healer may first begin to become aware of his woundedness while in the midst of his own personal psychotherapy or when having direct contact with patients in emotional pain during the internship phase of professional training. Lawrence Kirmayer (2003) identified five stages in the development of the wounded healer. Initially, he sees himself as quite different from those he helps, unaware of or reluctant to confront his own woundedness, seeking consciously to identify with the power of healing. Then there is his first "initiation trial," when he has his first confrontation with his woundedness. As the denial of his woundedness is lifted, he may be plagued by darkness and identify entirely with his wounds. He looks outside himself for the cure. Gradually, he comes to accept his woundedness and, in doing so, evokes his inner healer, which initially appears in a tentative way. He may doubt his own legitimacy or feel limited in his power, and may hope to be rescued by a powerful hero. Through remaining in contact with, not disconnected from, his inner wound, he becomes more able to descend again and again to the underworld of suffering. He comes to see this process, limited and incomplete as it is, as a way to continue. He knows his strengths and limitations to be one and the same. Remaining in touch with his wounds protect him from the threat of pride and arrogance.

This developmental sequence in which the healer opens a conduit between his own wounds and his inner healer allows a parallel development to occur in his functioning in the outer world. Initially the role of healer is foreign to him. He may be drawn to the practice of psychotherapy through altruistic-sounding reasons. Through his exposure to much suffering in an apprenticeship or clinical training, he becomes wounded again along fault lines already laid down by his own history. The apprentice healer comes to identify unconsciously with patients through their common wounds while, at the same time, he begins to worry about performing the role of healer, aware of the burden of expectations. He is forced to rely on his inner resources and begins to assume the healer role. He calls forth his inner healer to dress the patient's wounds. Many may stop at this stage, content to work with a configuration in which the healer's own active stance contains the wounds of both the patient and himself. But if he can continue to recognize his own vulnerability, the healer accepts the patient's own healing ability as an equal participant in the healing transaction. In this way, the patient can both wound and heal the healer.

Essentially this means that as we come to identify and accept our own inner woundedness and can empathize more fully with the patient, the experience changes us as healers as much as it changes the patient. The psychotherapist's wounds may be activated in certain situations, especially if his patient's wounds are similar to his own. For example, while teaching a graduate class in mental health counseling, Marcy, a very talented student whose internship placement was at an inpatient chemical dependency unit, became very disturbed when I said the Twelve Step programs such as A.A. and N.A., while extremely helpful to many, are not necessary for recovery, and that many patients recover without these programs (Fletcher 2013). Marcy stood up and very emotionally disagreed with me, proclaiming that she owed her life to A.A.. That may be, I said, but it does not mean that every alcoholic will find it as useful as you have. She insisted that if someone does not find the Twelve Steps helpful, it is because that individual is not using the program correctly. I pointed out that she was buying into the "party line," blaming the patient for his failure to use the program, and that if she did this at the chemical dependency unit, she would not be at all helpful to her clients. She could not hold up her way of recovery as the model that all should use; it is only one of several models.

From her own experience with anorexia, Carolyn Costin, advocate and activist in the field of eating disorders, became a therapist for those with eating disorders and founded several residential treatment centers. She warns that recovered clinicians must walk a fine line with their "insider" knowledge. Even though they think they understand what a client means or is going through because they have "been there and done that," it is critical that they understand that what worked best for them is not necessarily the best for the patient. She warns that self-disclosure in any form is a tricky part of our work as therapists and can quickly become a slippery slope (Costin 2002). Costin's suggestions are supported by the findings of Williams and Haverkamp (2015) who, in multiple interviews with eleven therapist-participants, found that these individuals thought their personal eating disorder histories had substantial ethical relevance in their day-to-day practice with eating disorder patients.

Why do we do this work?

Kassan (1996) wrote that probably all psychotherapists get asked occasionally how they can do this work, wondering if hearing all the unhappiness and pain gets them depressed. In response to the question "When patients ask how or why you do this work, what do you tell them?" one man said, "I usually say that I'm most alive when I'm working. That everybody's born to a purpose and I don't think I could do too much else in life" (op. cit., p. 197).

Another question was "What experiences in your background led you to choose this profession?" Some said that growing up, being the therapist was their role in the family. A woman social worker said:

> I came from a family that was disturbed in a number of ways, and no one talked about anything, and I was the emotional caretaker, and didn't get noticed for having any personal needs. So I'm very interested in secrets, and what makes systems work, and all that.
>
> (p. 393)

A male social worker said, "I was born into an alcoholic family, and I was a therapist from the age of 5" (p. 384). A female social worker said:

> At the time I went to school, I was working more with kids, and I was out of touch with what a disturbed kid I had been. I think it had to do with the disturbance in my own family. My father was never in any kind of treatment, but was a pretty paranoid guy, and that impacted very strongly on me. I didn't think at the time I went into the field that it was an influence, but I do now.
>
> (p. 395)

The experience of being a patient was the deciding factor for many in becoming a therapist. A male psychiatrist said:

> It has a good deal to do with the Holocaust, and the idea that such a crazy thing, such a mind-boggling, intolerable idea, motivated people and seemed to be the norm. I lost a lot of my family, so it became a very personal issue. I have followed the thread through my analysis. The idea of figuring out the *mishegas* (craziness) that we all suffered was an important motivation.
>
> (p. 395)

A male social worker wrote:

> My own experience as a patient at age thirty. I was very unhappy, and somatizing to beat the band. The world opened up, and there were dramatic results, even in my physical health. I was awed by my therapist's skill and training. She said I might have an aptitude for it, but I regarded that only as something nice to hear. Years later, another therapist, who was himself a Jesuit priest, told me that there was training available for someone like me who wasn't a doctor, which I didn't know.
>
> (pp. 387–388)

Bibliography

Adler, G. (1956). *Dynamic Aspects of the Psyche*. New York: Analytical Psychology Club.

Alexander, F. (1958). Unexplored Areas in Psychoanalytic Theory and Treatment—Part II. In: *The Scope of Psychoanalysis* (pp. 319–335). New York: Basic Books.

Aron, L. (1996). *Mutuality in Psychoanalysis*. Hillsdale, NJ: Analytic Press.

Bromberg, P. (1998). *Standing in the Spaces: Essays on Clinical Process, Trauma, and Dissociation*. Hillsdale, NJ and London: Analytic Press.

Buber, M. (1970). *I and Thou*. Trans. and notes by Walter Kaufman. New York: Charles Scribner's Sons.

Bullitt-Jonas, M. (1999). *Holy Hunger*. New York: Knopf.

Burton, A. (1972). *Twelve Therapists: How They Live and Actualize Themselves*. San Francisco: Jossey-Bass.

Carey, B. (2011). Expert on Mental Illness Reveals Her Own Fight. *The New York Times*, June 23, A1–A17.

Chessler, P. (2003). *Woman's Inhumanity to Woman*. New York: Plume.

Costin, C. (2002). Been There, Done That: Clinicians' Use of Personal Recovery in the Treatment of Eating Disorders. *Eating Disorders: The Journal of Treatment and Prevention*, *10* (2): 292–303.

Cotter, A. (2010). Limping the Way to Wholeness: Wounded Feeling and Feeling Wounded. In: L. Hockley & L. Gardner (eds.), *House: The Wounded Healer on Television: Jungian and Post-Jungian Reflections* (pp. 101–115). New York and London: Routledge.

Cousins, N. (1981). *Anatomy of an Illness: As Perceived by the Patient—Reflections on Healing and Regeneration*. New York: Bantam.

Eigen, M. (1998). Shivers. In: J. Reppen (ed.), *Why I Became a Psychotherapist* (pp. 77–88). Northvale, NJ: Jason Aronson.

Eigen, M. (1999). *The Psychoanalytic Mystic*. Binghamton, NY: E.S.F.

Elkins, D. (1998). *Beyond Religion: Eight Alternative Paths to the Sacred: A Personal Program for Building a Spiritual Life outside the Walls of Traditional Religion*. Wheaton, IL: Quest.

Farber, S. (2012). *Hungry for Ecstasy: Trauma, the Brain, and the Influence of the Sixties*. Lanham, MD: Jason Aronson/Rowman & Littlefield.

Farber, S. (2013). *Hungry for Ecstasy: Trauma, the Brain, and the Influence of the Sixties*. Lanham, MD: Jason Aronson/Rowman & Littlefield.

Farber, S. (2015). My Patient, My Stalker Empathy as a Dual-Edged Sword: A Cautionary Tale. *American Journal of Psychotherapy*, *69* (3): 331–355.

Farber, S. (in press). Becoming a Telepathic Tuning Fork: Anomalous Experience and the Relational Mind. *Psychoanalytic Dialogues*.

Flaherty, A. (2004). The Midnight Disease: The Drive to Write, Writer's Block, and the Creative Brain. New York: Houghton Mifflin.

Flaherty, A., & Post, N. (2000). *The Massachusetts General Hospital Handbook of Neurology*. Philadelphia: Lippincott Williams & Wilkins.

Fletcher, A. (2013). *Inside Rehab: The Surprising Truth about Addiction Treatment—and How to Get Help that Works*. New York: Penguin.

Frank, K. (2013). Out from Hiding. In: S. Kuchuck (ed.), *Clinical Implications of the Psychoanalyst's Life Experience: When the Personal Becomes Professional* (pp. 65–80). New York: Routledge.

Freud, S. (1912). Recommendations to Physicians Practising Psycho-Analysis. In: *The Standard Edition of the Complete Psychological Works of Sigmund Freud*, vol. 12 (pp. 109–120). London: Hogarth Press.

Friedman, L. (2005a). Is There a Special Psychoanalytic Love? *Journal of the American Psychoanalytic Association, 53* (2): 349–375.

Friedman, L. (2005b). Response to Martha Nussbaum. *Journal of the American Psychoanalytic Association, 53* (2): 385–388.

Fromm, E. (1960). *Psychoanalysis and Zen Buddhism.* New York: Harper & Brothers.

Galeazzi, G., Elkins, K., & Curci, P. (2005). The Stalking of Mental Health Professionals by Patients. *Psychiatric Services, 5*: 137–138.

Garcia-Amador, M., Colom, F., Valenti, M., Horga, G., & Vieta, E. (2009). Suicide Risk in Rapid Cycling Bipolar Patients. *Journal of Affective Disorders, 117* (1–2): 74–78.

Gilroy, P., Carroll, L., & Murra, J. (2002). A Preliminary Survey of Counseling Psychologists' Personal Experiences with Depression and Treatment. *Professional Psychology: Research and Practice, 33*: 402–407.

Goldberg, C. (1991). *On Being a Psychotherapist.* Northvale, NJ: Jason Aronson.

Groesbeck, C. (1975). The Archetypal Image of the Wounded Healer. *Journal of Analytical Psychology, 20*: 122–145.

Henry, W. (1971). *The Fifth Profession: Becoming a Psychotherapist.* San Francisco: Jossey Bass.

Hesse, E., & Van IJzendoorn, M. (1998). Parental Loss of Close Family Members and Propensities towards Absorption in Offspring. *Developmental Science, 1* (2): 299–305.

Hillman, J. (1967). Insearch: *Psychology and Religion.* New York: Scribners.

Hockley, L., & Gardner, L. (2010). *House: The Wounded Healer on Television: Jungian and Post-Jungian Reflections.* New York and London: Routledge.

Jamison, K. (1995). *An Unquiet Mind: A Memoir of Moods and Madness.* New York: Random House.

Jung, C. (1951). *Fundamental Questions of Psychotherapy.* Princeton, NJ: Princeton University Press.

Jung, C. (1954). On the Psychology of the Trickster-Figure. In: *The Archetypes and the Collective Unconscious* (*Collected Works of C. G. Jung*, vol. 9, Part 1) (pp. 255–274). Princeton, NJ: Princeton University Press.

Jung, C. (1955). *Modern Man in Search of a Soul.* New York: Harcourt Brace.

Jung, C. (1961). *Memories, Dreams, Reflections.* New York: Vintage.

Jung, C. (2012). *The Red Book: A Reader's Edition.* New York: Norton.

Kakar, S. (1982). *Shamans, Mystics, and Doctors: A Psychological Inquiry into India and Its Healing Traditions.* New York: Alfred A. Knopf.

Kaplan, A. (2006). Being Stalked—An Occupational Hazard? *Psychiatric Times, 23* (8).

Kassan, L. E. (1996). *Shrink Rap: Sixty Psychotherapists Discuss Their Work, Their Lives, and the State of Their Field.* New York: Jason Aronson.

Kernberg, O. (1996). Thirty Methods to Destroy the Creativity of Psychoanalytic Candidates. *International Journal of Psychoanalysis, 77*: 1031–1040.

Kerr, J. (1993). *A Most Dangerous Method: The Story of Jung, Freud, and Sabina Spielrein.* New York: Knopf.

Khantzian, E. (1985). The Self-Medication Hypothesis of Addictive Disorders: Focus on Heroin and Cocaine Dependence. *American Journal of Psychiatry, 142* (11): 1259–1264.

Kirmayer, L. (2003). Asklepian Dreams: The Ethos of the Wounded Healer in the Clinical Encounter. *Transcultural Psychiatry, 40* (2): 248–277.

Klein, M. (1946). Notes on Some Schizoid Mechanisms. *International Journal of Psycho-Analysis*, *27*: 99–110.

Kottler, J., & Carlson, J. (2005). *The Client Who Changed Me*. New York and Hove (U.K.): Routledge.

Kuchuck, S. (2013). *Clinical Implications of the Psychoanalyst's Life Experience: When the Personal Becomes Professional*. New York: Routledge.

Lesser, W. (1995). Book Review: *An Anthropologist on Mars: Seven Paradoxical Tales* by Oliver Sacks. *The New York Times*, February 19, A1–A31.

Levi-Strauss, C. (1964). *The Raw and the Cooked: Introduction to a Science of Mythology*. New York: Harper & Row.

Lipp, M. (1980). *The Bitter Pill—Doctors, Patients, and Failed Expectations*. New York: Harper & Row.

Marston, A. (1984). What Makes Therapists Run? A Model for Analysis of Motivational Styles. *Psychotherapy: Theory, Research, Practice, Training*, *21*: 456–459.

Mander, G. (2004). The selection of candidates for training in psychotherapy and counseling. *Psychodynamic Practice*, *10*: 161–172).

McGuire, W. (1994). *The Freud/Jung Letters: The Correspondence between Sigmund Freud and C. G. Jung*. Princeton, NJ: Princeton University Press.

Meloy, J. R. (1999). Stalking. An Old Behavior, a New Crime. *Psychiatric Clinics of North America*, *22* (1): 85–99.

Meloy, J. R., & Boyd. C. (2003). Female Stalkers and Their Victims. *Journal of the American Academy of Psychiatry and the Law*, *31* (2): 211–219.

Meloy, J. R., & Fisher, H. (2005). Some Thoughts on the Neurobiology of Stalking. *Journal of Forensic Sciences*, *50* (6): 1472–1480.

Merchant, J. (2011). *Shamans and Analysts: New Insights on the Wounded Healer*. London: Routledge.

Miller, A. (1979). The Drama of the Gifted Child and the Psycho-Analyst's Narcissistic Disturbance. *International Journal of Psycho-Analysis*, *60* (47): 58.

Miller, G., & Baldwin Jr, D. (1987). Implications of the Wounded-Healer Paradigm for the Use of the Self in Therapy. *Journal of Psychotherapy and the Family*, *3* (1): 139–151.

Nouwen, H. (1979). *The Wounded Healer: In Our Own Woundedness, We Can Become a Source of Life for Others*. New York: Image.

O'Connor, M. (2001). On the Etiology and Effective Management of Professional Distress and Impairment among Psychologists. *Professional Psychology: Research and Practice*, *32* (4): 345–350.

Remen, R. N. (1997). *Kitchen Table Wisdom: Stories that Heal*. New York: Riverhead Trade.

Roiphe, K. (2016). *The Violet Hour: Great Writers at the End*. New York: Dial Press.

Sacks, O. (1996). *An Anthropologist on Mars: Seven Paradoxical Tales*. New York: Vintage.

Sacks, O. (2015). *On the Move: A Life*. New York: Knopf.

Searles, H. (1979). The Patient as Therapist to His Analyst. In: *Countertransference and Related Subjects: Selected Papers* (pp. 380–459). New York: International Universities Press.

Slater, L. (2005). Three Spheres. In: L. Gutkind (ed.), *In Fact: The Best of Creative Nonfiction* (pp. 3–24). New York: Norton.

Smith, R. (1997). *The Wounded Jung: Effects of Jung's Relationships on His Life and Work*. Evanston, IL: Northwestern University Press.

Strean, H. (1993). *Therapists Who Have Sex with Their Patients: Treatment and Recovery*. New York and London: Routledge.

Sullivan, H. (1953). *The Interpersonal Theory of Psychiatry*. New York: Norton.

Sussman, M. (1992). *A Curious Calling*. Northvale, NJ: Jason Aronson.

Sussman, M. (1995). *A Perilous Calling: The Hazards of Psychotherapy Practice*. New York: Wiley.

Tillman, J. (2014). Patient Suicide: Impact on Clinicians. *Psychiatric Times*. Retrieved from http://www.psychiatrictimes.com/special-reports/patient-suicide-impact clinicians? GUID=E28D0073-CBF7-4EC0-8F95-A7F0BAFC4596&rememberme=1&ts=1301 2015

Truman, J., & Mustaine, E. (2011). When Social Workers Are Stalked: Risks, Strategies, and Legal Protections. *Clinical Social Work Journal, 39* (3): 232–242.

van der Kolk, B. (2014). *The Body Keeps the Score: Brain, Mind, and Body in the Healing of Trauma*. New York: Viking.

Walcott, D., Cerundolo, P., & Beck, J. (2001). Current Analysis of the Tarasoff Duty: An Evolution towards the Limitation of the Duty to Protect. *Behavioral Sciences and the Law, 19*: 325–343.

Williams, M., & Haverkamp, B. (2015). Eating Disorder Therapists' Personal Eating Disorder History and Professional Ethics: An Interpretive Description. *Eating Disorders: The Journal of Treatment and Prevention, 23* (5): 393–410.

Winnicott, D. (1958). Hate in the Countertransference. In: *Collected Papers: Through Paediatrics to Psychoanalysis* (pp. 194–203). New York: Basic Books.

Yalom, I. (2009). *Staring at the Sun: Overcoming the Terror of Death*. San Francisco: Jossey-Bass.

Chapter 3

The psychotherapist's occupational hazards

Sharon K. Farber

The occupational hazards of doing this work can impact the therapist and the patient severely, turning an otherwise good therapist into a wounding healer. They include the therapist's vulnerability to the patient's depression or anxiety, becoming traumatized by a patient's suicide or becoming suicidal themselves, falling in love with a patient, being physically attacked by a patient, being stalked by the patient, becoming vicariously traumatized in dealing with severely traumatized patients, feeling envious of a patient or colleague, and the overlooked problems in a long-term therapy that come from the therapist's decision to retire.

Vulnerability to depression, anxiety, and suicide

Treating the suicidal patient can become the therapist's worst nightmare. Having had one patient commit suicide can make him/her very anxious about another.

Jane Tillman (2014) interviewed twelve therapists whose patient had committed suicide and identified eight common themes, including traumatic responses such as dissociation, traumatic intrusion, avoidance, somatic symptoms associated with the suicide, and nightmares. Affective responses included crying, sadness, anger, grief, and fear or anxiety about the consequences. They spoke of treatment-specific relationships including their work with the patient, particularly the last session, and contact with the patient's family. Relationships with colleagues were complicated, including contacts with the therapist's personal analyst, supervisor, peers, and trainees. Many were concerned about being sued. Grandiosity, shame, humiliation, guilt, judgment, and blame were all spoken about. There was a sense of personal crisis, with doubts expressed about continuing their work. Some felt they were changed for the better in their work with patients while some felt changed for the worse.

There is a big difference between thinking about suicide and planning to do it and it is the critical job of the therapist to determine this.

> I'm very active in questioning them about it, and finding out what it is. Is there a plan, or is this just a vague feeling? I don't overreact to it. I do it in a very nonthreatening nonanxious kind of way. A patient told me that she left a

therapist because the therapist overreacted to her depression, and she was not suicidal, and she didn't want to have to take care of the therapist's anxiety. I'm very calm, because I have worked with very disturbed patients. I would cancel sessions and go with them to the emergency room.

(Kassan 1996, p. 166)

Therapists who treat depressed patients are vulnerable not only to the patient's depression, which can become introjected into the therapist by means of projective identification, but to his suicidality (Heath 1991). Jung explained that

It is a typical occupational hazard of the psychotherapist to become psychically infected and poisoned by the projections to which he is exposed. The peculiar emotional condition of the patient does have a contagious effect. One could almost say it arouses similar vibrations in the nervous system of the analyst, and therefore . . . psychotherapists are apt to become a little queer. One should bear that problem in mind. It very definitely belongs to the problem of transference.

(Jung, cited by Groesbeck 1975, p. 135)

Depressed therapists may be at risk of suicide. The incidence of suicide in therapists is high, suggesting that those who enter this field are particularly vulnerable or that the stresses of this work make us vulnerable, or both. In treating suicidal patients, our clinical judgment may become clouded by the countertransference hatred that suicidal patients evoke in us (Nagel 1989). As Winnicott told us in his paper on hate in the countertransference, "However much [the therapist] loves his patients he cannot avoid hating them, and fearing them, and the better he knows this the less will hate and fear be the motive determining what he does to his patients" (Winnicott 1958, p. 195). When we cannot identify and tolerate our own hateful wishes toward the patient, we end up becoming involved in a masochistic relationship with him which puts us at greater risk for suicide.

Falling in love with a patient and the erotic transference

When Kassan (1996) asked therapists if they had ever felt that they were falling in love with a patient and if they did, how they handled it, a male social worker said:

I did at one time early in my career feel like I was falling in love with a patient . . . It was a time when my marriage was very rocky and I was feeling very needy and unhappy. And this was a woman who was very much my type, that I could have easily dated if she had not been a patient. I dealt with it by discussing it in supervision. I don't think she knew. I was quite conscious of the need not to act it out in some way, and I don't think I did.

(Kassan 1996, p. 460)

Another male social worker said:

> I did, with one particular patient. I felt that if I had known this person in another context, I would have declared myself and I would have said this is how I feel and what do you think we can do about it. Instead, I sublimated it, and this was a patient who needed a lot of nurturing, so that's what I did with it.
>
> (op. cit., p. 460)

Not all therapists can handle this so well and instead get involved in a sexual relationship with a patient, thus becoming a wounding healer. An indispensable discussion of dealing with the therapist's erotic countertransference can be found in Andrea Celenza's (2014) *Erotic Revelations: Clinical Applications and Perverse Scenarios*.

Being attacked or stalked

When a woman who consulted me about domestic violence revealed that her husband, a construction worker, regularly beat their eleven-year-old son, I told her I had an ethical and legal obligation to report it to Child Protective Services, who would conduct an investigation. Later that evening, I discovered that someone had poured liquid concrete all over a car parked in front of my home office. Thinking she had told her husband, I suspected him, thinking he assumed the car was mine.

Being stalked by a patient is a very real occupational hazard for which our professional training does not prepare us (Farber 2015). Although those who work with psychiatric patients in inpatient treatment settings with more severely ill patients are at particular risk of becoming victims (Galeazzi et al. 2005), an Italian study found the rate of stalking in private mental health settings is higher than that in public settings and that the perpetrators of stalking are mainly women who mostly target mental health professionals in private practice (Meloy & Boyd 2003). Pope and Vasquez (2011) reviewed research indicating that almost one in every five psychologists reported having been physically attacked by at least one client. Over 80 percent reported having been afraid that a client would attack them. More than one out of four had summoned the police or security personnel for protection, and about 3 percent reported obtaining a weapon. Sixteen percent of social workers have been stalked by a client (Truman & Mustaine 2011).

Stalking is a very old behavior but a relatively new crime (Farber 2015; Meloy 1999) in North America, some European countries, Australia, and New Zealand (Meloy & Fisher 2005). Stalkers are criminals, something often ignored or not understood by mental health clinicians, law enforcement agencies, and the media. We are accustomed to thinking clinically about our patients. To cope effectively with a stalking patient, we must seek the help of forensic mental health experts and develop an ability to think forensically, a radical shift in how we think about patients, not at all easy to make. I discovered this when I was stalked for almost a year by a woman who wanted me to treat her; this was when there were no stalking laws, little literature on the subject, and when I was in no frame of mind to consider seeking it (Farber 2015). It was a horrific experience that induced a post-traumatic stress disorder and impaired my thinking more than I realized at the time. When it began, I knew little about stalking, equating stalkers with serial killers who stalked their prey, usually celebrities. Although not all stalkers are violent, I did not know this then. I muddled my way alone through this experience, then sought forensic advice, and years later, reading the literature on stalking helped me deconstruct this experience, convincing me that it is a very real occupational hazard (Kaplan 2006) for health and mental health clinicians. I came to understand why I had become such an enticing morsel for my stalker. Several years after it stopped, when I had some emotional distance from it, I wanted to understand how and why it happened and how and why it stopped. I reviewed my notes and collection of letters, photographs, and tapes which jogged my memory of this time, realizing that I had done some things that, once the stalking started, inadvertently served to maintain it.

Vicarious traumatization

"Trauma is contagious" (Herman 1992, p. 140), meaning that all therapists working with trauma patients run the risk of developing symptoms of vicarious traumatization. When we work with trauma survivors, we become changed. Our empathy for our patient can come with a cost. When we listen to patients' stories of the worst kind of victimization and sorrow, it can be overwhelming and fill us with disgust, fury, and helplessness. We often feel incompetent to respond and may feel angry at the patient for provoking such feelings in us. Repeated exposure to such stories of human cruelty may cause us to lose faith in the power of the therapeutic relationship and to feel far more personally vulnerable than ever (Herman 1992). As Vanderlinden and Vandereycken (1997) point out, under such circumstances it is easy for therapists to narrow the psychological world of patients to one of trauma and survival. When that occurs, therapists may become overly detached and dissociative to defend against the emotional impact, which may result in an identification with the offender and a tendency to blame the victim for what happened. Or the therapist may become so over-identified and empathic that he may try to rescue the patient or assume too much responsibility for his life (Farber 2000).

To prevent this, countertransference reactions need to be shared and processed with colleagues (Pearlman & Saakvitne 1995). Working with such patients can test our psychological strength to the maximum, making it necessary that therapists exercise certain preventive measures. Seeking consultation with supervisors and colleagues experienced in working with traumatized patients may keep the therapist from becoming vicariously traumatized by the work (McCann & Pearlman 1990) and from committing serious errors.

When treating such challenging patients, it is necessary to have a good balance in our professional and personal lives. We may need to reduce the number of trauma patients seen. Allowing a 24-hour availability for contact may be a needed temporary measure in the beginning of treatment or in specific times of crisis, but should resolve in due time. Both patients and therapists need a social support system to prevent the therapist from becoming the patient's only significant other. "The therapist's personal life should be emotionally rich and psychologically strong enough to nourish his or her professional life, and not the reverse" (Vanderlinden & Vandereycken 1997, p. 169).

Envy of patients or colleagues

Another "forbidden feeling" is envy of a patient or colleague, something we tend to deny. Envy is one of the most primitive and fundamental emotions, in which the subject envies the object for some possession or quality, while jealousy is based on love and aims at the possession of the loved object and the removal of the rival (Klein 1957). Envy can be a very destructive emotion when it is unconscious. When Kassan (1996) asked "Do you ever feel envious of your patients?", some could acknowledge it, mentioning most often envy of a patient's income or financial success. A female therapist said, "Once in a blue moon I have felt competitive with a female patient's financial success. I realize they earn more money than me, and I get a twinge" (op. cit., p. 467). Another female therapist said, "A lot of them have a lot more than I do, in terms of money. Some of my clients have a ton of money. Those are the only ones I feel envious of" (op. cit., p. 467).

Others were envious of a patient's professional achievements or career success. A male psychiatrist said, "I've been envious of certain patients' intellectual achievements" (op. cit., p. 467). A female therapist said, "Sometimes I'm envious of their lives. I have some clients who have pretty exciting lives" (op. cit., p. 467). Another female therapist envied patients' success in personal relationships. "When I was going through a very difficult breakup of a relationship, it was very hard for me to work with people in very positive, loving relationships" (op. cit., p. 467). Another woman said, "There have been times recently, because my husband died recently, when I've envied them running to the Hamptons and dating, all of that" (op. cit., p. 467).

A few envied the personal qualities of some patients. A male therapist said he envied "a certain social ease, a facility for being able to be extremely articulate and expressive, and be good storytellers and good joke tellers" (op. cit., p. 468). Another male therapist envied some male patients' ease with women. A female social worker said, "I have patients who are talented, or stunningly beautiful. How could you help but wish you could be like that sometimes?" (op. cit., p. 468). Another woman said, "Some people are very good about making very clear professional decisions, and are creative in their thinking, and I envy that" (op. cit., p. 468). A few older therapists envied patients their youth, freedom, or opportunity.

One woman said, "Certain backgrounds that some patients came from, certain opportunities they had that I wished I had had" (op. cit., p. 468).

Some felt envious and competitive toward other therapists. A male therapist said quite openly, "At conferences, I want to come in with a machine gun and shoot everybody" (op. cit., p. 497). Others felt competitive about income and professional success. One man said, "Everyone should be coming to me and not to other therapists, to begin with, that's number one. And other people make more money, they have more hours" (op. cit., p. 497). A female social worker said:

> Sometimes I'll think that someone else has such a big practice with great fees, and I'll envy that. But because of my background relative to my siblings, I've learned to translate that and try to figure out what they're doing to have what they have.
>
> (op. cit., p. 497)

Some felt envious of colleagues' writing skills, marketing ability, and intellectual abilities. Carolyn Ellman, writing about women's envy of other women, said, "Envy is a universal part of female development (with more or less destructive effects on a woman's personality" (Ellman 2000, p. 633). Phyllis Chessler said:

> While most women envy and compete only with each other—not with men—few women can survive without bonding to at least one or two other women. Women seek female approval as much as they seek male approval. Therefore, most girls and women deny even to themselves that they envy or compete, even indirectly, with those upon whom they also depend.
>
> (Chessler 2003, p. 15)

A female social worker said, "I will often envy someone who has come up with a brilliant idea or thought, and I'll also admire them" (Kassan 1996, p. 498). This conscious envy is not destructive and can provide motivation to be more creative, but when a woman's envy is unconscious, her fear of her destructive envy can prevent her from enjoying her own sexuality, aggression, and creativity (Ellman 2000). Therapists who receive recognition for their writing have to tolerate the often hateful envy of colleagues, no easy task. Writer Anne Lamott (1995) commented:

> Some wonderful, dazzling successes are going to happen for some of the most awful, angry, undeserving writers you know—people who are, in other words, not you . . . And you are going to want to throw yourself down the back stairs, especially if the person is a friend . . . Then I started to write about my envy. I got to look in some cold, dark corners, see what was there, shine a little light on what we all have in common. Sometimes this human stuff is slimy and pathetic . . . but better to feel it and talk about it and walk through it than to spend a lifetime being silently poisoned.
>
> (Lamott 1995, pp. 122–129)

Attachment difficulties in the decision to retire

Winnicott said, "In doing psychoanalysis I aim at Keeping alive, Keeping well, and Keeping awake" (Winnicott 1962, p. 166). Consciously or unconsciously, all patients will at some time ask themselves, "Will my therapist stay alive and is she capable of understanding me?" (Power 2015, p. 39). As the therapist's aging becomes increasingly more visible, the patient will have real or fantasied reasons for these fears.

In the previous chapter, one therapist said she loved her work so much that she would never retire. "I love it. I'll never retire, they'll have to drag me out by my heels. I get better as I get older" (Kassan 1996, p. 579). I felt much the same way until I came across *Forced Endings in Psychotherapy and Psychoanalysis: Attachment and Loss in Retirement* (Power 2015). Because we are wounded healers, our original attachment patterns tend to impact internally and on the people around us. At a time when our own attachment figures (parents and partners) are more likely to have died, our internal ability to soothe ourselves might be even more crucial if we are to explore and engage with the world. Those with strongly ambivalent or disorganized attachment patterns may try to get their attachment needs met through compulsive caregiving. There is anecdotal evidence that this group, who had an inverted caring relationship with their own parents, may be highly represented among therapists, thus making it very difficult for them to even consider retiring from practice.

Reading this book has shaken up some of my thoughts about retirement and created some changes in my thinking that make it easier to talk with patients about the inevitability of my demise. As we age, we may lose some of our cognitive abilities, thus interfering with our ability to do the work as we had been accustomed to (Dewald & Schwartz 1993). And of course, there is the increased risk of dying, and thus abandoning patients, a traumatic experience. Even Freud continued working until weeks before his death and Martin Bergmann worked until he was almost 101.

The question of if and when to retire is a very difficult one because it is something we tend not to talk about and do not want to think about. There is much denial about the need to retire. An anonymous correspondent asked in an anxious and urgent tone, "So, who is going to tell me I am past it; that my concentration, memory, and energy are not up to the work?" (op. cit., p. 47).

The last time I saw my analyst, I had the devastating experience of walking into his office at the appointed time, only to find that his waiting room and consulting room were dark. "What's going on?" I asked. He sat slumped over his desk, looking as if he had been taking a nap. He looked up, startled, and did not answer me so I turned on the lights myself. I was confused. This was not the lively, sharp-as-a-tack man who had helped me develop a safe and secure attachment to him, and then my husband and my son. After a few silent moments I told him that I could not stay there like this, and left. I called him a few days later and told him that I would not return and suggested that he no longer see patients because he was not functioning well enough. He was seventy-two. It was a terrible way to end such a long and trusting relationship. Had he made the decision to retire, I would have been spared this experience. Given the givens, I weathered it pretty well but I do not know about his other long-term patients. I would not want to do that to mine.

Until now, I do not think I would have even considered retiring. Anne Power has made me think about it and the ambivalence I feel now feels like such a burden. I do not want to arrange my professional life through the lens of my demise. So many of us do not regard retirement as a given, as a developmental phase of professional life (op. cit.) This denial of illness and death as part of aging was unfortunately modeled for us by Freud.

The day after reading Power's book I was able to broach the subject of my mortality with a long-term patient. She had called me twice the previous week when I was waiting for her, to tell me she'd be late for her appointment. I never received her call because my telephone died. (Death is intruding mercilessly!) When she said she wondered what had happened to me, I asked her what had gone through her mind about it. She could not say anything more about it but seemed relieved when I told her that we have seen each other get older together and perhaps it had occurred to her on some level that I'd become ill or died. That opened up the issue for us. We talked more about it. She was glad we had talked about it and I was too.

But I wish I did not feel impelled to think about it. Why can't I just live my life mindfully, in the present moment, without anticipating the future so much? Why can't I live my life like other people do, without such a well-developed conscience?

Lack of self-care

All too often, psychotherapists care more for their patients than they do for themselves, making their work more hazardous. Caring for the self is essential for all of us (Khantzian & Mack 1983).

References

Celenza, A. (2014). *Erotic Revelations: Clinical Applications and Perverse Scenarios.* New York and London: Routledge.

Chessler, P. (2003). *Woman's Inhumanity to Woman.* New York: Plume.

Dewald, P., & Schwartz, H. (1993). The Life Cycle of the Analyst: Pregnancy, Illness, and Disability. *Journal of the American Psychoanalytic Association, 41*: 207.

Ellman, C. (2000). The Empty Mother: Women's Fear of Their Destructive Envy. *Psychoanalytic Quarterly, 69*: 633–657.

Farber, S. (2000). *When the Body Is the Target: Self-Harm, Pain, and Traumatic Attachments.* Northvale, NJ: Jason Aronson.

Farber, S. (2015). My Patient, My Stalker Empathy as a Dual-Edged Sword: A Cautionary Tale. *American Journal of Psychotherapy, 69* (3): 331–355.

Galeazzi, G., Elkins, K., & Curci, P. (2005). The Stalking of Mental Health Professionals by Patients. *Psychiatric Services, 56* (2): 137–138.

Groesbeck, C. (1975). The Archetypal Image of the Wounded Healer. *Journal of Analytical Psychology, 20* (2): 122–145.

Heath, S. (1991). *Dealing with the Therapist's Vulnerability to Depression.* Northvale, NJ: Jason Aronson.

Herman, J. (1992). *Trauma and Recovery: The Aftermath of Violence, from Domestic Abuse to Political Terror.* New York: Basic Books.

Kaplan, A. (2006). Being Stalked—An Occupational Hazard? *Psychiatric Times, 23* (8): n.p.

Kassan, L. E. (1996). *Shrink Rap: Sixty Psychotherapists Discuss Their Work, Their Lives, and the State of Their Field.* New York: Jason Aronson.

Khantzian, E., & Mack, J. (1983). Self-Preservation and the Care of the Self-Ego Instincts Reconsidered. *Psychoanalytic Study of the Child, 38*: 209–232.

Klein, M. (1957). *Envy and Gratitude, and Other Works 1946–1963.* New York: Free Press.

Lamott, A. (1995). *Bird by Bird: Some Instructions on Writing and Life.* New York: Anchor.

McCann, L., & Pearlman, L. (1990). Vicarious Traumatization: A Framework for Understanding the Psychological Effects of Working with Victims. *Journal of Traumatic Stress, 3*: 131–149.

Meloy, J. (1999). Stalking: An Old Behavior, a New Crime. *Psychiatric Clinics of North America, 22* (1): 85–99.

Meloy, J., & Boyd, C. (2003). Female Stalkers and Their Victims. *Journal of the American Academy of Psychiatry and the Law, 31* (2): 211–219.

Meloy, J., & Fisher, H. (2005). Some Thoughts on the Neurobiology of Stalking. *Journal of Forensic Science, 50* (6): 1472–1480.

Nagel, S. (1989). Countertransference to Transference Acting Out of Suicidal Threats of a Borderline Personality Disorder. In: J. Masterson & R. Klein (eds.), *Psychotherapy of the Disorders of the Self. The Masterson Approach* (pp. 328–344). New York: Brunner/Mazel.

Pearlman, L., & Saakvitne, K. (1995). *Trauma and the Therapist: Countertransference and Vicarious Traumatization in Psychotherapy with Incest Survivors.* New York: Norton.

Pope, K., & Vasquez, M. (2011). *Ethics in Psychotherapy and Counseling: A Practical Guide.* New York: Jossey-Bass.

Power, A. (2015). *Forced Endings in Psychotherapy and Psychoanalysis: Attachment and Loss in Retirement.* New York and London: Routledge.

Tillman, J. (2014). Patient Suicide: Impact on Clinicians. *Psychiatric Times.* Retrieved from http://www.psychiatrictimes.com/special-reports/patient-suicide-impact-clinicians?GUID=E28D0073-CBF7-4EC0-8F95-A7F0BAFC4596&rememberme=1&ts=1301 2015

Truman, A., & Mustaine, E. (2011). When Social Workers Are Stalked: Risks, Strategies, and Legal Protections. *Clinical Social Work Journal, 39* (3): 232–242.

Vanderlinden, J., & Vandereycken, W. (1997). *Trauma, Dissociation, and Impulse Dyscontrol in Eating Disorders.* New York: Brunner/Mazel.

Winnicott, D. (1958). Hate in the Countertransference. In: *Collected Papers: Through Paediatrics to Psychoanalysis* (pp. 194–203). New York: Basic Books.

Winnicott, D. (1962). The Aims of Psycho-Analytical Treatment. In: *Maturational Processes and the Facilitating Environment: Studies in the Theory of Emotional Development* (pp. 166–178). London: Karnac.

Chapter 4

The hero's journey of post-traumatic growth

Sharon K. Farber

In scientific studies of the subject, adversity is associated with negative psychological outcomes such as anxiety, depression, post-traumatic stress disorder, and blunted emotional responding. Adversity has also been tied to the belief that the world is not benevolent and that life is not meaningful, the kind of thinking that is a recipe for a lack of kindness (DeSteno 2015). David DeSteno wanted to know whether adversity hardens hearts or warms them. The findings of his studies demonstrated that in many cases adversity elicits empathy and compassion in those who have experienced it.

> The reason, we suspect, is that compassion isn't as purely selfless as it might seem. While it might appear to be a response to the suffering of others, it is also a strategy for regaining your own footing—for resilience in the face of trauma. After all, having strong social relationships is one of the best predictors of psychological well-being in the long run, and so anything that enhances your bonds with others—like expressing compassion for them— makes you more resilient . . .
>
> In both studies, the results were the same. Those who had faced increasingly severe adversities in life—loss of a loved one at an early age, threats of violence or the consequences of a natural disaster—were more likely to empathize with others in distress, and, as a result, feel more compassion for them . . .
>
> Those who had faced increasingly severe adversities in life—loss of a loved one at an early age, threats of violence or the consequences of a natural disaster—were more likely to empathize with others in distress, and, as a result, feel more compassion for them.
>
> (op. cit., p. 9)

Boys, however, seem to be more negatively affected than girls to disadvantage (Miller 2015).

> Any disadvantage, like growing up in poverty, in a bad neighborhood or without a father, takes more of a toll on boys than on their sisters . . . Marianne Bertrand, . . . who with Jessica Pan has studied the gender gap, also found that

boys fare worse than girls in disadvantaged homes, and are more responsive than girls to parental time and resources. "Their findings were very consistent: Families that invest more in children are protective for boys." . . . But they said there were clues to why boys are extra sensitive to disadvantage. A big one is that impoverished households are more likely to be led by single mothers, and boys suffer from a lack of male role models . . . "Boys particularly seem to benefit more from being in a married household or committed household—with the time, attention and income that brings."

(op. cit., p. A3)

Post-traumatic growth

Ernest Hemingway (1994) said that the world breaks everyone, but afterwards, some of us are strong in the broken places. Although it is well known that post-traumatic stress disorder is a common outcome of trauma, what is not well known is that another outcome of trauma is post-traumatic growth (Rendon 2015), the story of the phoenix rising from its ashes.

> Trauma is a breaking point in a survivor's life. They are left transformed. Part of that change involves anguish, but research increasingly shows that suffering can catalyze life-altering growth. Survivors are forced to think differently about themselves and the world. "When you are near death, everything seems to crystallize," said Matt Cotcher, who had a large brain tumor removed in 2007—and after years of surgeries, rehabs and therapy, is now training to climb Mt. Kilimanjaro to raise money to fight brain cancer.
>
> (Rendon 2015, p. C3)

People react differently to the same painful events and some even respond relatively well. Paradoxically, the same experiences that lead others into psychosis and addiction can be what is transformative in others. Over the last few decades it has been found that that with the right circumstances and support, survivors can actually emerge from their trauma stronger, more focused, and with a new and clear vision for the future. In fact, between half and two-thirds of trauma survivors report positive changes—far *more* than suffer from PTSD (Rendon 2015). The psychotherapists who have contributed chapters to this book are examples.

There is a growing body of research documented globally on post-traumatic growth, the experience of positive change that occurs as a result of the struggle with very challenging life crises (Tedeschi & Calhoun 2004). These changes include greater appreciation of life and changed sense of priorities; warmer, more intimate relationships with others; a greater sense of personal strength; recognition of new possibilities or paths for one's life; and spiritual development. Post-traumatic growth occurs concurrently with the attempts to adapt to highly negative sets of circumstances that can engender high levels of psychological distress.

[In] the frightening and confusing aftermath of trauma, where fundamental assumptions are severely challenged, can be fertile ground for unexpected outcomes that can be observed in survivors: posttraumatic growth . . .

In the developing literature on posttraumatic growth, we have been finding that reports of growth experiences in the aftermath of traumatic events has outnumbered reports of psychiatric disorders. This is despite the fact that we are concerned with truly traumatic circumstances rather than everyday stressors. The widespread assumption that traumas often result in disorder should not be replaced with expectations that growth is an inevitable result. Instead, we are finding that continuing personal distress and growth often coexist. Although not prevalent in either clinical or research settings, there has been a very long tradition of viewing human suffering as offering the possibility for the origin of significant good . . .

Maslow (1970), for example, whose most influential work was originally published in the 1950s and 1960s, argued consistently that psychologists should expend much greater efforts in studying "people who are actually healthy" (p. 270) and the better and brighter aspects of human behavior and nature . . .

Posttraumatic growth describes the experience of individuals whose development, at least in some areas, has surpassed what was present before the struggle with crises occurred. The individual not only has survived, but has experienced changes that are viewed as important, and that go beyond what was the previous status quo. Posttraumatic growth is not simply a return to baseline—it is an experience of improvement that for some persons is deeply profound.

(op. cit., pp. 2–4)

Viktor Frankl (1997), a Viennese neurologist and psychiatrist, published *Man's Search for Meaning* in 1946, months after the end of World War II, telling of the horrors of life in Auschwitz, how the Nazis systematically dehumanized each prisoner until there was nothing left, and his own struggle to survive.

Then, one evening, almost by accident, Frankel discovered something that would save his life. As he marched back from a work detail that evening, he was in terrible pain. His feet were covered in sores, his shoes torn. With a bitterly cold wind bearing down on him, he obsessed over all the tiny things he needed to do in order to survive. If a piece of sausage were given to him, should he trade it for bread? Should he trade a cigarette for a bowl of soup? How could he find a piece of wire to replace the bit that had served as a shoe-lace? How could he get on good terms with the guard who might be able to assign him to a closer work detail? Then, in the midst of this complex calculus of survival, an image came to him. He saw a detailed and clear vision of himself giving a lecture after the war on the psychology of the concentration camp. And that changed how he viewed everything around him. "All that oppressed me at that moment became objective, seen as described from the remote viewpoint of science. By this method I succeeded in rising above the situation, above the sufferings of the moment," he wrote.

(Rendon 2015)

Frankl described a way of thinking about suffering, trauma, and their aftereffects quite different than how psychology tends to view psychopathology. For him, the suffering that can result from trauma is not always a malady to be cured, but rather, is an important sign of inner turmoil that is normal. In fact, he says, they are an achievement. They are problems demanding attention and can only be cured in the course of resolving the underlying conflict. In many cases, treating the symptoms only prolongs the illness. Frankl founded an entire branch of psychotherapy, logotherapy, focused on the idea of finding meaning in one's life, especially in one's suffering, focusing on meaning as the central driving force of a healthy life.

Stories of post-traumatic growth can be found in ancient history, religion, in the lives of our most celebrated people, and even in popular culture (Rendon 2015). One of the best-known stories appeared in 1939, only two illustrated pages long. It told the story of a young boy who watches helplessly as his parents are murdered by a robber. Days later, he is at his bedside praying to avenge their deaths by spending the rest of his life fighting all criminals. The boy is Bruce Wayne, who takes on the character of the superhero Batman to fight crime and protect the city of Gotham. As illustrated in that early comic strip, he is transformed by the brutal murder of his parents. Batman is not the only superhero to be transformed by loss. In the Spider-Man series Peter Parker begins using his powers to fight evil only after the tragic death of his uncle. The Green Lantern witnesses his father's death in a plane crash. The theme of loss and transformation is constant.

Those who developed the stories of the superheroes were inspired by real people. For Paul Levitz, who wrote for DC Comics for forty-two years, the tale of post-traumatic growth was grounded in the story of Theodore Roosevelt (Rendon 2015). Roosevelt, born to a powerful wealthy family, was confined indoors with severe asthma for much of his childhood. He had a very close relationship with his father, who often stayed up late at night with him when he was sick. When Teddy was in college his father died suddenly from cancer. To honor him, Teddy dedicated himself to public service. By the time he was twenty-four he was already a New York State assemblyman, and two and a half years later his first daughter, Alice, was born. Two days later Teddy's wife and mother died within hours of each other. Roosevelt withdrew from public life, left Alice with his sister, and went to live on a ranch in North Dakota, where he built a cabin and raised cattle. He went on long hunting trips, shooting grizzly bears. At times he rode alone on horseback for days through blizzards and below-zero temperatures, pushing himself to physical and psychological extremes. He became fearless, confronting gunmen threatening to kill him and hunting down cattle thieves. When he slowed down, he was overcome with grief.

Eventually Roosevelt returned to New York and ran New York City's police commission. He walked the officers' beats to ensure they were doing their jobs, exposed corruption in the force, and locked horns with corrupt political figures. He became a transformative force for reform, much as he did later as President. "People succeed in wonderful and dramatic ways in history . . . And that provides the inspiration for what the heroic journey can be" (op. cit., p. 35).

When Emily Samuelson, a contributor to this book, wrote that healing is a hero's journey, she exemplified Joseph Campbell's archetype of *The Hero*. In *The Hero's Journey*, Campbell (2014), inspired by Jung's concept archetypes of the collective unconscious, developed the archetype of *The Hero*, the person who goes out and achieves great deeds on behalf of the group, tribe, or civilization. Perhaps when Sigmund Freud developed his burning desire to become a hero, which you'll read about in the next chapter, he unconsciously knew that he was on a hero's journey.

Tedeschi and Calhoun have described how "the cognitive processing of trauma into growth appears to be aided in many people by self-disclosure in supportive social environments" (2004, p. 11). Supportive others can assist in post-traumatic growth by providing a way to craft narratives about the changes that have occurred and through offering perspectives that can be integrated into schema change (op. cit.). This book has provided a way to craft these narratives.

Tedeschi and Calhoun emphasize that the presence of post-traumatic growth does not necessarily mean a lessened degree of psychological distress. Consider what Rabbi Harold Kushner said in reflecting upon the death of his son:

> I am a more sensitive person, a more effective pastor, a more sympathetic counselor because of Aaron's life and death than I would ever have been without it. And I would give up all of those gains in a second if I could have my son back. If I could choose, I would forego all of the spiritual growth and depth which has come my way because of my experiences . . . But I cannot choose.
>
> (Tedeschi & Calhoun 2004, p. 10,
> citing Viorst 1986, p. 295)

Other research into resilience defined it in much the same way as post-traumatic growth. Fletcher and Sarkar said, "It is the study of psychological resilience that seeks to understand why some individuals are able to withstand—or even thrive on—the pressure they experience in their lives" (2012, p. 12). Many believe these qualities are predetermined, that either you have them or you do not. Fletcher and Sarkar found that not only is resilience necessary for succeeding in stressful situations, it is a skill that can be developed over time. Those who have experienced adversity early in life may adapt to it, steeling themselves to pressure they encounter as they get older.

This was found in the Grant Study, an innovative study of the human life cycle, for which Harvard recruited 268 of its strongest and most promising undergraduates, The program's originators thought medical research was too heavily weighted in the direction of pathology, and they wanted to chronicle the ways in which a group of the most capable individuals coped with their lives over the life span. Psychiatrist George Vaillant, who became the director of the study in 1938, had deep personal reasons for becoming a psychiatrist and wanting to understand just how people adapt to painful life circumstances. He revealed that when he was ten, his father killed himself, leaving him traumatized (Shenk 2009).

Almost forty years later, Vaillant interviewed the Grant Study men and found that for many who came from painful childhoods, later love in life could be emotionally corrective as can be the development of a successful career. Vaillant posed essential questions about the individual differences in confronting life's stresses. How can we successfully change those patterns of behavior that make us miserable, unhealthy, and reckless? Why do some of us manage so well with what life hands us, while others, who have had similar advantages or disadvantages, cope poorly or not at all? For each man Vaillant evaluated which defense mechanisms were more adaptive than others, classifying them into four categories: psychotic, immature, neurotic, and mature. Vaillant found that people mature by their adaptive processes and defense mechanisms evolving from lower to higher (Farber 2013; Vaillant 1977).

Gina Higgins (1994) had personal reasons for becoming a psychologist and wanting to understand how and why some people do well in life, despite their painful life circumstances. She has done well, unlike her brother, who committed suicide after having experienced prolonged sexual abuse. She found that resilient people have developed the ability to use their adverse experiences for their steeling effect, allowing them to function far better than expected, which helps them complete the critical developmental tasks that face them as they grow. What Nietzsche said may be true, that whatever does not kill us makes us stronger (Farber 2013).

When Higgins did her doctoral dissertation, studying what resilient adults have in common, she came to the same conclusion as Vaillant. She sought out and selected forty subjects who were chosen for their extreme past hurt and current health, using human capacities that lie dormant in many of us. She found that these people had above-average to superior IQs; exceptional talents, including creativity and other inner resources (and had developed many of them); attained higher economic levels than their families of origin; showed high levels of ego development; were able to sustain empathically close relationships in childhood, adolescence, and adulthood, including those they formed with individuals who came to serve as parental surrogates. They often maintained a great deal of political and social activism. Frequently they had siblings who were highly emotionally disturbed. Looking at them from a more psychodynamic perspective, they remain fiercely committed to reflection, new perspectives, and ongoing therapy (Higgins 1994).

Higgins found that resilience evolves over time. Even conditions such as schizophrenia and bipolar disorder, for which there is strong evidence of heritability, are molded by environmental influences and the brain's plasticity (Doidge 2007). Resilience "best captures the active process of self-righting and growth that characterizes some people so essentially" (Higgins 1994, p. 1). An impressive strength of the resilient is their ability to acknowledge and experience significant psychological pain and still maintain their ability to *love well*, creating and sustaining relationships marked by reciprocity and concern for the other as well as the self. They form and take part in relationships that can survive, even thrive, on discord, disillusionment, frequent anger, and frustration, and successfully negotiating these conflicts. They have developed a way of relating to others in a manner which does not usually sacrifice the truth and understanding with which they perceive them. They usually succeed in their efforts to recognize and distinguish others' needs and characteristics. They have unexpected strengths and a capacity to love, despite being exposed to hatred. Resilient people do more than survive adversity; with the right kind of help they can actually thrive and love and transcend it.

Resilience can be cultivated, Higgins found, pointing out that psychotherapists, teachers, counselors, and other surrogates should never underestimate their possible corrective impact on a child or adult. Given that adversity harms boys more than girls, especially those growing up in single mother homes (Miller 2015), when the surrogate for a boy is a man, this provides an advantage:

> So many of the resilient said that their hope was continually bolstered by the sudden kindness of strangers, even for just brief moments, and integrated into the broader fabric of resilient faith over time. The gratitude with which the resilient recalled their surrogates was enormous. "Enormous reparative potential resides in the bread-and-butter basics of caring about the young and listening closely to their lives. You can do this in any capacity: babysitter, teacher, therapist, neighbor, relative, clergy, coach, butcher, baker, or candlestick maker."
>
> (Higgins 1994, p. 324)

Building on Alexander's (1958) concept of the corrective emotional experience, Hartman and Zimberoff (2004) identified over twenty types of corrective experiences, and suggest that they all fit into one of three categories: (1) building ego strength through the release of shame and reclaiming worthiness; (2) building agency through the release of helplessness and reclaiming personal power; and (3) building authenticity through the release of dissociation and identification and reclaiming self-reflective identity.

Most of Higgins' resilient subjects were in psychotherapy for prolonged periods of time and so it should be no surprise that so many of them became psychotherapists themselves. Gina Higgins is one of them. So am I. So are many respected colleagues. Higgins said, "At Harvard I once heard someone remark that all dissertations are veiled autobiographies. Perhaps this is true of all committed professional work, varying mostly in the transparency of the veil" (Higgins 1994, p. xviii). "The resilient capacities in ourselves and others are reparative mechanisms that can propel you forward at any phase in the life cycle" (Farber 2013, p. 316). Therapists who undertake an intensive, lengthy psychotherapy often return to it for a briefer period of time when in need.

How do the wounded become resilient?

Among the many resilient human beings who found her way into Higgins' study is Anya, a psychologist, happily married for twenty-eight years, and mother of two psychologically healthy sons. As a child she was the victim of a satanic cult and forced to become a prostitute. How can it be possible that she was deeply respected by the seasoned clinician who referred her to the study and was considered quite healthy by her therapist? Having dissociated her cult abuse memories, she began to recall them when she was forty-six. Unlike many satanic cult survivors, she has never had any significant psychopathology, did not marry a compromised person, and did not reproduce anything remotely resembling catastrophic experiences in her children's lives. Both her therapist and colleagues verify that none of her relationships outside her family and the cult have ever been abusive. "Anya's past could make you wonder why she is still ambulatory, let alone resilient" (Higgins 1994, p. 10).

Anya explained that what gave her hope was a man in the cult who befriended and protected her, and when the cult leaders discovered this, they hanged him, forced her to watch, and blamed her. This man, extraordinarily enough, was a pedophile who stumbled unknowingly into the cult, probably because he was a pedophile rather than a sadist. He tried to help Anya by inflicting less pain on her than he might have, and for Anya this was life-preserving and life-affirming. He threatened to leave the cult because it was so sadistic and pretended to do the sadistic things to Anya that they expected him to do. He liked Anya and forming such attachments were not allowed. His efforts must be understood within the context of what Anya experienced in her family. When Anya was three, her mother colluded in her and her sister's physical and sexual abuse by their father, a prominent San Francisco psychoanalyst. Anya remembers when her third sister was born but soon disappeared. Anya presumes it was by sacrifice. When she was eighteen, her other sister was diagnosed as schizophrenic and killed herself. Soon after, Anya fell in love with her husband and left the family.

Anya's pedophile had became a locus of hope, the only locus of hope she had. "We prefer to think of hope as a soft-robed goddess, but some find it even— ironically, *chillingly*, in a pedophile" (op. cit., p. 105). Anya fought to preserve her soul and did this by imagining a host of benevolent spiritual children with protective powers, who were charged with guarding her integrity. She asked them who they were and they said that they were there to protect her, to which she responded, "Well, why didn't you do a better job?" (op. cit., p. 108). They explained that they could not cross over into her real life but that they were there to protect her spirit and that she could call on them whenever she wanted. Anya's dissociation was so severe that she may well have had dissociative identity disorder. These imagined protectors helped her to develop a life for herself as a wife, mother, and a wounded healer.

Creating a new narrative

The stories we tell about who we are are extremely important. They can trap us in a victim's life or can open the door to something new and transformative (Rendon 2015). If we define ourselves as victims of adversity, we must create a new story of our life. Once we allow ourselves to imagine it, then we might be able to create it. The wounded healer must create a new and better narrative for his life. Talking or writing expressively about difficult experiences forces a survivor to translate them into language, especially important with traumatic memories (Pennebaker 1991; Rendon 2015).

> Life-threatening events activate the amygdala, the brain's fear center. Those memories are red hot with emotion but can lack language or context. Writing helps survivors to label the experience, attaching language to it that allows survivors to understand and process the event instead of leaving it as some alert drifting adrift in our neural wiring. Once that's done, people can assign it meaning, some level of coherence, and give the event a structure and place in their lives. Representing the experience with language is a necessary step toward understanding the experience, Pennebaker argues.
>
> (Rendon 2015, p. 116)

Writing can be more effective than talking to an empathic listener because it forces one to really think through an event and its consequences in a more detailed and thorough way than talking about them. As we write we become observers, regarding our lives with a certain detachment and distance. Because we tend to talk faster than we write, writing slows it all, allowing us to reframe the problems in our life as challenges.

One hero's journey

Michael Eigen, psychoanalyst and author, went into analysis to heal the wounds of a traumatic childhood. Being a patient made him want to become an analyst. His writing has helped him make sense of his experience.

> My younger brother was killed by a truck when he was almost 11 and I was 21. My mother never really fully recovered and to say I felt guilty does not even come close. I suspect I became an analyst partly to bring my brother back to life. This is one reason why I have been attracted to the impossible and worked so long with patients who had been given up on by others—the psychotic . . ., the unwanted, undeveloped, malignant, recalcitrant or otherwise maimed self . . . and the dead.
>
> (Eigen 1998, p. 81)

He suffered from terrible feelings of aloneness but eventually felt himself as one among many threads woven into the great human tapestry, providing him with the empathy needed to help anguished or depressed others become threads in the same tapestry (Eigen 1998; Farber 2013).

> Nowadays, more and more people come in and actually say that they don't feel alive . . . I remember certain people I've met in my life, like Winnicott, Allen Ginsberg, or the rebbe Menachem Schneerson. When I was with them, I felt it was okay to be the sort of person I am. With them it was okay for me to be somehow off the map, beyond the map; it was okay for there to be in life such a person as I was. In that passage, then, I was trying to encode, for whomever it might reach, something like a message in a bottle. Floating on the sea, it then might reach some people, who would hear the message that it's okay for them to be the sort of alone person they are. And by some miracle, by making room for such a message, some of these people, through the course of years, have tapestried out. They've found themselves situated in a larger tapestry that makes room for the sorts of being they were and are, whereas earlier there didn't seem to be any place for them.
>
> (Eigen 1997, pp. 99–101)

> After years of reciting permutations of my traumatic upbringing, I began losing interest in how hurt I was. The wound that never heals meets the fire that never goes out in never-ending ways. I became less interested in my past than in getting on with my life . . . As time went on, I got more interested in what went on in therapy for its own sake, as a process of soul making. Therapy is not only a soul searchlight. Interactions between patient and therapist actually create being and new nuances of being.
>
> (Eigen 1998, p. 84)

References

Alexander, F. (1958). Unexplored Areas in Psychoanalytic Theory and Treatment—Part II. In: *The Scope of Psychoanalysis* (pp. 319–335). New York: Basic Books.

Bollas, C. (1997). *Freely Associated: Encounters in Psychoanalysis with Christopher Bollas, Joyce McDougall, Michael Eigen, Adam Phillips, Nina Coltart*. London and New York: Free Association.

Campbell, J. (2014). *The Hero's Journey: Joseph Campbell on His Life and Work*. Novato, CA: New World Library.

DeSteno, D. (2015). The Funny Thing about Adversity. *The New York Times*, October 18, n.p.

Doidge, N. (2007). *The Brain that Changes Itself: Stories of Personal Triumph from the Frontiers of Brain Science*. New York: Penguin.

Eigen, M. (1997). Michael Eigen. In: A. Molino (ed.), *Freely Associated: Encounters in Psychoanalysis with Christopher Bollas, Joyce McDougall, Michael Eigen, Adam Phillips, Nina Coltart* (pp. 93–126). London and New York: Free Association.

Eigen, M. (1998). Shivers. In: J. Reppen (ed.), *Why I Became a Psychotherapist* (pp. 77–88). Northvale, NJ: Jason Aronson.

Farber, S. (2005). Free Association Reconsidered: The Talking Cure, the Writing Cure. *Journal of the American Academy of Psychoanalysis and Dynamic Psychiatry, 33* (2): 249–273.

Farber, S. (2013). *Hungry for Ecstasy: Trauma, the Brain, and the Influence of the Sixties.* Lanham, MD: Jason Aronson/Rowman & Littlefield.

Fletcher, D., & Sarkar, M. (2012). Psychological Resilience: A Review and Critique of Definitions, Concepts, and Theory. *European Psychologist, 18*: 12–23.

Frankl, V. (1997). *Man's Search For Meaning.* New York: Pocket Books.

Hartman, D., & Zimberoff, D. (2004). Corrective Emotional Experience in the Therapeutic Process. *Journal of Heart-Centered Therapies, 7* (2): 3–84.

Hemingway, E. (1994). *A Farewell to Arms.* London: Arrow.

Higgins, G. (1994). *Resilient Adults: Overcoming a Cruel Past.* San Francisco: Jossey-Bass.

Maslow, A. (1970) Motivation and Personality. New York: Harper.

Miller, C. (2015). A Disadvantaged Start Hurts Boys More Than Girls. *The New York Times*, October 22.

Pennebaker, J. (1991). *Opening Up: The Healing Power of Confiding in Others.* New York: Avon.

Rendon, J. (2015). *Upside: The New Science of Post-Traumatic Growth.* New York: Touchstone.

Shenk, J. (2009). What Makes Us Happy? *The Atlantic* (June): n.p.

Tedeschi, R., & Calhoun, L. (2004). Posttraumatic Growth: Conceptual Foundations and Empirical Evidence. *Psychological Inquiry: An International Journal for the Advancement of Psychological Theory, 15* (1): 1–18.

Vaillant, G. (1977). *Adaptation to Life.* Boston and Toronto: Little, Brown.

Viorst, J. (1986). Necessary Losses. New York: Simon & Schuster.

Chapter 5

The overt and covert Freud

Prototype of the wounding healer

Sharon K. Farber

Sigmund Freud's ideas thoroughly altered our view of human beings as rational and conscious. He has been called psychiatry's greatest hero by some and its most calamitous rogue by others (Lieberman 2015). To some orthodox Freudians Freud remains an impervious hero who could do no wrong, while, at the other extreme, he has been condemned as a fabricator (Roazen 1971).

> This Freud was extremely ambitious. He denied what he knew in order to be treated as an eminent German doctor. He was also determined to deflect the pervasive anti-Semitism in Vienna away from himself and his creation. We can say that there was a revealed or overt Freud and a concealed or covert Freud.
>
> (Berke 2015, p. xii)

Freud said that "when a man is endowed with power it is hard for him not to misuse it" (Freud 1937, p. 249). Ironically, Freud misused his power, turning against those dearest to him. He can be described as a traumatizing narcissist (Shaw 2014), using a relational system of subjugation to dominate others. His first playmate was his nephew John, whom he loved and hated, a relational pattern that continued throughout his life, marking his significant relationships (Donn 1988).

> My emotional life has always insisted that I should have an intimate friend and a hated enemy. I have always been able to provide myself afresh with both, and it has not infrequently happened that the ideal situation of child-hood has been so completely reproduced that friend and enemy have come together in a single individual—though not, of course, both at once or without constant oscillations.
>
> (Freud 1900, p. 521)

Freud's followers endowed him with great power, feeding his sense of entitlement, leading him to abuse his power and transgress the same boundaries he warned others about. One patient described Freud's attitude as being "Do as I say, not as I do" (Roazen 1971, p. 124). Many of his early circle followed suit. Jung used his own patients for his own psychological needs. He treated Sabina Spielrein for hysteria when she was eighteen, then became her lover; he also treated Toni Wolff, then had an affair with her as well (Kerr 1993). Otto Rank had an affair with his patient Anaïs Nin. And it goes on and on until the present.

Freud suffered multiple traumas in childhood and later, resulting in chronic anxiety and depression. His early letters to Fliess reported migraine symptoms, pain all over his body, abdominal distress, and heart palpitations. "The chief patient I am preoccupied with is myself" (Masson 1985, p. 261). He became his most important patient, immersing himself in his new techniques and associating to the elements in his dream life and communicating them to Fliess.

Freud's "passionate desire was to become a great man, to achieve fame, to be, in his own words, a hero" (Breger 2000, p. 2), about whom biographies would be written. Ernest Jones was Freud's most well-known biographer and wrote a three-volume biography that idealized Freud (Jones 1953, 1955, 1957). Our knowledge of Freud is due largely to his own ambitious promotion of the psychoanalytic movement, aided by Jones, his second-in-command. Their relationship was essentially an opportunistic one.

Despite or perhaps because of Freud's severe traumatization, he had a blind spot about trauma, regarding sexuality as the root of all psychopathology. After graduation from the University of Vienna, he worked as an assistant in the laboratory of physiologist Ernst Brucke, the happiest years of his student days. He had no contact with women during these years, was shy and afraid of women, and was a virgin when he married at thirty, an indication of the extent of his inhibitions (Breger 2009).

Freud has been highly criticized for

> presuming that because our sexual urges are so strong they must make their way into every single one of our decisions. Neuroscience, as well as casual introspection, tells us otherwise: that our desire for wealth, acceptance, friendship, recognition, competition and ice cream are all independent and equally real impulses, not merely lust in costume.
>
> (Lieberman 2015, p. 44)

Both Wilhelm Reich and Sándor Ferenczi thought Freud was relatively impotent, suffering from sexual inhibitions which account for the nature of some of his central ideas (Roazen 1993). His very potent libidinal energy was used in the service of promoting the psychoanalytic movement.

Freud's theory of the unconscious was the culmination of a cultural process extending over several centuries, and many of his discoveries had been anticipated by previous thinkers (Whyte 1962). Although he had no concrete evidence of the existence of the unconscious or of neurosis, he developed his theory from inferences derived from his patients' behavior, his own self-analysis, and the Kabbalah. Yes, this "godless Jew" (Gay 1987) was influenced by mystical Judaism. Anti-Semitism, poverty, and a history of traumatic losses early in life played major roles in forming his personality and theories.

Ernest Jones and Sigmund Freud: made for each other

Brenda Maddox, Jones' biographer, called him Freud's wizard, the colossus of the international psychoanalytic movement, who "drew much criticism for his alleged arrogance, autocracy, dishonesty" (Maddox 2007, p. 2).

Jones moved the center of psychoanalysis from Vienna to London, bringing its influence to New York, Toronto, and Boston. He wrote many books and articles, founded the British Psycho-Analytical Society and the *International Journal of Psycho-Analysis*, editing it for many years. As the president of the International Psychoanalytic Association he organized the rescue of many Jews, including Freud, from the Nazis, to resettlement in Britain and elsewhere.

Considered irresistible to women, it was believed Jones slept with many adult patients. He went on trial after four mentally defective girls complained that he sexually assaulted them. He had to resign from London's West End Hospital after examining female patients without a third person present. This essentially ended his career as a physician, motivating him to promote himself as a psychoanalyst (Maddox 2007). It was in Jones' self-interest to curry favor with Freud and advance psychoanalysis. Freud called Jones "the liar from Wales" (Roazen 1993) and told Ferenczi, "Jones makes trouble all the time, but we know his worth well enough" (Maddox 2007, p. 2). As Jones' reputation grew, he set up the new International Psycho-Analytic Press in London, along with a psychoanalytic bookshop. He was invited to broadcast on the BBC in 1932, the same year he became president of the International Psychoanalytic Association.

The traumatized Freud

Freud was born into a large extended family in Catholic Freiberg, the first-born son of Jacob and Amalia Freud. Amalia was a domineering, insensitive woman. When observing his son Martin's wife, Esti, with her three- or four-month-old son, Freud chastised her for cuddling him too much, saying that excessive parental tenderness was harmful because it tended to accelerate sexual maturation. "Another way of looking at it would be that Freud was suspicious of mother love" (Roazen 1993, p. 154). When his mother died, Freud did not even attend her funeral, sending his daughter Anna as his representative (Roazen 1993).

His father was a merchant and salesman but could afford only a single rented room. The family lived in poverty, relying on money sent from relatives in England. When Freud was eleven months old, Amalia became pregnant with a second son. The newborn child was named after Amalia's younger brother, who had died of tuberculosis at age twenty, just a month previously. The infant died of an infection around six months after birth. Amalia had seven more babies, a pattern in which she was constantly pregnant and losing new babies. Amalia was undoubtedly depressed and emotionally unavailable after the deaths of her brother and children. Freud must have become frightened that he too would get sick, then die or disappear and that he would lose those whom he needed the most. Living in such cramped conditions Freud was exposed to the intimate details of his parents' lives: their reactions to the deaths of his infant brothers, their anxiety about poverty, their sexual relationship, the births of other babies, nursing, and infant care. Jacob's two adult sons from his first marriage, one of whom was married and had two children, lived with them and joined him in the family business, which required the participation of many family members, including Amalia. This meant Freud was left with a nursemaid. When he was nine or ten his uncle Josef, Jacob's younger brother, was caught in a counterfeit money scandal, and was sentenced to ten years in prison. Jacob, already a failure as a breadwinner, had further shamed the family.

Freud was very attached to his nursemaid, who may have abused him sexually. Freud revealed in a dream that she was his "instructress in sexual matters . . . that she washed him in reddish water in which she had previously washed herself" (Krull 1986, p. 120). Through bathing in water bloodied by her menses, Freud became a dirty Jew. Themes of religion and travel are also connected to her. She took Freud to church; he returned preaching about what he had heard. She was the first person who thought highly of his abilities, thus fostering his ambition. She encouraged him to steal coins to give to her. His mother told him that she was really a thief who had stolen all the coins and toys that had been given to him. She was arrested and sentenced to prison, another profound loss for Freud. These early losses created fears around absence and death, expressed in anxiety dreams about his mother's death.

Freud's fear of travel is tied to his first train trip at age three, when Jacob's business collapsed and his family relocated to Vienna. Arriving at the train station, Freud was filled with fear when the gas-jet lights illuminating the station reminded him of souls burning in hell, a belief acquired accompanying his Catholic nursemaid to church. He was terrified that the train would take his parents, leaving him behind. His train phobia does not seem related to seeing his mother naked in her train compartment when he was three, as he believed. He could not actually recall seeing his mother naked on the train; "he just supposed that he must have and that he then pushed the image down into his unconscious. From this supposition he generalized that all train phobia derives from repressed sexual desire" (Stossel 2014, p. 236). As an adult, when traveling by train with his family, he booked a separate compartment because he was ashamed to have them witness his fits of anxiety. He arrived at train stations hours before departure, symptomatic of his terrible fear of being left behind.

He longed to go to Rome, the legendary dwelling place of the Messiah. In a letter to Fliess, he wrote, "Incidentally my longing for Rome is deeply neurotic. It is connected with my school-boy hero worship of the Semitic Hannibal" (Masson 1985, p. 285). It may also be connected with his ambivalence about Christianity.

Vienna continued growing as Europe's cultural capital (Bettelheim 1991). Jews came to identify more with German culture than their Jewishness. It was a time when cultures clashed and melded, providing an opportunity his family

was eager to take advantage of. Despite its anti-Semitism, Vienna had an allur-
ing liberalism, promoting a unique interest in mental illness and sexual problems, a fascination that extended throughout society. Despite Jews coming to
dominate professions like medicine and law, in many medical specializations
their advancement was very difficult. Freud's tenure at the university occurred
during a time of rampant anti-Semitism. Freud felt like an alien and sought out
"intellectual fathers."

Cocaine helped him manage his anxiety. Touted in his day as a wonder
drug, it was often used as a mood enhancer and was even an ingredient in
household products. Freud experimented with it, thinking he might find medical uses for it that would make him famous. It lifted him out of his depressed
state, making him feel more alive and energetic (Stossel 2014). He wrote his
famous paper "On Coca" (Freud 1884) at twenty-eight, speaking glowingly
of its therapeutic benefits. Merck & Company and Parke, Davis & Company,
leading producers of cocaine-based pharmaceuticals, paid him to write about
their products.

Libido theory, *drekkologie,* and Freud's retreat from the seduction theory

Freud spent his happiest years studying the nerve cells of crayfish early in his
career (Gay 1988) and was relatively old before making his greatest discoveries.
At almost fifty, his sex drive had diminished considerably, something referred
to in many letters to Fliess. "I stand for an infinitely freer sexual life, although
I myself have made very little personal use of such freedom" (E. Freud 1960,
p. 308).

Why would someone so free to think about sexuality be so constricted sexually? Why would this man so invested in promoting psychoanalysis as scientific
become so interested in mysticism and the occult? The roots may lie in Freud's
deep interest in Hassidic Judaism, a mystical form of orthodox Judaism which
took on a strong erotic element and promoted ideas about telepathy and the
like. Although we tend to think of Freud as a secular Jew, more recent studies
show that he emerged from a deeply religious Hassidic background in Galicia,
with generations of distinguished rabbis and scholars on both sides of his family (Bakan 2004; Berke 2015; Krull 1986). He was familiar with Hebrew and
Yiddish.

When the fifth Lubavitcher Rebbe, Rabbi Shalom Dov Ben Schneerson, sought
Freud's help for depression in 1903, it stimulated Freud's secret longings to return
to his Hassidic roots (Gay 1988). Freud became very interested in Hassidism and
the discipline involved. The Rebbe replied, "The discipline of Hassidus requires
that the head explains to the heart what the person should want, and that the heart
(should) implement in the person's life that which the head understands" (Berke
2015, p. 12). Freud asked, "Are not the head and the heart two continents that are
completely separated? Does not a great sea divide them?" (op. cit., p. 12). The

Rebbe responded that the task was to build a bridge to span these two continents. Freud concluded that "The head grasps what the heart is unable to contain, and the heart cannot tolerate" (op. cit., p. 13). Meeting with the Rebbe may have planted the seed leading to Freud's theory of hysteria. When he came to recognize that hysteria's theatrical physical symptoms were induced by repudiated dissociated memories that were converted into physical symptoms, the seed for this too may have been planted by the Rebbe. Freud learned that the Rebbe had the immense psychic powers of a medium, induced by going into trance states to access paranormal states in himself and others (Berke 2015). When Freud wrote about telepathic processes and other uncanny phenomena, this concept too may have originated from his relationship with the Rebbe.

Freud's sexual inhibitions may also be traced to Hasidism, in which it is believed to be a blessing to have joy in life, found in their singing, dancing, ecstatic worship, and marital sexual relationships, but at the same time, extramarital intercourse and masturbation are considered perverse (Bakan 2004; Farber 2012). The notion of sexuality as the source of all energy is found in the Kabbalah's major document, the Zohar, which regards the Shekinah as the female counterpart of God. And so the "Kabbalist saw in sexual relations between a man and his wife a symbolic fulfillment of the relationship between God and the Shekinah" (Bakan 2004, p. 272).

Freud secularized the Kabbalah's mysticism to formulate psychoanalytic theory (Berke 2015). Kabbalah's domain is the soul. According to Bettelheim (1983), Freud's many references to the soul have been removed from the Strachey translation; he demonstrates that the word *psychoanalysis* essentially means soul-study. Ferenczi called psychoanalysis the Kabbalah of the twentieth century (Berke 2015).

Michael Eigen tells us that one of the themes in the Kabbalah is that we are broken.

> To tear even three letters from a page of Torah, put them in your mouth and taste, your tongue will burn like the child Moses with a holy fire that never goes out. The fire that never goes out meets the wound that never heals.
>
> (Eigen 2012, p. vi)

Rabbi Nachman of Breslov, founder of Hasidism, was a Hassidic master. He felt at times very close to God, at other times quite distant. As a child he spoke to God in heartfelt pleas and continued to do so. Eigen (2012) tells us that Nachman turned speaking to God into a kind of psychoanalytic method, pouring his heart out, a free association expression, a talking cure.

In 1934, when Freud requested prominent Kabbalist Rabbi Dr. Alexandre Safran, chief rabbi of Geneva, to visit him to discuss the relationship between his concepts of the life and death instincts and Judaism, he learned his concepts corresponded with Talmudic concepts of the *yetzer-ra* (the evil inclination) and the *yetzer-tov* (the good inclination) found in the Zohar (Berke 2105). Freud had secret longings to return to his Hassidic roots (Gay 1988). Other psychoanalytic ideas that can be traced to the Kabbalah include the concept of methods of dream interpretation and the significance of reparation. The concepts of *tikkun olam*, repairing the world, and psychoanalysis (Berke 2015) are complementary.

Despite Jacob Freud's renunciation of his Hassidic origins, they may have remained with him as taboos against masturbation and extramarital affairs which he communicated to Sigmund. He warned him that masturbation would be punished with castration (Krull 1986). When one of Freud's sons told him of his concerns about masturbation, Freud warned him about it (Roazen 1971). A crucial turning point in the development of psychoanalysis came soon after Jacob's death, when Freud renounced the seduction theory, for which some blamed Freud for sowing the seeds of false memory syndrome (Mollon 2000).

Although it was boldly stated that the ultimate cause of hysteria is always the seduction of a child by an adult (Breuer & Freud 1895), when faced with what seemed like an epidemic of sexual abuse in Vienna's best families, Freud commented on an episode implicating his own father (van der Kolk 2014). It was a critical time in Freud's personal life and scientific thought when he renounced the seduction theory, saying these reports were produced by fantasies, not real events, thus facilitating the discovery of the Oedipus complex, infantile sexuality, and thus, psychoanalysis.

As Breger said:

> As he pursued his self-analysis he would have had to apply these ideas to himself as well as to his patients. But this proved too dangerous, so he invented a half-truth, the Oedipal theory, which he then used to account for his own neurosis as well as everyone else's . . .
>
> It was at precisely this time, when he was re-experiencing his early traumas, that he turned away from the unbearable emotions associated with them and substituted his theory of the Oedipus complex.
>
> (Breger 2009, p. 95)

Not only did Freud abandon the seduction theory, he also abandoned the reality of all childhood trauma. Krull (1986) believed this renunciation was based on his deep-rooted fear of violating his father's taboo against delving into the family's history. Was the secret about Jacob's "perverse" masturbation? Or about Jacob's sexual molestation of Freud?

Freud's dream associations revealed details too forbidden to mention to Fliess, referred to as *dreck*, which means 'feces' in German and Yiddish. He sent Fliess the latest installments of his "*Drekkologie*" (dream-book), so called because "I can hardly tell you how many things I (the new Midas) turn into—filth (*Dreck*) . . . I am sending you today No. 2 of the *Drekkological* reports . . . No. 1 . . . contains wild dreams . . ." (Krull 1986, p. 64). The forbidden subject was invariably his own sexuality.

Although he revealed to Fliess that he believed masturbation was "the one major habit, the primary addiction, and that it is only as a substitute . . . that the other addictions—to alcohol, morphine, tobacco, and the like—come into existence" (Masson 1985, p. 287). Krull suggests Freud's dirty secret, which he refused to explore, was that in lieu of a sexual relationship with his wife, he relieved himself by masturbating.

Almost all photographs of Freud show him holding a cigar (Gay 1988). Cigars can boost mood and stimulate memory and alertness. Freud's nicotine habit began with smoking cigarettes, then cigars exclusively. He typically smoked twenty cigars daily, twenty-five toward the end of his life. One cigar may be equivalent to a pack of cigarettes. When it was suggested that his cigar habit signified an unconscious phallic fetish, it is said that Freud uttered: "Sometimes a cigar is just a cigar."

When his habit began producing symptoms of the cancer that killed him, initially a growth on his jaw and palate, he told no one for fear that his physician would order him to give up cigars. When it grew too large to be neglected, he had thirty-three surgeries, losing a large part of his jaw and acquiring a prosthesis, but never gave up cigars. He smoked until he died at eighty-three. Sometimes a cigar is more than a cigar.

Freud's burning desire to become a hero

The legend of the Wandering Jew is about a Jew who taunted Jesus on the way to the crucifixion and was then cursed to wander the earth until the Second Coming. Jews became "resident aliens" wherever they lived, having an ill-fated and historically ineradicable relationship with their Christian hosts, living in central and eastern Europe among hostile cultures in small communities called *shtetls*. As Orthodox Judaism declined in favor of modernization, Freud's father renounced the religion of his Hassidic forefathers (Carroll 2010). Later, Sigmund reinvented himself, transformed from despised traumatized Jew to glorious hero. He destroyed his intimate papers to trick his biographers into seeing him as a hero, as he told his fiancée in 1885.

> I have destroyed all my notes of the past fourteen years, as well as letters, scientific excerpts and manuscripts of my papers . . . As for the biographers, let them worry. We have no desire to make it too easy for them. Each one of them will be right in his opinion of "The Development of the Hero," and I am already looking forward to seeing them go astray.
>
> (E. Freud 1960, pp. 140–141)

Freud continued destroying old personal documents and falsifying much personal history in order to become a hero. He would have been pleased that the number of his biographies exceeds the number of books he wrote, and exceeds biographies about Darwin, Einstein, and Marx (Oring 1984).

Freud was ambivalent about whether psychoanalysis was a form of treatment, thus a branch of medicine, or a psychology, which would free him to reach his goal, philosophy. He was interested in the philosophy of the mind, not treatment. "I knew no longing other than that for philosophical insight, and I am now in the process of fulfilling it as I steer from medicine over to psychology. I became a therapist against my will" (Masson 1985, p. 180).

Freud's first hero was his father. It was a turning point in his life when Jacob fell off that pedestal. Although early on Freud admired his father and they had a mutually caring and supportive relationship, there was an early reversal of father–son roles, with Sigmund becoming the premature adult who would achieve great things, while Jacob became more and more childlike and helpless. There was the pivotal moment when they walked together in Vienna and Jacob wanted to show his son how much better things were for Jews since the time he was a poor peddler. He told him how, when proudly wearing his beaver hat in the *shtetls* of Galicia, a gentile had crossed his path and deliberately knocked his hat into the gutter, jeering, "Jew, get off the pavement" (Freud 1900, p. 197). Twelve-year old Sigmund asked indignantly, "What did you do?" Jacob simply said that he stepped into the gutter and picked up his hat. Sigmund was severely disappointed in him, leading him to write that he could think of no need in childhood as strong as the child's need for a father's protection (Freud 1930). His father was no longer his hero, leading him to identify his whole life with dominating heroes such as Napoleon, Alexander the Great, Hannibal, Oedipus, and Moses. It was better to live as a powerful hero than the person he was, a poor traumatized Jewish boy in a crowded Viennese ghetto (Breger 2000).

Freud's ambition succeeded in creating a movement led by those whose personal analysis he oversaw in some way. The fights he had with Alfred Adler and Carl Jung remain in people's minds, particularly because they each successfully founded separate schools of psychoanalytic thought. Because many documents about Freud had been sealed by the Freud Archives until the turn of the century, much accumulated documentation has become publically available, evoking a renewed expansion of Freud studies (Roazen 1971).

Freud's blind spot about trauma

Despite traumatic losses early throughout his life, Freud had a blind spot about the role played by trauma in his life and his theories. Although aware of dissociative processes in his patients' suffering from hysteria (Freud 1910), and recognizing that their somatic symptoms were induced by psychological trauma, he subsequently dismissed the dissociative processes Breuer (Breuer & Freud 1895) believed to be at the root of hysteria. The result in psychoanalysis is an emphasis on conflict and repression at the expense of trauma and dissociation (Farber 2013). Some think Freud's abandonment of his seduction theory sowed the seeds of false memory syndrome (Mollon 2000). Philip Bromberg said, "Part of our work as analysts facilitates the restoration of links between dissociated aspects of self so that the conditions for intrapsychic conflict and its resolution can develop" (Bromberg 1998, p. 13).

The Interpretation of Dreams is considered Freud's greatest work, often described as disguised autobiography. The creation of psychoanalysis originated largely through his own self-analysis (Mahony 2002), mainly through analyzing his own dreams. His self-analysis resulted in brilliant insights and discoveries: sexual conflicts, emotional events of infancy and early childhood. Freud developed a method of interpreting dreams and described many manifestations of the unconscious, from neurotic symptoms to events of everyday life. In addition, Freud developed a treatment method that became the predecessor of modern psychotherapy. Many of his theories are overstated, overly generalized, and filled with personal biases such as the universality of the Oedipus complex, sexuality as the driving force for all human action, penis envy, and men's fear of their inner femininity (Breger 2000). There was no convincing evidence for these concepts; they stemmed from Freud's personal needs and blind spots derived from his self-analysis.

Freud's emphasis on the libido and infantile sexuality shocked his contemporaries and reinforced a stereotype of the Jew as sexual pervert.

> A Jew was, so to speak, the wrong person to announce that the sexual instinct was a far more subtle and significant factor in mental life than had ever been supposed; and the fact that in Central Europe, at least, anti-Semitism was so strong—only Jews could be found to support the new views confirmed the suspicions of outsiders.
>
> (Jones 1959, pp. 207–211)

Freud's Jewish identity reflected in his Jewish jokes

Like many comedians whose humor serves as manic defense (Farber 2013), this depressed, anxious man loved to tell jokes. Native American author Sherman Alexie said, "The two funniest tribes I've ever been around are Indians and Jews, so I guess that says something about the inherent humor of genocide" (Alexie 2004, p. 15). One of the main functions of humor is sublimation of aggressive and sexual thoughts that are prohibited from being openly expressed (Freud 1905b, 1911a). Freud has been described as an excellent raconteur who enjoyed making a point with anecdotes and jokes in his correspondence as well. Although Freud knew the pain of anti-Semitism, he could joke about it.

Five years after publication of *The Interpretation of Dreams* (Freud 1900, 1905b), Freud revealed in *Jokes and Their Relationship to the Unconscious* how the "joke-work" is intimately related to the "dream-work." It is significant that Freud began collecting Jewish jokes at the same time that he began his self-analysis. Oring (1984) explored this to determine what aspects of his character and Jewish identity were revealed in his collection of Jewish jokes, a manuscript which seems to no longer exist. He found that Freud frequently identified with the characters and themes in his jokes, which held significant associations to his dreams and found that there was a strong relationship between the jokes' messages and Freud's own state of mind.

> Freud's conflict over his Jewish identity generated the energy that allowed him to invent psychoanalysis and organize the psychoanalytic movement. Without the barriers, without the shame, without the conflict, the invention might not have been forthcoming. Conflict is at the core of Freud's theory of psychodynamics, so it should not come as a surprise if we find it at the root of his own identity.
>
> (Oring 1984, p. 78)

The *Schnorrer* jokes are pessimistic, recalling the manifest misery of the Jews (Gay 1987). The *Schnorrer* is someone with an air of entitlement, a beggar with limitless *chutzpah* (nerve) who will get money from another any way he can. Freud loved telling *Schnorrer* jokes, identifying with the *Schnorrer*. Freud lived in poverty earlier in his life and even after marrying, lived on borrowed money. At times he behaved and felt like an intellectual *Schnorrer*, taking the ideas of others and presenting them as his own, denying his indebtedness and dependence.

Freud wrote his *Kuck* jokes, a short series of jokes about the occult, reflecting his ambivalence about his belief in the occult.

> Frederick the Great heard of a preacher in Silesia who had the reputation of being in contact with spirits. He sent for the man and received him with the question "You can conjure up spirits?" the reply was: "At your Majesty's command. But they don't come."
>
> (Oring 1984)

The *Schadchen* (marriage broker) jokes reflect Freud's hostility to the repressive quality of the institution of marriage, and the demise of his sexuality before he was fifty.

> We suspect that following the birth of his children and coincident with the beginning of Freud's most creative period of writing and research, there was a general withdrawal of Freud's libido from . . . Martha and a redirection of his energies to the development of psychoanalysis . . . His selection of the metaphor of a fiancée for his psychoanalytic research suggests the transfer of his libido from Martha to "his new wife-to-be—psychoanalysis." And yet the hostility of the old relationship seems to carry over.
>
> (op. cit., pp. 29–30)

The *Ostjude* is the stereotyped dirty Jew, combining every pejorative, shunned by Germans and German Jews alike. *Ostjude* jokes are about food caught in unruly beards, unwashed bodies, and obsessive religiosity. "A barber appeared every morning to trim his beard and, if necessary, his hair" (Roazen 1971, p. 236), as if to rid him of *Ostjude* qualities. Although named Schlomo Sigismund at birth, Sigismund was a stereotypical character in Viennese anti-Jewish jokes and he later changed his name to Sigmund. Including jokes about dirty Jews helped Freud distance himself from them. However, it was from these same Jews that Freud was immediately descended.

Freud's ambivalence about being Jewish was most powerfully expressed in *Moses and Monotheism* and his jokes about it (Oring 1984). The four basic themes in Freud's story were that Moses was an Egyptian, not a Jew; that the mono-theism given to the Jews was derived from the Egyptian worship of Aren; that Moses was murdered by the Israelites in the wilderness and the strict monotheism he taught was under the Semitic worship of Yahweh, and that Moses' murder was repressed, thus creating enormous guilt among the Jews. That is, the anti-Semitism Jews have experienced for centuries is partly a result of their refusal to acknowledge and atone for this murder, suggesting "that the anti-Semitic persecu-tions they had endured . . . were the result of not having acknowledged the under-lying truth in the Christian mythology of deicide" (op. cit., p. 101). Freud delayed publishing it for several years, perhaps because he had reservations about it. In a letter to Arnold Zweig, he described it as "An historical novel that won't stand up to criticism" (op. cit., p. 95). He was right; Jews dismissed the book, with some regarding it as anti-Semitic. It was discredited historically by scholars.

The joke about the Egyptian Moses, which no one seemed to find funny, is as follows:

> The boy Itzig is asked in grammar school, "Who was Moses?" and answers, "Moses was the son of an Egyptian princess." "That's not true," says the teacher. "Moses was the son of a Hebrew mother. The Egyptian princess found the baby in a casket." But Itzig answers, "Says she!"
>
> (op. cit., p. 91)

Baptism was the usual route ambitious Jews took to overcome obstacles to advancement (Oring 1984). Although Freud was ashamed to further his career in this way, he was also ashamed of his unconscious wish to identify as a Christian. Yet when colleague Max Graf, sensing an increase in Vienna's anti-Semitism, asked Freud if he should baptize his son, Freud advised:

> If you do not let your son grow up as a Jew, you will deprive him of those sources of energy which cannot be replaced by anything else. He will have to struggle as a Jew, and you ought to develop in him all the energy he will need for that struggle.
>
> (Oring 1984, pp. 70–71)

When Freud claimed to be "a godless Jew" (Gay 1987), he proclaimed that being a Jew was part of his personal identity. His nephew Harry argued that he was not really an atheist. "Sigmund Freud consciously felt himself a Jew, but he was thoroughly anti-religious, though by no means an atheist. It is just that he did not think much of rites and dogma" (op. cit., pp. 3–4). While not abandoning atheism, Freud began seeing Judaism's belief in an invisible God as a source of introspection and a capacity for abstract thinking, a triumph of intellect over faith.

> Freud in fact advertised his unbelief every time he could find, or make, an opportunity. "My language is German. My culture, my attainments are German. I considered myself German intellectually, until I noticed the growth of anti-Semitic prejudice in Germany and German Austria. Since that time, I prefer to call myself a Jew."
>
> (Gay 1988, p. 448)

He was a member of the B'nai Brith and addressed the group many times. He declared himself a Jew more assertively in historically troubled times (Gay 1987). As may be true in most marginalized groups, a certain self-hatred mingled with pride.

The end of Freud's life

Like so many German Jews, Freud had a false sense of security and did not take seriously the anti-Semitic threat, even when Karl Lueger, a virulent anti-Semite, was elected mayor of Vienna in 1897. He thought Catholicism was the real enemy, representing what he most despised about religion (Carroll 2010). In fact, John Cornwell, in *Hitler's Pope*, wrote about Pope Pius XII, originally Eugenio Pacelli, that evidence was found

> that from an early stage in his career Pacelli betrayed an undeniable antipathy toward the Jews, and that his diplomacy in Germany in the 1930s had resulted in the betrayal of Catholic political associations that might have challenged Hitler's regime and thwarted the Final Solution.
>
> (Cornwell 2000, p. xi)

Pacelli found in Hitler a good negotiating partner for his Reich concordat, a Church–State treaty between the papacy and Germany, which imposed a moral duty for German Catholics to obey the Nazi rulers.

Like so many Jews smitten with German culture, he could not believe the stories of Nazi horrors were true, and so resisted fleeing Vienna to escape. It was not until his daughter Anna was detained by the Gestapo in 1938 that, with Jones' help, he emigrated to London, effectively snuffing out the psychoanalytic movement almost overnight in Europe (Lieberman 2015). Freud's apartment at Bergasse 19 was used by the Nazis as a transit station for Jews expelled from their apartments and relocated there before their final deportation to the death camps; Freud's five sisters died in concentration camps (Freud 2007).

Both famous and ordinary people gave Freud and his family a very warm reception in London. Finally, and shortly before his death, he said, "For the first time and late in life I have experienced what fame means" (Gay 1988, p. 632). His cancer ate its way through his cheek, smelling so bad that his favorite dog shrank from him. Days before his death, when his physician Schur described him as being "far away," there were bits of wit. When they heard a broadcast proclaiming this to be the last war, Schur asked if he believed it, and Freud replied dryly, "My last war" (Gay 1988, p. 650). Then the jokes stopped. Freud prepared carefully for his death. On September 19, 1939 he sent for Jones to say good-bye and on September 21 reminded Schur of an old promise.

> "Schur, you remember our 'contract' not to leave me in the lurch when the time had come. Now it is nothing but torture and makes no sense . . . Talk it over with Anna, and if she thinks it's right, then make an end of it."
>
> (Gay 1988, p. 651)

Schur convinced her it was pointless to keep her father alive and, on the day Freud chose to die, injected him with morphine; Freud fell into a coma and died on September 23, the Sabbath and Yom Kippur, the Day of Atonement (Berke 2015; Gay 1988).

> There are several Jewish primary sources that point to the special merit a person has when dying on the Sabbath, and especially Yom Kippur . . . According to the Talmud, dying on the Sabbath, the Day of Rest, is a good sign, for then the soul of the deceased will go immediately into Heaven. Dying on Yom Kippur is a good sign because repentance has begun.
>
> (Berke 2015, pp. 182–183)

Freud's family decided that Jones should write his biography (Maddox 2007). When Jones died and was cremated at Golders Green in 1958, his ashes were interred close to those of Freud (Jones 1959).

Psychoanalysis, the Jewish science

A psychoanalytic stereotype that contains a kernel of truth is that when the patient asks the analyst a question, the analyst responds talmudically, asking him what he thinks about it. Aron and Henik (2015) described inquiry and questioning as defining features of both psychoanalysis and the Jewish tradition. A question invites inquiry, analysis, discussion, debate, multiple meanings, and interpretation that continues across the generations.

This relationship is pertinent to those who become therapists, more than half of whom are Jews. A study of 4,300 therapists found them so similar in terms of cultural origin, social class, religious background, political affiliation, and influences on their choice of profession and specialty, that they were classified as the fifth profession (Henry et al. 1971). This study found these values, while not exclusively Jewish, include the love of wisdom, the love of learning, the ethos of *tikkun olam*, or healing the world, and *tzedakah*, acts of generosity which sustain others in a life of dignity, which have roots in the Kabbalah (Bakan 2004; Berke 2015). At the root of *tzedakah* is the striving for justice for all. A value originally transmitted through Jewish spiritual leaders is transmitted today through social, cultural, and political organizations. Jewish mothers are known to tell their children that it is a *mitzvah*, a blessing, to help people. Many children celebrating their Bar or Bat Mitzvah will devote some time to community service.

Freud and the talking cure

Although Freud is regarded as the father of psychoanalysis, it was Josef Breuer, Freud's colleague and mentor, who was the true father of the discipline (Breger 2000, 2009). Many of the essential features of psychoanalysis were invented by Breuer (Breuer & Freud 1895). Although "On the Psychical Mechanism of Hysterical Phenomena" was coauthored, the case of Anna O, the first case in *Studies in Hysteria*, is entirely Breuer's work (Breger 2009).

"Anna O." was the pseudonym of Bertha Pappenheim, an intellectually gifted 21-year-old whose illness lasted over two years. She had physical and psychological disturbances; despite a thorough neurological examination, all the tests were normal. Her right arm and leg were severely paralyzed. Her eye movements were peculiar and her vision was restricted. She had trouble holding her head up, eating, and drinking, and had a severe cough. She had difficulty speaking or understanding her native language; she seemed confused and delirious, often muttering a few words to herself. Her emotional intensity and lability, extreme anxiety and depression, and the presence of what seemed to be two different selves indicated that she may have suffered from dissociative identity disorder.

After hearing Anna O. mutter a few words, Breuer put her into a trance and, improvising, uttered the same words to her, inducing her to free associate to them. Verbalizing her fantasies seemed to free her, bringing her back to normal mental life for a few hours. Although Breuer called it the cathartic method, the sanction to talk freely through free association was a revolutionary ethos of unprecedented honesty (Thompson 2001) and became the fundamental rule of psychoanalysis (Farber 2005). Anna O. was thus the first psychoanalytic patient and Breuer's method was the real start of psychoanalysis as a therapy and theory.

When Breuer and Freud met in 1877, Breuer, an established physician, became Freud's mentor and friend, and was generous with the praise, support, and openness that Freud needed. They developed a very close relationship. In the lectures he gave on his trip to the U.S. Freud gave Breuer full credit for inventing free association, the basic rule of psychoanalysis; however, after his drive for fame had become more powerful, Freud increasingly took credit in subsequent publications as the sole inventor of psychoanalysis, discarding many of Breuer's ideas and treatment methodologies (Breger 2009). And so we have come to believe that Freud was the founder of the psychoanalytic method. Breuer had embarked on a journey that led him to make some of the most important contributions to modern neural science: that unconscious mental problems exist, that unconscious mental conflict can evoke psychiatric symptoms, and that these symptoms can be alleviated when the memory of the underlying unconscious cause is brought into consciousness. Breuer concluded that:

> each individual hysterical symptom immediately and permanently disappeared when we had succeeded in bringing clearly to light the memory of the event by which it was provoked and in arousing its accompanying affect, and when the patient had described that event in the greatest possible detail and had put the affect into words.
>
> (Breuer & Freud 1895, p. 6)

Anna O. called it "the talking cure" and referred to it jokingly as mental chimney sweeping. She and Breuer discovered that the roots of her illness lay in traumatic past events, a discovery that resonated powerfully with Freud's own problems with mood lability, anxiety, migraine headaches, and gastrointestinal symptoms, interesting him in conversion hysteria. Breuer thought that a split-off portion of consciousness, mediated by a process of autohypnosis, was at the center of hysteria, a process in which the patient unwittingly induces a dissociated trance state in himself that allows the physical expression of that which could not be expressed in words (Breuer & Freud 1895; Farber 2000). Although both agreed that hysterics suffer largely from "reminiscences," painful memories of a traumatic nature, they disagreed on the phenomenon of dissociation, which Breuer believed was the root of hysteria (Breuer & Freud 1895).

Freud began minimizing the shattering effects of trauma in favor of the centrality of repressed sexual factors, finding a sexual root for virtually everything. For Breuer, it was a matter of scientific difference when he gently disagreed, stating that Freud overvalued sexuality. Freud, demanding complete agreement, turned on him brutally, saying he was glad to be rid of him. He stopped hypnotizing patients and asked them to relate anything which came to their minds, no matter how unpleasant, foolish, trivial, or irrelevant it might seem, then helped them connect their hysterical symptoms to trauma in their past (Freud 1900). By the time *Studies in Hysteria* was released, Freud presented himself as the founder of "the talking cure," thus betraying Breuer (Breger 2009). Breuer's daughter-in-law recalled that when Breuer was an old man, he was walking in the street and saw Freud approaching. He instinctively opened his arms in greeting. Freud walked by as if he did not see him (Breger 2009). Freud drove away the people in his life most important to him: Breuer, Adler, Jung, Rank, Fliess, and Ferenczi, which demonstrates the limits of Freud's self-analysis. One can only wonder what Freud's life and work might have been like if he had had the benefit of a personal psychoanalysis.

Freud and the writing cure

Although Freud did not invent the "talking cure," he benefitted greatly from the "writing cure" (Farber 2005). At thirty-one, Freud began a seventeen-year correspondence with his physician friend Wilhelm Fliess, during which his self-analysis emerged and was recorded in his dream-book, yielding some of his most revolutionary works: *Studies on Hysteria*, *The Interpretation of Dreams*, and *The Aetiology of Hysteria*. So absorbing was his self-analysis that during this time, he had not even one "talking cure" (Mahony 2002).

His self-analysis was conducted for the most part in writing—a huge body of letters and records of his associations—and was the source of Freud's theory, meaning that his self-analysis was quite literally a writing cure (Mahony 1987, 2002). "No activity, including clinical analysis, could match the act of writing for the unique benefits that it offered to Freud . . . He called reflection and writing work" (Mahony 2002, pp. 886–887). "Freud was never that keen about being a therapist. He preferred being a writer, and writing about why he preferred being a writer" (Freud & Phillips 2002, pp. viii–ix). Like most committed writers, Freud did not choose to write; he was driven to write (Farber 2013; Mahony 2002).

After discarding Breuer, Freud joined forces with Fliess, who was not a cautious scientist and whose theories were as sweeping as Freud's. Both had theories about sexuality and homosexuality. An otolaryngologist, Fliess believed that because the nasal and genital tissue were similar, problems with the nasal membranes were responsible for many illnesses throughout the body and that sexual difficulties or cardiac symptoms could be treated by applying cocaine to the nasal membranes or by nasal surgery. Fliess seemed like a bold scientific genius to Freud, who joined him in almost killing Freud's patient, Emma (Irma) Eckstein, with a bungled surgery on her nose and too much cocaine. Freud wrote about this in "The Dream of Irma's Injection" (Freud 1900), glossing over his malpractice. Fliess operated on Freud's nose twice. Freud became quite dependent on him and the cocaine he prescribed, maintaining their long-distance friendship by exchanging over three hundred letters, in which Freud's flattery and overvaluation of Fliess grew dramatically. He addressed him as "my only Other" (Breger 2009, p. 88). When Fliess did not reply immediately to a letter, Freud's self-esteem was affected. Freud wrote not only about scientific matters but about his marriage and sex life. "We are now living in abstinence" (Masson 1985, p. 54). Freud spoke of the homosexual element of his friendship with Fliess (op. cit.).

Freud stands among the few most prolific great writers of history (Farber 2005; Mahony 2002). Although many of the early analysts, Erickson and Sterba in particular, were attracted to Freud as a writer (Mahony 1987), the English-speaking world has not read Freud as the writer he was because the Strachey translation, on Ernest Jones' instructions, deliberately cast his writing in a very scientific light while denying the creative artist in him. Adam Phillips' editions of several of Freud's works with new translations has balanced this picture, presenting Freud not only as a scientist and philosopher but also as a writer (Flem 2003).

When Freud put his trust in free association, he was following not only Breuer but also his intuition, the source of which can be traced to Ludwig Börne, the first boyhood author in whose work Freud became absorbed (Farber 2005; Freud 1926; Jones 1953). Borne wrote an essay in 1823, "The Art of Becoming an Original Writer in Three Days," which Freud took to heart and which also has become today's standard advice for writers who rely on "free writing," the written form of free association (Farber 2005).

> Here follows the practical prescription I promised. Take a few sheets of paper and for three days in succession write down, without any falsification or hypocrisy, everything that comes into your head. Write what you think of yourself, of your women, of the Turkish War, of Goethe, of the Fonk criminal case, of the Last Judgment, of those senior to you in authority—and when the three days are over you will be amazed at what novel and startling thoughts have welled up in you. That is the art of becoming an original writer in three days.
>
> (Borne, cited in Jones 1953, pp. 156–157)

From the age of fifteen, Freud wrote "everywhere, all the time" (Farber 2005; Flem 2003, p.128), playing with words, like a child at play (Freud 1908). He hated constraints and deadlines, but knew that even though he did not want to, he had to learn moderation and rein in the wish to write feverishly, every minute (Flem 2003). Freud relied on his extensive literary skills to create a new heroic self and conduct his self-analysis. In 1919 he wrote to Ferenczi of Borne's influence that "He could well have been the source of my originality" (Mahony 1987, p. 160). Borne's influence even extended to the modality of Freud's self-analysis.

From early on, Freud knew the therapeutic benefits of writing. He wrote an extraordinary volume of material throughout his career, even while his body was ravaged with cancer. While writing he gained a desired space and freedom from the pain life imposed upon him, and it helped him recover from the necessary feelings of passivity and receptivity of his clinical hours (Mahony 2002). Alternating between darker and lighter moods, he said that he did some of his best writing when mildly depressed or in bad health, and had to learn to trust his moods (Flem 2003; Mahony 1987). The benefit of his depression was that it was the impetus for creativity, something he wrote about in *Mourning and Melancholia* (Freud 1917).

> One strenuous night last week, when I was in the stage of painful discomfort in which my brain works best, the barriers suddenly lifted, the veil dropped, and it was possible to see from the details of neurosis all the way to the very conditioning of consciousness. Everything fell into place, the cogs meshed, the thing really seemed to be a machine which in a moment would run of itself.
>
> (Mahony 1987, p. 5)

A year later, he spoke of writing a book on dreams; then, having begun his self-analysis, said he intended to force himself to write the book to get himself out of a bad mood (Jones 1953). In June 1898, he confided to Fliess that his dream-book was nearly finished, written as if in a dream (Farber 2005).

Freud asked his patients to free-associate out loud, the equivalent of asking them to play with words. He preferred writing case histories that read like short stories (Breuer & Freud 1895). The first volumes of his *Collected Works* appeared in 1925, and in 1930 he was awarded the Goethe Prize for literature. Although pleased with the award, he thought the cash prize too small and too late in coming; he was disappointed that he had not received the more prestigious Nobel Prize (Breger 2000). He wrote to Sterba and Stekel that he was always writing novels in his mind and his natural inclination was to become a novelist so that he could better record for posterity all that his patients were telling him (Farber 2005; Flem 2003; Mahony 1987).

Freud wrote six papers on technique between December 1911 and July 1914, and then every ten years or so, around 1914 and 1925, he wrote about the actual practice of psychoanalysis. To read these papers is to read Freud's growing disillusionment with psychoanalysis as a treatment. "It is one of the secrets of psychoanalysis that Freud was not overly impressed by its curative powers" (Freud & Phillips 2002, p. xi).

Freud (1900) had writer's block while analyzing the dream of Irma's injection, and had the realization that he needed to engage in a self-analysis by applying the free association method to himself. This was the most tortuous part of his writing career, reflected in his many letters to Fliess, his critical reader and ambivalently revered "Other" (Masson 1985). His self-analysis was conducted in large part in writing—papers, letters, recording his associations—which meant that his self-analysis was quite literally a writing cure (Mahony 1987, 2002). He had been friends with Ferenczi more than twenty-five years and wrote more letters to him than anyone else, 1,250 in all. "No activity, including clinical psycho-analysis, could match the act of writing for the unique benefits it offered to Freud; this is an overlooked fact" (Mahony 2002, pp. 886–887).

In fact, Freud was never really interested being a therapist, and preferred being a creative improviser. He was making it up as he went along—the rules, techniques, and theories. Keep in mind that there were no precedents for him to follow, no psychoanalytic training institutes or supervisors, or other system of checks and balances. At the beginning, psychoanalysis

> had no texts, no institutions, and no rhetoric . . . The first practitioners of psychoanalysis were making it up as they went along . . . [it] began then, as a kind of virtuoso improvisation within the science of medicine; and free association—the heart of psychoanalytic treatment—is itself ritualized improvisation.
>
> (Phillips 1997, pp. 3–4)

Studying Freud's personal concept of writing and how he used it sheds light on a significant aspect of his relationship with others as well as his sense of his own heroic greatness (Mahony 2002). Freud's motivations for writing were to convey information, to convince or amuse. Sometimes he engaged in expressive self-purposive writing, for example in his many letters to his fiancée Martha Bernays and later to Fliess. There was the financial motivation to finish the *New Introductory Lectures* to support his psychoanalytic publishing house. He was motivated to complete *Totem and Taboo* to surpass Carl Jung "in his own mythological reserve and thereby subject that rebellious son to a paternally administered castration" (Mahony 1987, p. 159)." Another aim in writing was to discover and achieve insight, aims that he had in adolescence, when he took up Borne's advice about becoming an original writer.

Freud violated all the rules he had laid down for others

The way Freud conducted his practice and his written instructions for psychoanalysis became the template upon which generations of psychoanalysts modeled themselves. The assumption was that if Freud did it, it must be the right thing to do. All too often, however, there was a tremendous discrepancy between what Freud said to do in his papers on technique and what he actually did. His technical papers include "Recommendations to Physicians Practising Psycho-Analysis" (Freud 1912), "Further Recommendations on the Technique of Psychoanalysis" (Freud 1913), "On Narcissism" (Freud 1914a), "On the History of the Psycho-Analytic Movement" (Freud 1914b), "Remembering, Repeating, and Working through" (Freud 1914c), and "Introductory Lectures on Psychoanalysis" (Carey 2004; Freud 1916). He also published five famous case histories: Dora (Freud 1905a), Little Hans (Freud 1909a), Rat Man (Freud 1909b), the Schreber case (Freud 1911b), and Wolf Man (Freud 1919b). Roazen tells us that even if we were to accept Freud's version of these case histories uncritically, we need to wonder how representative they were of his methods (Freud 1905a, 1905b, 1909b).

In practice, however, Freud violated the boundaries he cautioned others about. Although there is an ethical opposition to dual relationships in psychotherapy (Pope 1991), Freud flaunted his ethic and his contemporaries followed suit. Although Freud warned Ferenczi that kissing his patients might lead to a sexual relationship (Lazarus & Zur 2002), he had a sexualized relationship with his own daughter by analyzing her. Freud socialized with and had business relationships with patients. It is fascinating that Freud's granddaughter, Miriam Sophie Freud, who prefers using her middle name, is a social worker who knew little about psychoanalysis, yet she coauthored a paper on dual relationships and boundary violations in social work (Freud & Krug 2002).

Freud wrote about the "wild analyst," not realizing he was one himself.

> There was, to put it mildly, an uneasy relationship for Freud between theory and practice . . . Freud, of course, was the first wild analyst in the sense that he was never psychoanalysed by anyone else. Like many of the early analysts he had no psychoanalytic training because there was no psychoanalytic training available . . . Freud, as the founder, seemed uniquely placed to be the legitimator, answerable to no one else, of his own invention.
>
> (Freud & Phillips 2002, p. xi)

Roazen, a psychoanalytic historian, was the first non-psychoanalyst whom Anna Freud allowed to access the British Psychoanalytical Institute's archives. He was the first to raise sensitive issues about Freud's routine boundary violations as well as the previously silenced stories of Freud's analysis of his own daughter and the story of Victor Tausk's suicide, acknowledged publicly when Roazen (1990) wrote about it in 1969 in *Brother Animal: The Story of Freud and Tausk*. "Tausk's struggle with Freud was misunderstood at the time and has since been repressed out of loyalty to the master" (Roazen 1993, p. xxxvi).

> In 1969 I knew that I was violating a taboo by opening up this issue (Anna's analysis by Freud), but I never realized, even in 1975 when I discussed it at greater length in my *Freud and His Followers*, that the silence over what Freud had done would persist . . . Even Anna Freud's official biographer in 1988 handled the matter with kid gloves.
>
> Among orthodox Freudians, I found deep resentment for my having betrayed "the cause" through publishing *Brother Animal . . .* For a remarkable number of people, the only legitimate way to write about Freud is by proposing propaganda that not only idealizes the first psychoanalyst but simultaneously serves to promote the business of contemporary psychoanalysis. The historical Freud must be, from their point of view presented in such a way . . . that buttresses the self-image of today's practicing analysts. But this means we are deprived of Freud as a model of originality and daring who should . . . be used to challenge rather than support our preconceptions.
>
> (Roazen 1990, pp. xv–xvii)

Roazen had made the politically incorrect discovery that

> Freud violated all the rules he had laid down for others: he treated some patients free of charge, even though he had stated that there had to be a financial incentive for the patient to recover; he was known to have invited patients to his home for a meal or served them food in his office, even though he had advised against an analyst's becoming too familiar with his patients; and as long as he could talk freely, and without the pain of his later illness, Freud was said to have "chattered."
>
> (Roazen 1993, p. 108)

In effect, Freud made the whole psychoanalytic movement into a kind of extended family. He committed serious indiscretions and boundary violations, becoming a wounding healer with some. Freud could be a good therapist when treating patients who did not challenge him or develop a negative transference. He thrived on patients who were openly grateful and idealizing, who gratified his narcissistic wish to be a hero.

Because Freud was a neurologist and wanted to triumph in the medical world, he favored followers who were physicians, who were more likely to promote the advancement of psychoanalysis. Wilhelm Stekel, a physician and writer, was one of the first patients Freud analyzed. During his treatment he suggested Freud hold a discussion group to discuss his ideas, a suggestion that altered history. The initial meeting was attended by Stekel, Max Kahane, Rudolf Reitler, and Alfred Adler. Kahane and Reitler were childhood friends. Alfred Adler was the only recruit with any clout in the medical field. They met every Wednesday evening in Freud's living room, and became known as the Wednesday Psychological Society. According to Stekel, these earliest meetings featured "complete harmony among the five, no dissonances; we were like pioneers in a newly discovered land, and Freud was the leader. A spark seemed to jump from one mind to the other, and every meeting was a revelation" (Lieberman 2015, p. 51).

Freud's circle included many non-physicians (an opera producer, a bookseller, an artist, a novelist) as well as physicians, who tended to be internists and general practice doctors. They gathered around a table at 8:30 pm. Formal presentations began at 9, after which was fifteen minutes of socializing. Cigars and cigarettes were laid out and smoked in great quantities. Black coffee and cakes were served. Max Graf, a musicologist, described the mood: "There was the atmosphere of the founding of a religion in that room, and Freud himself was its new prophet" (Lieberman 2015, p. 51).

Freud's pattern of wounding those important to him

Freud had not written about his special approach until he found himself disagreeing with Adler, Stekel, and Jung, and began writing in order to distinguish his form of treatment from their "heretical" views. He never really considered any new advance, dismissing it immediately as heresy, a remarkable contradiction to his view that skepticism is a critical component of the practice of science, requiring "a capacity for skepticism but also . . . for skepticism about one's skepticism" (Mayer 1996, p. 724). Ernest Jones (1959) wrote:

> The word "movement" . . . is characterized by the ardent desire to promulgate . . . beliefs that are accounted exceedingly precious; it is akin to what nowadays is called "propaganda." It was this element that gave rise to the general criticism of our would-be scientific activities that they partook rather of the nature of a religious movement and amusing parallels were drawn.

Freud was of course the Pope of the new sect, if not a still higher Personage, to whom all owed obeisance; his writings were the sacred text, credence in which was obligatory on the supposed infallibilists who had undergone the necessary conversion, and there were not lacking the heretics who were expelled from the church.

(Jones 1959, p. 205)

When opinions within the movement became a thorn in the side of the International Psychoanalytic Association and Freud's relationship with Jung was greatly strained, Freud became quite anxious that the movement might not survive. "Jones then made a crucial move which has been seen as a deliberate manoeuvre to displace Jung in the Freudian power structure. Jung abdicates from his throne, he declared to Freud" (Maddox 2007, p. 101). Knowing that Freud had already lost Adler and Stekel, he proposed that a small select group of analysts analyzed by Freud represent Freud's pure theory and oversee and defend the psychoanalytic movement. Jones made no mention of Carl Jung as a possible member of the Committee, even though Jung and Freud had not yet severed their ties. Freud loved the idea and insisted that "The Committee" be strictly secret (Maddox 2007; Oring 1984). The five original members were Jones, Karl Abraham, Sándor Ferenczi, Otto Rank, and Hanns Sachs.

From the beginning, Freud's followers, generally a generation younger than Freud, yearned to know the answers to life's larger questions which were not readily answered in science or medicine. They were attracted to psychoanalysis and came to feel like comrades in arms for a noble cause (Breger 2000). Many had their own psychological difficulties and were searching for cures for their own anxieties and conflicts, which they discussed at meetings of the Vienna Psychoanalytic Society. If they were looking for the father they never had, Freud held out the promise of being that father. It was well known within this tight group that he did not live up to the proclaimed ideals he held up for others. They maintained a conspiracy of silence about this, binding them in a passionate allegiance that made them feel superior to outsiders and free to go their own way in violating various taboos. Freud could permit himself the technical liberties as daring as the practices he criticized his opponents of indulging in.

Freud, as the creator of psychoanalysis, felt free himself to chuck this or that aspect of what he had recommended in print, confident that he knew best what was or what was not critical to the best interests of psychoanalysis.

(Roazen 1995, p. xxii)

It was the best interests of the movement that Freud cared about, not the best interests of the patient.

The movement spread widely between the end of World War I and the beginning of Nazism, with an international psychoanalytic congress held every two years in Europe's major cities. By the 1920s the European institutes and their American and English counterparts were training more and more analysts, and new journals were founded. Shortly after Hitler's ascent, a bonfire of psychoanalytic books, including all of Freud's, was burned in Berlin. Goring, Hitler's second in command, took over the German Society for Psychotherapy, purging it of all its Jewish and psychoanalytic features and remaking it as the Reich Institute for Psychological Research and Psychotherapy (Lieberman 2015).

"Do as I say, not as I do"

Freud spent his vacations with several patients, including Kata Levy, a psychoanalyst who seemed to be enmeshed in the world surrounding Anna Freud, a frank violation of his admonition that the analyst is to be "opaque to his patients and, like a mirror, should show them nothing but what is shown to him" (Freud 1912, p. 118). While Freud was staying with her family in the mountains, he volunteered to analyze Kata, to which she replied:

> Surely you are on vacation, Professor Freud, and do not want to be bothered by analyzing me. But Freud surprised her by saying straightforwardly that he had begun to analyze Anna, and that he would just as soon have both of them at the same time.
>
> (Roazen 1993, p. 110)

Despite his warning that "in psychoanalytic treatments the intervention of relatives is a positive danger" (Freud 1916, pp. 458–459), Freud treated his sister-in-law, Ruth Mack-Brunswick, who was held in great esteem within the psychoanalytic movement, as well as her brother Mark Brunswick, a musician, and her brother-in-law David Brunswick, a psychologist-psychoanalyst. For a while all three were in treatment with Freud simultaneously. His motives were thought to be a mix of his own personal, professional, financial, and therapeutic needs. The Brunswicks were extremely wealthy. Freud also simultaneously treated James Strachey, editor-in-chief of the *Standard Edition*, and his wife, Alix. He also analyzed people he knew socially, some of whom spent considerable time within his household. Freud often let his patients know which of them he preferred; for years he solicited contributions from them to support a favorite former patient, the Wolf Man.

Freud's narcissism allowed him to set up precedents for followers Strachey, Riviere, and Winnicott, by allowing his British analysands/followers to edit and translate his work. Soon after beginning treatment of the Stracheys, Freud got them to translate *A Child Is Being Beaten*. He analyzed Joan Riviere at the same time that he consulted with her on matters of translation. Both James Strachey and Riviere continued the precedent Freud established with their own patients. Donald Winnicott had his first two analyses with Strachey (1923 to 1933) and Riviere (1933 to 1938), and was Masud Khan's analyst from 1951 to 1966; during this time Khan edited Winnicott's books and essays.

Freud's analysis of his own daughter

When Freud's libido had subsided early in his life and Martha, at the early age of 35, expected or hoped to enter menopause, she conceived Anna, her last child, instead, an unwanted pregnancy (Roazen 1990, 1993). Five months before her birth, Freud dreamt the founding dream of psychoanalysis. Anna's birth and the birth of the psychoanalytic movement were intertwined. He and Martha were disappointed that Anna was not a boy. Having born five children in eight years, Martha had had enough of infants. She never really loved Anna, taking little responsibility for her needs. Her primary caretaker or "psychological mother" was her Catholic nursemaid, just as her father's had been.

Freud had wanted to transfer the leadership of psychoanalysis to his sons but was disappointed that none of them did well professionally. Some of his disciples thought he neglected his sons, referring to his disciples as his sons (Roazen 1993). He turned to Anna, developing an unusually close relationship with her, enjoying her mischievous nature. She became ardently attached and devoted to him. He groomed her to become his most zealous follower, a role she filled splendidly.

The rules are there to be broken when there is good reason for doing so, but Freud felt entitled to break the rules without explaining why. He broke the rules because he had the power to do so and it suited his needs. Freud's analysis of Anna from 1918 to 1922 and then from 1924 to 1925 was his worst boundary violation, an incestuous treatment, stimulating her sexual fantasies about him (Rachman 1993). Hers was more than a training analysis; Anna was a suitable case for treatment. At a time when analyses typically lasted several months, Anna's was an unusually long one that never resolved her flight from her sexuality and her unshakeable focus on her father.

> Her low self-esteem had long led her to a flight into fantasy. Anna told herself "nice stories," extended complicated daydreams that first accompanied and then substituted for masturbatory pleasure. These nice stories in which she often played a heroic and self-sacrificial male role left her feeling depleted and "dumb," unable to make decisions. What she called her "night life," which she recorded for her father from 1915 on, was on the other hand distressingly turbulent. There are repeated and violent dreams of going blind, "of shooting, killing or dying," she writes to him in 1919; of defending her father from enemies and finding her sabre broken . . . Striving to defend or serve the father figure and failing to do so is a recurrent theme. The underlying wish of both night life and nice stories is manifest in a dream of 1915: "Recently

I dreamt that you are a king and I a princess; that people want to separate us by means of political intrigues. It was not pleasant and very agitating."

(Appignanesi & Forrester 1992, pp. 279–280)

Rebecca Coffey (2014) comments:

Imagine . . . being drawn by your father into an erotic power play. Imagine that he psychoanalyzes you for a total of about one thousand clinical hours.

When doing so, keep in mind that your father has also defined the birth of civilization as the moment mankind realized that incest is *verboten*. This means that even if the verbal foreplay of your psychoanalysis makes you occasionally feel (way too) heterosexual, nothing that is aroused is going to be consummated.

What might have happened to your sexuality and sense of self during those years of analysis?

What might have happened to your love for your father?

What might have happened to your sibling relationships and to your relationship with your mother? By the time that lengthy analysis had ended, where might you stand emotionally in relation to your family, given that you were the only family member with whom your father ever expressed an inclination to transgress?

How would you feel about your youth and your possibilities? How would you feel about your life choices?

(Coffey 2014, p. xiv)

Although Freud was aware of his ambivalence about Anna's becoming involved with another man, about her celibacy and suppressed sexuality, he was reluctant to let her grow up (Appignanesi & Forester 1992). He was as addicted to her as he was to cigars (Young-Bruehl 1988). Anna was less ambivalent than her father. Having grown up observing the nature of her parents' marriage, becoming her father's psychoanalytic heir was far more attractive than becoming someone's wife. From the age of fourteen, Anna sat in on the Wednesday evening meetings.

She was shy and pretty but had poor self-esteem. The bachelors in Freud's circle had their eye on her, especially Otto Rank. She was said to have been in love with three of them but her intense tie to her father made her fearful of male attention (Roazen 1971; Young-Bruehl 1988). When she traveled to England at eighteen and received a very warm reception from Ernest Jones, Freud (1905c) anxiously warned her never to be alone with him.

Freud (1937) thought a woman's castration complex, resulting from lacking a penis, was central to her personality development, a view initially refuted by Edith Jacobson in 1937 (Jacobson 1976). He believed the girl turns to her father as her new love object, from whom she hopes to obtain a penis, thus ending the pre-Oedipal homosexual phase. How could Anna have resolved her Oedipal complex if her father was her analyst?

To what extent did Freud consider that if Anna were not so acutely aware of her father's expectations of her, she might have had an opportunity to love another man, marry, and have children? (Anna expressed her maternal feelings toward the children she taught and the children of the Hampstead nurseries.) Did this courageous explorer of human sexuality consider that his intense interest in Anna joined with her deep need to be loved, thus complicating the development of her sexuality?

Freud was virulently opposed to female homosexuality, believing that the female's object choice should find its way to the opposite sex and that mothers should ensure that they curtail their daughters' pubertal masturbation (Freud 1905c, 1909a, 1909b).

> [It] is only through committed consort with a man that a woman can gain moral and emotional fortitude. Lesbians don't enjoy intimacy with men. And so, in Sigmund Freud's world, the very act of making love with another female sets a woman on a path towards breakdown. Published excerpts from Anna's diaries and correspondence suggest that she began having intensely romantic feelings for women by her early twenties. Undeniably, by the time she was thirty she had begun a monogamous relationship with Dorothy Burlingham, heir to the Tiffany fortune. Neither woman ever publicly acknowledged the relationship as sexual. But it did continue, merrily, committedly, and concertedly for more than five decades.
>
> (Coffey 2014, p. xii)

After three years of analysis, Freud recognized that Anna's analysis was not progressing well and asked Lou Andreas-Salome to "partner" him in it. The relationship between Anna and Andreas-Salome was one of discussion and consultation, with Andreas-Salome stretched out on a divan and Anna seated at her feet (Young-Bruehl 1988). Anna often identified with strong male characters or took a male role in her fantasies and dreams. Anna knew her extreme closeness to her father tempted her to deceive him in her analysis. She spoke with Andreas-Salome about continuing her analysis with her father.

> The reason for continuing . . . was not the entirely orderly behavior of my honorable inner life: occasional unseemly intrusions of the daydreams combined with an increasing intolerance—sometimes physical as well as mental—of the beating fantasies and of their consequences (i.e. masturbation) which I could not do without.
>
> (Young-Bruehl 1988, p. 122)

When Freud had two major operations on his jaw there was a two-year break in Anna's analysis. She became his chief nurse, secretary, and spokesperson. Although Anna did not take over the organization of domestic life, in other ways she replaced her mother, sharing the bed with Freud (Coffey 2014). When he felt well enough, he suggested that they resume their analytic work together; she gratefully accepted.

In *A Child Is Being Beaten* Freud (1919c) explored the association between pleasure and suffering, as well as the nature of memory versus fantasy. Mahony suggests Anna was the child being beaten (A. Freud 1922). Freud wrote it when Anna's analysis was fully under way. The present tense in the title, says Mahony, reflects Freud's concurrent clinical activity with Anna (A. Freud 1922). In a home-grown version of the return of the repressed, and in a fatherly professional twist of the seduction theory, Freud was carrying out an iatrogenic seduction and abuse of his daughter, increasing her beating fantasies. In 1922, Anna wrote a paper, "Beating Fantasies and Daydreams." Late in her life, when she became concerned about inquiries by prospective biographers, she claimed the clinical material came from her own analytic practice. which was impossible because when she wrote the paper, she had no analytic practice; the paper was written six months before she even saw her first patient. She wrote the paper because she wanted to attend the September 1922 International Congress in Berlin as a member of a psychoanalytic society. Writing to Eitingon, head of the Berlin Society, she asked if she submitted the paper whether the Berlin Society would accept her on the basis of this work (Young-Bruehl 1988).

> But it is at least clear from her various correspondences that "Beating Fantasies and Daydreams" was modeled—in general . . . on her own case . . . In the three parts of her essay, Anna Freud presented three stages in the development of her subject's beating fantasy. The first was the creation of the beating fantasy, which was itself a substitute for an incestuous father–daughter love scene . . . the climax of which coincided with masturbatory gratification.
>
> (Young-Bruehl 1988, p. 103)

Rachman (1993) suggests that Freud's background of childhood trauma become reenacted in his psychological seduction of his daughter as he projected his uncon-scious erotic feelings onto Ferenczi, who was rumored to have engaged in sexual behavior with patients (Celenza & Gabbard 2003).

Freud referred to Anna as his faithful Antigone, the daughter of the blind Oedipus (Roazen 1971, pp. 437–438). He seemed to be as blind as Oedipus to what he was doing to her. She needed her own identity: she needed something and someone of her own and found it in Dorothy Burlingham, who came to Vienna from America with her four children in search of psychoanalysis. Anna arranged for Freud to analyze her. Her biographers have essentially ignored this relation-ship which lasted more than five decades (Burlingham 1989; Coffey 2014) and finally gave Anna some independence from her father, putting him more in the background of her life. After World War I, Anna became a key player in the insti-tutionalization of psychoanalysis.

Freud and countertransference

Freud's dislike of America seemed to have been acted out against his American patients, to whom he gave a particularly hard time. Ruth Mack-Brunswick, an American and a favorite of Freud's, was an exception, as was her brother Mark. Freud warned Mark at the beginning of treatment that he would not get anywhere in the analysis unless he stopped masturbating, which Mark thought was quite puritanical. A later analysis with Robert Bak, who was "strictly Freudian" about masturbation, went much better (Roazen 1971).

Although aware of countertransference arising in the analyst, Freud insisted the analyst recognize this in himself and completely overcome it through self-analysis. As the so-called founder of psychoanalysis, Freud never had the benefit of a training analysis or his own personal analysis. He believed the training analysis was not as important as the development of the candidate's therapeutic creativity (Roazen 1971). As late as the early 1920s, there was no control or training analysis, conducted by a candidate in training under supervision of a more experienced analyst.

Helene Deutsch saw the value of countertransference in that it could help the analyst identify with the patient's problems. When she suggested it would be a good idea for the analyst to take some active steps to dissolve the transference, Freud asked "How?" "By showing he is not perfect," she answered, an idea that angered Freud. He responded, "You mean to show not only the patient is a swine, but I too?" (Roazen 1971, p. 153).

Before World War I, Jung proposed that psychoanalysts be required to undergo their own training analysis, a proposal which may have been meant as a criticism of Freud as suffering from unanalyzed unconscious conflicts (Roazen 1971). By 1925, the consensus was that all prospective analysts must be analyzed. Two years before his death, Freud's thinking had changed sufficiently that he wrote that not only should every prospective analyst undergo a training analysis but that he should return to his own analysis periodically (Freud 1937). Once again, it was "Do as I say, not as I do." Freud had never had an analysis and was not about to start. Ferenczi, like Jung, had objected that Freud felt he was the only one who did not need to be analyzed (Roazen 1993). He said that Freud as an old man did "not love anyone, only himself and his work" (Roazen 1993, p. 205; Ferenczi & Dupont 1995, p. 160).

Expelling the heretics

All the major figures who broke off their relationships with Freud, including Alfred Adler, Wilhelm Stekel, Carl Jung, and Sándor Ferenczi, had central disagreements with Freud on the failure to accept the ubiquitous nature of sexual motivation and the Oedipus complex. Almost all significant new developments in theory and therapy originated in those who worked outside the psychoanalytic mainstream: Adler, Jung, Rank, Ferenczi, the neo-Freudians (Karen Horney,

Erich Fromm, Harry Stack Sullivan, Eric Erickson, John Bowlby, Heinz Kohut, and the relational and intersubjective theorists (Breger 2009).

Anthropologist Elliott Oring (1984) thought that Freud's wish to escape his past was gratified to a degree in his creation of a "science" which allowed individuals to seek the freedom he never obtained for himself. Oring suggested that psychoanalysis can be viewed as a sublimation of Freud's conflict over his Jewish identity. He pointed out Freud's identification with Moses, founder of a new religion. The psychoanalytic movement was organized like a religion, with Freud its strict founder, like Moses, full of wrath. He was also its god, allowing no deviation from his teaching and requiring worship. Instead of faith and charity, Freud's religion espoused honesty, which was to be obtained by free association (Oring 1984).

Freud's followers were almost entirely Jewish and so it was quite a coup when Carl Jung, son of a Protestant pastor, reached out to him and became the first psychiatrist in his inner circle. Having Jung at the helm of psychoanalysis made it far more than a Jewish sect in anti-Semitic Vienna. Jung was brilliant and he and Freud shared an interest in the occult, an interest about which Freud was quite conflicted and which played a part in their relationship eventually breaking up.

Jung probably played the most substantial intellectual role in Freud's life. When they met in 1906, they talked for thirteen hours.

> Freud . . . , self-assured at the age of fifty-one, sat smoking cigars, picking up from time to time one little figure or another from the small collection on his desk and gazing with growing wonder upon the voluble and enthusiastic man whose ideas seemed so nearly to match his own. The loneliness of the years fell away as the men talked on past midnight, as the tall young Swiss, unself-conscious and unknowing, laid claim to Freud in a way that no one ever would again.
>
> (Donn 1988, p. 7)

So began the start of an powerful collaboration that lasted six years. From their first meeting, it seemed clear to Jung that Freud was obsessed with sexuality and fearful of the spiritual and the occult. He said that when Freud spoke of his libido theory,

> his tone became urgent, almost anxious, and all signs of his normally critical and skeptical manner vanished. A strange, deeply moved expression came over his face, the cause of which I was at a loss to understand . . . I can still recall vividly how Freud said to me, "My dear Jung, promise me never to abandon the sexual theory. That is the most essential thing of all. You see, we must make a dogma of it, an unshakeable bulwark . . ." In some astonishment I asked him, "A bulwark against what?" To which he replied, "Against the black tide of mud"—and here he hesitated for a moment, then added—"of occultism."

> This was the thing that struck at the heart of our friendship. I knew I would never be able to accept such an attitude.
>
> (Jung 1961, p. 150)

Freud relied on Jung more and more, writing him constantly, often every week. If Jung did not reply immediately, he would get a telegram asking what had gone wrong (McGuire 1974). Realizing there was something about his personality that many people did not like, Freud wrote to Jung:

> I have always felt that there is something about my personality, my ideas and manner of speaking, that people find strange and repellent, whereas all hearts open to you. If a healthy man like you regards himself as an hysterical type, I can only claim for myself the "obsessional type," each specimen of which vegetates in a sealed-off world of his own.
>
> (McGuire 1974, p. 82)

Freud regarded Jung as his adopted eldest son, his crown prince, and successor. In 1909, a decisive year for their relationship, Jung was invited to lecture on his association experiment at Clark University in Worcester, Massachusetts, while independent of this, Stanley Hall, president of Clark, paid tribute to Freud's writings and invited Freud and Jung to receive honorary doctorates at Clark's twentieth anniversary celebration. Freud and Jung traveled together to Clark. They each spoke to an audience which included twenty-seven distinguished psychiatrists, neurologists, and psychologists.

America liked Freud very much. Although Freud disliked American bourgeois culture, there is a legend that when they went to Dreamland, the amusement park in Coney Island, Freud declared that this was the only part of America that interested him. A year after Freud's Clark lectures were delivered, they were published, a critical point marking his acceptance in North America. Freud was very moved by his enthusiastic reception. "In Europe I felt like someone excommunicated; here I saw myself received by the best as an equal" (Gay 1988, p. 207).

Their trip to the U.S. lasted seven weeks, transforming a warm relationship into a deeper friendship, which "had all the savor of life at the edge of the frontier" (Donn 1988, p. 116). Jung wrote that they were together every day and analyzed each other's dreams. During this time Jung became aware of how keenly he felt the difference between Freud's intellectual attitude and his own. He found that Freud interpreted Jung's dreams incompletely or not at all.

> They were dreams with collective contents, containing a great deal of symbolic material. One in particular was important to me, for it led me . . . to the concept of the "collective unconscious" and thus formed a kind of prelude to my book, *Wandlungen und Symbole der Libido* . . .
>
> While I was working on this book, I had dreams which presaged the forthcoming break with Freud.

When I was . . . approaching the end of the chapter "The Sacrifice," I knew in advance that its publication would cost me my friendship with Freud. For I planned to set down in it my own conception of incest, the decisive trans-formation of the concept of libido, and various other ideas in which I differed from Freud . . . I knew that he would never be able to accept any of my ideas on this subject . . .

For two months I was unable to touch my pen, so tormented was I by the conflict. Should I keep my thoughts to myself, or should I risk the loss of so important a friendship? At last I resolved to go ahead with the writing—and it did indeed cost me Freud's friendship. After the break with Freud, all my friends and acquaintances dropped away. My book was declared to be rubbish; I was a mystic, and that settled the matter.

(Jung 1961, pp. 158–167)

Their relationship is reflected in their correspondence,

[in] the gradual warming of mutual regard, confidence, and affection, the continual interchange of professional information and opinions, the rapidly elaborating business of the psychoanalytical movement, the intimate give-and-take of family news, and at length the emergence of differences, disagreements, misunderstandings, injured feelings, and finally disruption and separation.

(McGuire 1974, p. xix)

Although European psychoanalysis was often done by non-medical or lay ana-lysts, in the U.S. the I.P.A.-approved psychoanalytic training institutes all employed exclusively medical analysts (Freud & Eitingon 2004). Ferenczi initi-ated the establishment of the International Psychoanalytic Association and Jung became Chairman for Life. However, considerable tension developed between Freud and Jung as they disagreed about libido and religion. In the midst of their difficulties, Freud fainted twice in Jung's presence when he sensed that Jung unconsciously wished him dead (Donn 1988). Before severing their relationship Jung very straightforwardly criticized him, saying that

Your technique of treating your pupils like patients is a *blunder*. In that way you produce either slavish sons or impudent puppies . . . If you should ever rid yourself entirely of your complexes and stop playing the father to your sons and instead of aiming continually at their weak spots, took a good look at your own for a change, then I will mend my ways . . . I shall continue to stand by you publicly while maintaining my own views, but privately shall start tell-ing you . . . what I really think of you. I consider this procedure only decent.

No doubt you will be outraged by this peculiar token of friendship, but it may do you good all the same.

(McGuire 1974, pp. 534–535)

Less than a year later Jung (1961) wrote to Freud:

> It has come to my ears ... that you doubt my *bona fides*. I would have expected you to communicate with me directly on so weighty a matter. Since this is the gravest reproach that can be leveled at anybody, you have made further collaboration impossible.
>
> (op. cit., p. 550)

They met for the last time in 1913 when Jung gave a talk on introverted and extraverted types in analytical psychology for the Fourth International Psychoanalytical Congress in Munich, introducing some fundamental concepts which distinguish his work from Freud's. Freud was enraged but came to feel grief-stricken over their lost relationship, as was Jung. Jung's colleague C. A. Meier spent an hour alone with Freud in Vienna. The only topic of conversation was Jung. Freud was full of questions about him. He still cared (Donn 1988). The two men had loved each other deeply.

Jung was devastated and felt his life slipping away. Months after his relationship with Freud ended, Jung began a period which has been considered a form of creative illness (Ellenberger 1970), similar to that undergone by shamans, religious mystics, and some artists, such as van Gogh, Strindberg, and Nietzsche. He began painting and began what he called his confrontation with the unconscious. He was flooded with a stream of visions so severe that it brought him to the edge of madness. He could not work and resigned his position at the University of Zurich; he could not read a scientific book. Yet he managed to see five analytic patients a day. He put a gun in his nightstand and said when he could no longer bear it, he would shoot himself. It has been suggested that this period of Jung's life was one of creative regression, At eighty-four, he said of that long trek,

> The journey from cuckoo land to reality lasted a long time. In my case Pilgrim's Progress consisted in my having to climb down a thousand ladders until I could reach out my hand to the little clod of earth that I am.
>
> (Dunne 2012, p. 3)

For the next decade he documented these events in his private journals, which ultimately were recorded in *The Red Book* (Jung 1909).

Jung developed most of his ideas after he had the courage to leave Freud (Storr & Stevens 1998). He established a system of treatment called analytical psychology, regarding the self as the unifying principle within the psyche, a view similar to the Kabbalistic idea of the soul. He returned to studying myth, philosophy, and religion, finding objective parallel to what he had experienced and elaborated in *Psychological Types* (Jung 1976). Here he began to organize his ideas about the structure and function of the psyche and to examine the basis of his differences from Freud. For the rest of his life he was preoccupied with the dynamics of personal transformation and growth. He developed his own approach to dreams, regarding them not as the expression of repressed wishes but as natural functions of the psyche, performing self-regulatory functions. He saw the nature of the treatment very differently than Freud, in part a reaction against the stereo-type of the classical analyst, sitting silent and aloof behind the couch. He did away with the couch, preferring that patient and analyst sit facing each other because it made it easier for them to experience themselves as colleagues, working on a shared task. Jung disagreed with the practice of seeing patients intensively over long periods. When possible he preferred to see patients twice or once a week, stopping treatment every ten weeks to encourage the patient to experience his own self-reliance (Storr & Stevens 1998).

Those trained relationally might be surprised to learn that in addition to Ferenczi (Harris & Kuchuck 2015), it was Jung who originated the relational concept. He offered what was a radical proposal at the time,

> that analysis was a dialectical procedure, a two-way exchange between two people who are equally involved. Although this was a revolutionary idea when he first suggested it, it is a model which has influenced psychothera-pists of most schools, though many seem not to realize that it originated with Jung . . .
>
> Jung greatly extended the Freudian view of the transference, for he under-stood that the doctor–patient relationship is an archetypal relationship which has been with us since the beginning of time.
>
> (Storr & Stevens 1998, pp. 96–111)

When he was sixty-eight Jung suffered a second creative illness, resulting from near-fatal emboli in his heart and lungs, and had a near-death experience in the hospital, which he recorded in detail (Farber 2012; Jung 1961). He made a full recovery and, like others who had a near-death experience, was no longer afraid of death (Farber 2013). He threw himself back into his writing.

When Freud published *On the History of the Psychoanalytic Movement* a year after their split (Freud 1914b), he suggested that Jung was anti-Semitic, evoking enormous controversy that continues to this day (Maidenbaum 2002; Martin & Maidenbaum 1991). Anti-Semitism was openly acceptable in Europe at that time, as it seems to be today; this was the culture Jung grew up in. Stevens points out that by contemporary standards Jung was not racist or anti-Semitic but was humane, broad-minded, and liberal, and ahead of his time in advocating the decriminalization of homosexuality, joining Freud in his views on infantile sexuality, and advancing the subversive idea that inside each man was an intact female personality, and a male personality inside every woman, which should be made conscious, integrated, and lived (Storr & Stevens 1998).

It was only fifty years ago that the Vatican issued the *Nostra Aetate*, perhaps the most important moment in modern Jewish–Christian relations. It refutes the charge that the Jews are responsible for Jesus' death, an accusation used for centuries to justify the persecution of Jews. It was not until 2000 that

Pope John Paul II apologized and asked forgiveness for wrong done to Jews, Gypsies, and others. Jung often said that great lights had great shadows; these accusations cast an enormous shadow around him. When Jung published "The Role of the Unconscious" (1970), in which he distinguished between a Jewish and German (Aryan) psychology, this was used as proof of his anti-Semitism. An international conference was held on the subject in New York, sponsored by the C. G. Jung Foundation and co-sponsored by the Postgraduate Center for Mental Health and the Union of American Hebrew Congregations, ultimately producing two books (Maidenbaum 2002; Martin & Maidenbaum 1991), featuring even-handed discussion by contributors. Jung had even predicted the Nazi eruption as early as 1918. "As the Christian view of the world loses its authority, the more menacingly will the 'blond beast' be heard prowling about in its underground prison, ready at any moment to burst out with devastating consequences" (Storr & Stephens 1998, p. 121).

When Stekel developed ideas that conflicted with Freud's about dream symbolism, psychic conflict, and technique, Freud became very dismissive of him, calling him an intolerable swine (Berke 2012). By 1919, Alfred Adler, who had been one of Freud's closest disciples, had also fallen out with Freud. Freud could not tolerate Adler's theories of the inferiority complex and personality, and gave an ultimatum to all members of the Vienna Psychoanalytic Society to drop Adler or face expulsion. Freud denounced Adler and Jung as heretics, driving Adler away but turning him into a celebrity. Both founded separate schools of psychoanalytic thought. When Stekel died suddenly of a cerebral hemorrhage in Aberdeen and Arnold Zweig said he was very moved by the news, Freud triumphantly wrote:

> I don't understand your sympathy for Adler. For a Jew boy out of a Viennese suburb a death in Aberdeen is an unheard-of career in itself and a proof of how far he had got on. The world really rewarded him richly for his service in having contradicted psychoanalysis.
>
> (Jones 1957, p. 208)

After the split with Freud, Jones, who had been Jung's understudy as "Freud's gentile," took Jung's place as the psychoanalytic crown prince and honorary Jew (Maddox 2007). He joked that he was a *shabbes goy*, a gentile who does the work Jews are not permitted on the Sabbath. The first volume of Jones' biography appeared to a mixed reception just as psychoanalysis was reaching the peak of its post-war wave, which swept over the U.S. most strongly and over Great Britain too. Its enthusiastic reception was a sign of the fascination with behavior and sexuality as well as with the curiosity about what Freud, the man, was like. Despite the fantastic reception, the biography received numerous complaints about Jones' effort to present himself in the best possible light, including one from Brill's widow and Max Schur. Jones also omitted any mention of Victor Tausk's suicide (Roazen 1993) and hid the fact that he had deliberately engineered the break with Jung in order to advance himself as Freud's crown prince (Paskauskas 1988). Jones' descriptions of Ferenczi's deterioration and last illness, although following exactly what Freud had written, described Ferenczi as paranoid and homicidal; this caused much angry protest, calling this description a myth and travesty. Similarly there were complaints by followers of Otto Rank. When he recorded Freud's compliment about how well Jones had chaired the Berlin psychoanalytic congress, he omitted Freud's reproach in the same letter: "As you ask for my judgment on the way you conducted the Congress I will suppress my habitual frankness with old friends and plainly say that you suffered it to drift occasionally with too weak a hand" (Paskauskas 1988).

Victor Tausk was one of Freud's most gifted early supporters. He was a brilliant psychiatrist, making him attractive to Freud, but he became almost completely forgotten in the history of psychoanalysis. We heard about him only when Roazen published *Brother Animal: The Story of Freud and Tausk* in 1969. Although Freud found Tausk's original ideas exciting, Freud became angry because Tausk had arrived at these ideas before Freud had done so himself. Roazen thinks that the reason that Tausk became almost completely forgotten is that Tausk was so original that Freud feared that Tausk, who was keenly interested in certain of Freud's ideas, might elaborate on some of them even before Freud had done so. He accused Tausk of stealing his ideas.

Freud resented Tausk's ambition and having a mind of his own, and felt very uncomfortable around him. As ambitious as Tausk was, he wanted to be Freud's shining star. His great dream was to be analyzed by Freud and Freud refused him, a great narcissistic blow. Although Freud tried to work out a compromise by recommending he go into analysis with Helene Deutsch, this did not work out well. She was five years younger than Tausk and, at that time, a nobody in psychoanalysis who had recently begun her own analysis with Freud. The referral was flattering to Deutsch but insulting to Tausk. Nonetheless, Tausk agreed and in his sessions with her, spoke almost entirely about Freud, voicing his thoughts that the trouble between them came from Freud's personal difficulties. He knew he had original ideas before Freud had them but was devastated that Freud would not acknowledge this. And Freud thought that Tausk was taking his ideas without acknowledging the source. And according to Roazen, each had a good basis for believing as he did (Roazen 1971, 1990).

> Each man believed he was unique and a genius and feared being destroyed by the other . . . Near the end of March 1919, after three months, Freud called a halt to the incestuous situation. He explained to Deutsch that Tausk had become an interference in her own analysis . . . Freud forced her to choose between terminating Tausk's analysis with her and discontinuing her own analysis with Freud. To Deutsch it did not constitute a realistic choice but an order. Tausk's treatment ended immediately. At this stage . . . Freud could not waste time on people who muddied his waters. Tausk wanted too much from him and was easily offended. Tausk's attitude toward Freud was

neurotically dependent, and Freud found it easier simply to get rid of him than to risk being—as Freud saw it—swallowed by him. Of course, he could well afford to dispense with an early supporter like Tausk, now that so many new pupils were flocking to him from all over the world.

(Roazen 1971, p. 319)

In 1919, Tausk tied a curtain cord around his neck, put his army pistol to his right temple, and shot himself, blowing off part of his head and strangling himself as he fell. In Freud's official obituary, praising Tausk's contributions to psychoanalysis, he blamed his death on the stresses he experienced during World War I, suggesting he shouldered no part in his suicide. In a letter he wrote ten days after Tausk's death to Swiss psychoanalyst and Christian pastor Oskar Pfister, he said, "Tausk has committed suicide. He was a highly gifted man but was a victim of fate, a delayed victim of the war" (Roazen 1990, p. 138). He wrote to Lou Andreas-Salome, with whom Tausk had had an affair, expressing his relief that Tausk was finally gone. He was quite honest about his cold feelings. "I confess I do not really miss him; I had long taken him to be useless, indeed a threat to the future" (Roazen 1971, p. 321).

Ferenczi was Freud's "favorite son" (Rachman 1993), his most gifted patient and protégé. Known as the *infant terrible* of psychoanalysis, he too had a mind of his own. He wanted Freud to analyze him, which Freud scornfully refused to do. He offered to analyze Freud, which Freud also refused, insisting his self-analysis was enough (Aron & Henik 2015; Kuchuck 2015).

Although Ferenczi's and Rank's work emphasized the ongoing attachment and separation issues in the patient–analyst relationship, Freud seemed unaware of the power of attachments and separations in his work, dropping patients or threatening to do so, with little awareness of how this affected them. "In fact, the traumatic separations he inflicted on those who were close to him . . . run like a red thread through the history of psychoanalysis" (Breger 2000, p. 318).

Rank's theory of birth trauma collided with Freud's blindness to such issues, resulting in a break between them, while Ferenczi's experiments with technique anticipated many modern developments in psychoanalysis, including the relational approach, putting him on the same collision course with Freud. Ferenczi was very interested in treating very ill patients; some of his findings are landmarks in the history of understanding borderline and psychosomatic patients.

Ferenczi understood psychoanalysis as a radically mutual endeavor in which unconscious communication between patient and analyst flows in both directions.

Within his intense, tenuous relationship with Freud, Ferenczi (1949) experimented with active techniques, frequent and explicit counter-transference disclosures, and reciprocal analysis of patients. In his paper "Confusion of Tongues between Adults and the Child" (Ferenczi 1949), Ferenczi presented new evidence that led him to reconsider Freud's original seduction hypothesis, which Freud later renounced. The paper engendered such controversy and so enraged Freud that he refused to shake Ferenczi's hand. This irreparable rift caused much of

Ferenczi's writing to be withheld from translation or otherwise stifled. He was accused of being mentally ill and was shunned.

Freud's break with Ferenczi became a defining moment in the evolution of psychoanalysis, ushering in the relational school. Ferenczi's work continues to influence psychoanalytic theory and practice, and covers many major contemporary psychoanalytic topics (Harris & Kuchuck 2015).

Hanky-panky with Freud's correspondence

Anxious about the possible damage that could be done to the psychoanalytic movement, Anna Freud hated historians and biographers invading her family's privacy. Jones gave in to her pressure to suppress Freud's reactions to Tausk's death in his biography (Roazen 1993). Tausk's death, her analysis by her father, and other matters had not been heard of because of Anna Freud's censorship. Both her analysis by her father and Tausk's suicide remained skeletons in the closet until publication of *Brother Animal* in 1971 when Roazen wrote, "Perhaps the most extraordinary illustration of Freud's allowing himself privileges he might have condemned in any other analyst was his analyzing his youngest child, Anna" (Roazen 1990, p. 100).

> Once I had published *Brother Animal*, Anna Freud and at least some of her doctrinally orthodox allies deemed that I should be discouraged, if not controlled . . . *Brother Animal* was misunderstood as an assault on Freud's character, and one which supposedly blamed Freud for Tausk's suicide.
>
> (Roazen 1993, pp. 103–104)

In his biography, Jones never hinted at the fact that Freud had analyzed his own daughter (Roazen 1993), information Roazen inadvertently stumbled on. Melanie Klein, A. A. Brill, and Ernst Kris tried to observe their children clinically and treated them analytically (Roazen 1993). Eduardo Weiss told Roazen he was considering analyzing one of his sons and wrote to Freud for advice. Freud mentioned that his analysis of Anna was successful but was less optimistic about analyzing a son. Weiss knew he was venturing on dangerous ground politically by telling this to Roazen because he and Anna were on very good terms with each other. He was the founder of the psychoanalytic movement in Italy; Freud had even written a preface to one of Weiss' books. But after Weiss' book containing Freud's letters to him appeared just a year after *Brother Animal* (Weiss 1970), Anna was furious and listed her objections to Kurt Eissler, who established the Freud Archives and was also most protective of Freud. The Archives was the main conduit through which Freud's material wound up in the U.S. Library of Congress, which must abide by any restrictions the Archives imposed on access. Although "starting with *Brother Animal*, there was an end to the hanky-panky with Freud's correspondence" (Roazen 1993, p. 94), Anna later blocked publication in Britain of Freud's letters to Weiss (Roazen 1993). In 1974 Anna wrote to Eva Rosenfeld, "All I can say is that Roazen is a menace whatever he writes" (Roazen 1993, p. 201; Young-Bruehl 1988, p. 434).

> Anna Freud felt free to pencil out anything she chose in Freud's published correspondences; in spite of this arbitrariness, somehow the historical fraternity has not been able to challenge her almost-unquestioned North American public understanding. I first raised the issue of censorship of Freud's letters in a 1968 book of mine; no reviewer, even in professional journals, took notice of what I had said. Then in 1969 my book *Brother Animal: The Story of Freud and Tausk* gave an appalling example of an excision from a Freud letter in connection with the suicide of Victor Tausk. Since then, there has been no more such tampering with Freud's letters. Because entire passages had been dropped without any indication of their deletion, "complete" new editions of Freud's letters to Abraham, Pfister, and Zweig, for example, are now necessary; for the earlier ones are all chopped up in ways that are historiographically incomprehensible.
>
> (Roazen 1993, p. 94)

The wounding healer and its consequences

After Freud's positive reception at Clark, America welcomed psychoanalysis. Nowhere was it embraced more fervently than in Hollywood. Actors, directors, producers, and their families spent some time in psychoanalysis, making it a shared ritual (Farber & Green 1993). Movie stars made public disclosures about their life-altering experiences in treatment, and many of the treating psychiatrists disclosed information about patients that should have remained private and confidential. Some insinuated themselves into all aspects of their patients' lives. Milton Wexler celebrated the double occasion of his eightieth birthday and the scientific research foundation he created with family, friends, and patients, many of whom made large donations to his foundation. As his practice became filled with wealthy celebrities, it became completely intertwined with the work of his foundation. The party's M.C. was comedian Elaine May, known for satirizing psychoanalysis with Mike Nichols. May married her analyst, David Rubenfine, who was consequently stripped of his position as training analyst at the New York Psychoanalytic Institute, and then linked up with Wexler and other "maverick" analysts.

As a result of Marilyn Monroe's suicide, her analyst, Ralph Greenson, was thrust into the public spotlight. When Greenson began treating her, he decided she needed a less formal environment than the usual office setting, and so began seeing her in his home study. Sometimes her sessions lasted five hours. She was usually the last appointment of the day and Greenson often invited her to stay for dinner with his family, who embraced her. She often helped his wife Hildi in the kitchen. Hildi regarded Marilyn as a waif, calling her husband's treatment "adoption therapy."

Cultic aspects of psychoanalytic institutes

Many analysts who deviated from the "party line" have noted institutional attempts at mind control. Shengold (1989) coined the term *soul murder* to describe mind control, the deliberate attempt to destroy the separate identity of another person, his soul remaining in bondage to someone else. Adam Phillips (1997) said, "When psychoanalysts spend too much time with each other, they start believing in psychoanalysis. They begin to talk knowingly, like members of a religious cult" (p. xiv). Kernberg (1996) said that too often psychoanalytic education becomes an indoctrination process rather than open scientific exploration. Psychoanalytic training programs can readily become plagued by subtle or pronounced authoritarian practices, instilling fear and fostering blind obedience to the leaders (Farber 2013; Kirsner 2000). "Most psychoanalytic institutes are unfree associations of psychoanalysts where the spirit of free inquiry has been replaced by the inculcation of received truth and the anointment of those who are supposed to possess knowledge" (Kirsner 2000, p. 10).

This blind submission can seep into the therapeutic relationship, preventing training candidates and their patients from developing creative, authentic, and meaningful experiences. Kernberg (1996) cites many existing problems within organized psychoanalysis in Europe, Latin America, and North America, including boundary violations, sexual abuse, financial exploitation, arbitrariness, and antisocial behavior, problems often involving training analysts which were known and tolerated.

When Martin Bergmann was denied training at the New York Psychoanalytic Institute because he was not a psychiatrist, he organized non-institutional psychoanalytic study groups, one of which I participated in for several years. He remained critical of institutional psychoanalysis throughout his life. Steven Reisner recalled a day, early in his analysis, when he brought up the possibility of finding an institute for further training. Bergmann's response was: "Haven't you been infantilized enough?" (Reisner, private correspondence, January 30, 2014). Emanuel Berman's (2004) relational view of psychoanalytic training demonstrates how generations of psychoanalytic candidates have either idealized a "proper analytic identity," turning it into a persecutory ideal, or rebelled against these standards.

Freud's ambivalence about the occult

Ever since Freud claimed psychoanalysis was a science, anything smacking of the occult was to be avoided. Although Freud wrote to French mystic Romaine Rolland that mysticism and the occult were dangerous, nonetheless, they fascinated him (Farber, unpublished paper; Freud 1960), as his collection of Jewish jokes about telepathic communication and other occult phenomena reflect (Freud 1941). He also was most interested in Jewish mysticism and the Kabbalah (Berke 2015).

As early as 1912, Freud described the communication that must exist in the psychoanalytic relationship, and said that the analyst "must turn his own unconscious like a receptive organ towards the transmitting unconscious of the patient. He must adjust himself to the patient as a telephone receiver is adjusted to the transmitting microphone" (Freud 1912, pp. 115–116). This description of unconscious affective communication (Arizmendi 2008) describes telepathic communication (Farber in press; Gooch 2007).

He anticipated Bromberg's relational concept, a paradigm of dissociated communication between patient and analyst which can be understood as a form of telepathic communication (Bromberg 1998, 2011; Farber in press). Freud's attraction to the occult drew him to Jung and his ambivalence about it played a part in severing their relationship. The psychic field between the two was always highly charged, producing both paranormal and very human phenomena (Moss 2014).

An incident occurred on their last evening in Freud's study that jarred both of them (Jung 1961):

> the famous account of two poltergeist bangs in Freud's study when he and Jung were talking together. Jung had specifically asked Freud for his views on precognition and parapsychology in general. Freud then launched into a vehement rejection of these matters, in the shallowest of terms. Jung, angered by this unjustified snub, bit back a strong retort. However, Jung says that he now experienced a curious sensation, as if his diaphragm was made of iron and was glowing red-hot. There was then a loud bang from the bookcase, so loud as to frighten both men. Jung remarked that this was an example of the phenomena he had been referring to, and added that there would now be another bang. Sure enough, as he said the words, the second bang went off in the bookcase. Freud was very shaken. Perhaps Freud himself was the "medium" for that occult phenomena, or perhaps it was Jung; or possibly it was the two of them reacting together.
>
> (Gooch 2007, pp. 155–156)

Toward the end of their friendship, Jung wrote to Freud:

> If there is a "psychoanalysis" there must also be a "psychosynthesis" which creates future events according to the same laws . . . That last evening with you has, most happily, freed me inwardly from the oppressive sense of your paternal authority.
>
> (McGuire 1974, p. 216)

A decade after their split, Freud was able to say that he was not one of those who dismiss the study of the occult as unscientific (Gay 1988). He began publishing papers about telepathy and other occult phenomena. He was invited in 1921 to be co-editor of three periodicals devoted to the study of occultism; although he refused, he wrote that if he could live his life over again, he would devote himself to psychical research rather than to psychoanalysis (Farber in press). His first and most forthright paper was "Psycho-Analysis and Telepathy" (1941) which he planned to read to the 1922 International Psychoanalytic Congress, but Jones (1957) persuaded him to consider the harmful consequences for psychoanalysis; consequently, the article was published posthumously in 1941. Other papers include "Dreams and Telepathy" (Freud 1922), "Some Additional Notes on Dream Interpretation as a Whole" (Freud 1925) and "Dreams and Occultism" (Freud 1933). He regretted that his study of religion did not include the experience of the mystics and saints (Farber in press; Jones 1957).

Jung tried to rescue Jewish psychotherapists from the Nazis. Although Jung tried to help Freud escape from Vienna and offered him $10,000, Freud rejected his offer, saying "I refuse to be beholden to my enemies" (Breger 2000, p. 359).

Hero worship

I suppose we all have a need to worship a hero or guru, someone who embodies our own undeveloped potential. Freud is the hero of so many psychoanalysts and was mine too. When the need to worship a hero exists along with another's narcissistic need to be worshipped (Shaw 2014), we can all too readily put that person on a pedestal, thus disconnecting ourselves from our own potential. Most of Freud's early followers comprised a conspiracy of silence, fostering the generational transmission of hero worship. His narcissism forbade anyone to challenge him. Although Freud was brilliant, he was human, something he had difficulty acknowledging.

Lou Andreas-Salome acknowledged how Freud's achievements were connected to his limitations: "Confronted by a human being who impresses us as great, should we not be moved rather than chilled by the knowledge that he might have attained his greatness only through his frailties?" (Roazen 1971, p. 322). Freud never had the benefit of a personal psychoanalysis. Although I was shocked and disillusioned to discover the ways his behavior created a template for the wounding healer, nonetheless I will be forever grateful to him. Despite Freud's all-too-human flaws, psychoanalysis has become a living and evolving theory of mind which has saved and transformed the lives of many.

References

Alexie, S. (2004). What You Pawn I Will Redeem. In: L. Moore & K. Kenison (eds.), *The Best American Short Stories 2004* (pp. 1–21). Boston and New York: Houghton Mifflin.
Appignanesi, L., & Forrester, J. (1992). *Freud's Women*. New York: Basic Books.
Arizmendi, T. (2008). Nonverbal Communication in the Context of Dissociative Processes. *Psychoanalytic Psychology*, 25 (3): 443–457.
Aron, L., & Henik, L. (2015). *Answering a Question with a Question: Contemporary Psychoanalysis and Jewish Thought*, vol. 2. Brighton, MA: Academic Studies Press.

Bakan, D. (2004). *Sigmund Freud and the Jewish Mystical Tradition*. New York: Dover.

Berke, J. (2012). *Why I Hate You and You Hate Me: The Interplay of Envy, Greed, Jealousy and Narcissism in Everyday Life*. London: Karnac.

Berke, J. (2015). *The Hidden Freud: His Hassidic Roots*. London: Karnac.

Berman, E. (2004). *Impossible Training: A Relational View of Psychoanalytic Education*. New York and London: Routledge.

Bettelheim, B. (1983). *Freud and Man's Soul: An Important Re-Interpretation of Freudian Theory*. New York: Vintage.

Bettelheim, B. (1991). *The Informed Heart: The Human Condition in Modern Mass Society*. London: Thames & Hudson.

Breger, L. (2000). *Freud: Darkness in the Midst of Vision—An Analytical Biography*. New York: Wiley.

Breger, L. (2009). *A Dream of Undying Fame: How Freud Betrayed His Mentor and Invented Psychoanalysis*. New York: Basic Books.

Breuer, J., & Freud, S. (1895). On the Psychical Mechanism of Hysterical Phenomena: A Preliminary Communication. *Standard Edition*, vol. 2 (pp. 1–17).

Bromberg, P. (1998). *Standing in the Spaces: Essays on Clinical Process, Trauma, and Dissociation*. Hillsdale, NJ and London: Analytic Press.

Bromberg, P. (2011). *The Shadow of the Tsunami and the Growth of the Relational Mind*. London and New York: Routledge.

Burlingham, M. (1989). *Last Tiffany: A Biography of Dorothy Tiffany Burlingham*. New York: Atheneum.

Carey, B. (2004). With Toughness and Caring, a Novel Therapy Helps Tortured Souls. *The New York Times*, July 13.

Carroll, M. (2010). Psychoanalytic Theories of Religion and the "Catholic Problem." In: B. Beit-Hallahmi (ed.), *Psychoanalysis and Theism: Critical Reflections on the Grünbaum Thesis* (pp. 81–98). Lanham, MD: Jason Aronson.

Celenza, A., & Gabbard, G. (2003). Analysts Who Commit Sexual Boundary Violations. A Lost Cause? *Journal of the American Psychoanalytic Association*, 51 (2): 617–636.

Coffey, R. (2014). *Hysterical: Anna Freud's Story*. Berkeley, CA: She Writes Press.

Cornwell, J. (2000). *Hitler's Pope: The Secret History of Pius XII*. New York: Penguin.

Donn, L. (1988). *Freud and Jung: Years of Friendship, Years of Loss*. New York: Scribner.

Dunne, C. (2012). *Carl Jung: Wounded Healer of the Soul: An Illustrated Biography*. London: Watkins.

Eigen, M. (2012). *Kabbalah and Psychoanalysis*. London: Karnac.

Ellenberger, H. (1970). *The Discovery of the Unconscious: The History and Evolution of Dynamic Psychiatry*. New York: Basic Books.

Farber, S. (2000). *When the Body Is the Target: Self-Harm, Pain, and Traumatic Attachments*. Northvale, NJ: Jason Aronson.

Farber, S. (2005). Free Association Reconsidered: The Talking Cure, the Writing Cure. *Journal of the American Academy of Psychoanalysis and Dynamic Psychiatry*, 33 (2): 249–273.

Farber, S. (2013). *Hungry for Ecstasy: Trauma, the Brain, and the Influence of the Sixties*. Lanham, MD: Jason Aronson/Rowman & Littlefield.

Farber, S. (in press). Becoming a Telepathic Tuning Fork: Anomalous Experience and the Relational Mind. *Psychoanalytic Dialogues*.

Farber, S., & Green, M. (1993). *Hollywood on the Couch: A Candid Look at the Overheated Love Affair between Psychiatrists and Moviemakers*. New York: William Morrow.

Ferenczi, S. (1949). Confusion of Tongues between Adults and the Child. The Language of Tenderness and the Language of Passion. *International Journal of Psychoanalysis, 30*: 225–230.

Ferenczi, S., & Dupont, J. (1995). *The Clinical Diary of Sándor Ferenczi*. Cambridge, MA: Harvard University Press.

Flaherty, A. (2004). *The Midnight Disease: The Drive to Write, Writer's Block, and the Creative Brain*. New York: Houghton Mifflin.

Flem, L. (2003). *Freud the Man: An Intellectual Biography*. New York: Other Press.

Freud, A. (1922). Beating Fantasies and Daydreams. In: *Introduction to Psychoanalysis: Lectures for Child Analysts and Teachers, 1922–1935. Early Writings*, vol. 1. New York: International Universities Press.

Freud, E. (1960). *Letters of Sigmund Freud*. New York: Basic Books.

Freud, S. (1884). *Über Coca* (On Coca). In: R. Byck (ed.), *Cocaine Papers* (pp. 47–73). New York: Stonington.

Freud, S. (1900). The Interpretation of Dreams. In: *The Standard Edition of the Complete Psychological Works of Sigmund Freud*, 4: 1–610. London: Hogarth Press.

Freud, S. (1905a). Fragment of an Analysis of a Case of Hysteria. In: *The Standard Edition of the Complete Psychological Works of Sigmund Freud*, 8: 9–236. London: Hogarth Press.

Freud, S. (1905b). Jokes and Their Relation to the Unconscious. In: *The Standard Edition of the Complete Psychological Works of Sigmund Freud*, vol. 8 (pp. 9–236). London: Hogarth Press.

Freud, S. (1908). The Creative Writer and Daydreaming. In: *The Standard Edition of the Complete Psychological Works of Sigmund Freud*, 8: 143–153. London: Hogarth Press.

Freud, S. (1909a). Analysis of a Phobia in a Five-Year-Old Boy. In: *The Standard Edition of the Complete Psychological Works of Sigmund Freud*, 10: 1–149. London: Hogarth Press.

Freud, S. (1909b). Notes upon a Case of Obsessional Neurosis. In: *The Standard Edition of the Complete Psychological Works of Sigmund Freud*, 10: 158–318. London: Hogarth Press.

Freud, S. (1911a). Formulations on the Two Principles of Mental Functioning. In: *The Standard Edition of the Complete Psychological Works of Sigmund Freud*, 12: 215–226. London: Hogarth Press.

Freud, S. (1911b). Psychoanalytic Notes on a Case of Paranoia. In: *The Standard Edition of the Complete Psychological Works of Sigmund Freud*, 12: 1–79. London: Hogarth Press.

Freud, S. (1912). Recommendations to Physicians Practising Psycho-Analysis. In: *The Standard Edition of the Complete Psychological Works of Sigmund Freud*, vol. 12 (pp. 109–120). London: Hogarth Press.

Freud, S. (1913). Remembering, Repeating and Working through. Further Recommendations on the Technique of Psycho-Analysis II. In: *The Standard Edition of the Complete Psychological Works of Sigmund Freud*, 12: 109–120. London: Hogarth Press.

Freud, S. (1914a). On Narcissism: An Introduction. In: *The Standard Edition of the Complete Psychological Works of Sigmund Freud*, 14: 73–104. London: Hogarth Press.

Freud, S. (1914b). On the History of the Psycho-Analytic Movement. In: *The Standard Edition of the Complete Psychological Works of Sigmund Freud*, 14: 7–65. London: Hogarth Press. London: Hogarth Press.

Freud, S. (1914c). Remembering, Repeating and Working through. Further Recommendations to Physicians Practicing Psychoanalysis. In: *The Standard Edition of the Complete Psychological Works of Sigmund Freud*, 12: 145–156. London: Hogarth Press.

Freud, S. (1916). Introductory Lectures on Psychoanalysis, Parts I and II. In: *The Standard Edition of the Complete Psychological Works of Sigmund Freud*, vol. 15 (pp. 15–239). London: Hogarth Press.

Freud, S. (1917). Mourning and Melancholia. In: *The Standard Edition of the Complete Psychological Works of Sigmund Freud*, 17: 217–256. London: Hogarth Press.

Freud, S. (1919a). The Uncanny. In: *The Standard Edition of the Complete Psychological Works of Sigmund Freud*, 17: 217–256. London: Hogarth Press.

Freud, S. (1919b). From the History of an Infantile Neurosis. In: *The Standard Edition of the Complete Psychological Works of Sigmund Freud*, 17: 3–122. London: Hogarth Press.

Freud, S. (1919c). A Child is Being Beaten. In: *The Standard Edition of the Complete Psychological Works of Sigmund Freud*, 17: 15–204. London: Hogarth Press.

Freud, S. (1922). Dreams and Telepathy. In: *The Standard Edition of the Complete Psychological Works of Sigmund Freud*, 18: 197–220. London: Hogarth Press.

Freud, S. (1925). Some Additional Notes on Dream Interpretation as a Whole. In: *The Standard Edition of the Complete Psychological Works of Sigmund Freud*, 19: 125–138. London: Hogarth Press.

Freud, S. (1926). Inhibitions, Symptoms, and Anxiety. In: *The Standard Edition of the Complete Psychological Works of Sigmund Freud*, 20: 87–174. London: Hogarth Press.

Freud, S. (1930). Civilization and Its Discontents. In: *The Standard Edition of the Complete Psychological Works of Sigmund Freud*, 21: 64–145. London: Hogarth Press.

Freud, S. (1933). Dreams and Occultism. In: *The Standard Edition of the Complete Psychological Works of Sigmund Freud*, 30: 31–56. London: Hogarth Press.

Freud, S. (1937). Analysis Terminable and Interminable. In: *The Standard Edition of the Complete Psychological Works of Sigmund Freud*, 23: 209–253. London: Hogarth Press.

Freud, S. (1941). Dreams and Telepathy. In: *The Standard Edition of the Complete Psychological Works of Sigmund Freud*, 18: 197–220. London: Hogarth Press.

Freud, S. (1960). *Letters of Sigmund Freud*. Ed. E. Freud. New York: Basic Books.

Freud, S. (2007). *Living in the Shadow of the Freud Family*. Westport, CT: Praeger.

Freud, S., & Eitingon, M. (2004). *Briefwechsel 1906–1939*. Tübingen: Edition Diskord.

Freud, S., & Krug, S. (2002). Beyond the Code of Ethics, Part I: Complexities of Ethical Decision Making in Social Work Practice. *The Journal of Contemporary Social Services, 83* (5): 474–482.

Freud, S., & Phillips, A. (2002). *Wild Analysis*. New York: Penguin Modern Classics.

Gay, P. (1987). *A Godless Jew: Freud, Atheism, and the Making of Psychoanalysis*. New Haven, CT: Yale University Press.

Gay, P. (1988). *Freud: A Life for Our Time*. New York: Norton.

Gooch, S. (2007). *The Origins of Psychic Phenomena: Poltergeists, Incubi, Succubi, and the Unconscious Mind*. Rochester, VT: Inner Traditions.

Harris, A., & Kuchuck, S. (2015). *The Legacy of Sándor Ferenczi*. New York and London: Routledge.

Henry, W., Sims, J., & Spray, S. (1971). *The Fifth Profession: Becoming a Psychotherapist*. New York: Jossey-Bass.

Jacobson, E. (1976). Ways of Female Superego Formation and the Female Castration Conflict. *Psychoanalytic Quarterly*, *45*: 525–538.

Jones, E. (1953). *The Life and Work of Sigmund Freud, Volume 1, 1856–1900: The Formative Years and the Great Discoveries*. New York: Basic Books.

Jones, E. (1955). *The Life and Work of Sigmund Freud, Volume II, 1901–1919: Years of Maturity*. New York: Basic Books.

Jones, E. (1957). *The Life and Work of Sigmund Freud, Volume III, 1919–1939: The Last Phase*. New York: Basic Books.

Jones, E. (1959). *Free Associations: Memories of a Psycho-Analyst*. New York: Basic Books.

Jung, C. (1961). *Memories, Dreams, Reflections*. New York: Vintage.

Jung, C. (1970). The Role of the Unconscious. In: *Civilization in Transition* (*Collected Works of C. G. Jung*, vol. 10) (pp. 3–28). Princeton, NJ: Princeton University Press.

Jung, C. (1976). *Psychological Types* (*Collected Works of C. G. Jung*, vol. 6). Princeton, NJ: Princeton University Press.

Jung, C. (2012). *The Red Book: A Reader's Edition*. New York: Norton.

Kernberg, O. (1996). Thirty Methods to Destroy the Creativity of Psychoanalytic Candidates. *International Journal of Psychoanalysis*, *77*: 1031–1040.

Kerr, J. (1993). *A Most Dangerous Method: The Story of Jung, Freud, and Sabina Spielrein*. New York: Knopf.

Kirsner, D. (2000). *Unfree Associations: Inside Psychoanalytic Institutes*. New York: Other Press.

Krull, M. (1986). *Freud and His Father*. New York: Hutchinson.

Kuchuck, S. (2015). On the Therapeutic Action of Love and Desire. In: A. Harris & S. Kuchuck (eds.), *The Legacy of Sándor Ferenczi* (pp. 223–234). London and New York: Routledge.

Lazarus, A., & Zur, O. (2002). *Dual Relationships and Psychotherapy*. New York: Springer.

Lieberman, J. (2015). *Shrinks: The Untold Story of Psychiatry*. New York: Little, Brown.

Maddox, B. (2007). *Freud's Wizard: Ernest Jones and the Transformation of Psychoanalysis*. New York: Da Capo

Mahony, P. (1987). *Freud as a Writer*. New Haven, CT: Yale University Press.

Mahony, P. (2002). Freud's Writing: His (W)rite of Passage and Its Reverberations. *Journal of the American Psychoanalytic Association*, *50* (3): 895–907.

Maidenbaum, A. (2002). *Jung and the Shadow of Anti-Semitism: Collected Essays*. Berwick, ME: Nicolas-Hayes.

Martin, A., & Maidenbaum, A. (1991). *Lingering Shadows: Jungians, Freudians, and Anti-Semitism*. Boston, MA: Shambhala.

Masson, J. (1985). *The Assault on Truth: Freud's Suppression of the Seduction Theory*. New York: Penguin.

Mayer, E. (1996). Subjectivity and Intersubjectivity of Clinical Facts. *The International Journal of Psychoanalysis*, *77*: 709–737.

McGuire, W. (ed.) (1974). *The Freud/Jung Letters: The Correspondence between Sigmund Freud and C. G. Jung*. Princeton, NJ: Princeton University Press.

McKinney, F. Free writing as therapy. Psychotherapy: Theory, Research, and Practice *13* (2): 183–187.

Mollon, P. (2000). *Freud and False Memory Syndrome*. New York: Totem.

Moss, R. (2014). When Jung Made Freud Swoon. Retrieved from www.mossdreams.com

Oring, E. (1984). *The Jokes of Sigmund Freud: A Study in Humor and Jewish Identity.* Philadelphia, PA: University of Pennsylvania Press.

Paskauskas, R. A. (1988). Freud's Break with Jung: The Crucial Role of Ernest Jones. *Free Associations, 1*: 7–34.

Phillips, A. (1997). *Terrors and Experts.* Cambridge, MA: Harvard University Press.

Pope, K. (1991). Dual Relationships in Psychotherapy. *Ethics and Behavior, 1*: 21–34.

Rachman, A. (1993). Ferenczi and Sexuality. In: L. Arom & A. Harris (eds.), *The Legacy of Sándor Ferenczi* (pp. 81–100). Hillsdale, NJ: Analytic Press.

Rank, O. (1996). *A Psychology of Difference.* Princeton: Princeton University Press.

Roazen, P. (1971). *Freud and His Followers.* New York: New American Library.

Roazen, P. (1990). *Brother Animal: The Story of Freud and Tausk.* New York: Da Capo.

Roazen, P. (1993). *Meeting Freud's Family.* Amherst, MA: University of Massachusetts Press.

Roazen, P. (1995). *How Freud Worked: First Hand Accounts of Patients.* Northvale, NJ: Jason Aronson.

Shaw, D. (2014). *Traumatic Narcissism: Relational Systems of Subjugation.* New York and London: Routledge.

Shengold, L. (1989). *Soul Murder: The Effects of Childhood Abuse and Deprivation.* New Haven, CT: Yale University Press.

Storr, A., & Stevens, A. (1998). *Freud and Jung: A Dual Introduction.* New York: Barnes & Noble.

Stossel, S. (2014). *My Age of Anxiety: Fear, Hope, Dread, and the Search for Peace of Mind.* New York: Knopf.

Thompson, M. (2001). The Enigma of Honesty: The Fundamental Rule of Psychoanalysis. *Free Associations, 8* (47): 390–434.

van der Kolk, B. (2014). *The Body Keeps the Score: Brain, Mind, and Body in the Healing of Trauma.* New York: Viking.

Weiss, E. (1970). *Sigmund Freud as a Consultant.* New York: Intercontinental Medical Book Corporation.

Whyte, L. (1962). *The Unconscious Before Freud.* London: Tavistock.

Young-Bruehl, E. (1988). *Anna Freud: A Biography.* New Haven, CT: Yale University Press.

Chapter 6

The wounding healer psychotherapist and the self-wounding healer

Sharon K. Farber

The wounding healer hurts not only his patient but also his remaining patients, whose trust he has betrayed. If he is affiliated with a psychoanalytic institute, he traumatizes candidates and can rupture the institute. He blackens the name of his profession and his family's name.

The wounding healer is not aware of the depth of his own wounds. He is usually not malevolent but unconscious of his own countertransference and how it can dominate his work. To remain empathically connected with the patient requires the therapist to revisit areas of his own emotional vulnerability: "We must come to this work centered and fortified, past injuries largely healed and mourned, our present desires largely sated" (Celenza 2010, p. 1).When the therapist cannot do this and suffers a great blow to his narcissistic vulnerability, this can lead a competent or even admirable therapist to becoming a wounding healer.

"This will never happen to me": the therapist's vulnerability to sexual boundary violations

Celenza and Gabbard (2003) studied data from the evaluation and/or treatment of over 200 cases, most of whom were not psychopaths but one-time transgressors. They found the typical characteristics of the therapist who engages in sexual misconduct are qualities that are to some extent present in analysts generally. In comparison to the psychopathic predator, the one-time offender seeks help for his problem and feels genuine remorse, and can, with the right treatment, be rehabilitated (Celenza 2007; Strean 1993).

Celenza and Gabbard are convinced it is misguided to dismiss every analyst who has made a serious error in judgment; that many, perhaps most transgressors, are open to rehabilitation efforts. They insist the temptation to deny this universal vulnerability is a replication of the kind of vertical splitting or compartmentalization that makes one vulnerable to sexual misconduct in the first place. Recovery depends upon the transgressor's attitude toward the transgression itself as well as his openness to and capacity for rehabilitation (Celenza 2007).

Does the transgressor appreciate the extent of harm he has inflicted on the victim, his colleagues, the institutional context, and finally the profession itself? Is she open and constructively self-critical such that rehabilitation is viable? Are *you* open to the possibilities or do you believe once a person has violated their ethics, he or she cannot be trusted ever again?

(op. cit., pp. 111–112)

When the therapist is in a vulnerable state, the patient may sense it and may feel responsible for tending to the therapist's needs, and so a role reversal may occur when it is unclear who the patient is or where the boundaries are. We can become especially vulnerable when we are not aware of our hateful feelings toward our patient that coexist in the countertransference along with our loving feelings. We need to be able to tolerate both without acting on them. "However much [the therapist] loves his patients he cannot avoid hating them, and fearing them, and the better he knows this the less will hate and fear be the motive determining what he does to his patients" (Winnicott 1958, p. 195). Unanalyzed countertransference hatred can erode away the positive affective relationship required to promote a relationship of safety and trust. When the analyst cannot tolerate his hateful countertransference feelings, it can motivate him to have sex with his patient while convincing himself he is doing it out of love. Unfortunately, because training in the mental health professions has become much less psychodynamic, there has been a decline in training about transference and countertransference in general, and more specifically about intense countertransference reactions. Further, often supervisors are reluctant to address trainees' sexual feelings in a straightforward way (Celenza 2007).

When a psychotherapist runs into difficulty in treatment, introspection and self-examination are needed. When that is not sufficient, a consultation with a respected colleague can be enormously helpful, but unfortunately when therapists are most at risk of becoming sexually involved with a patient, they are the least likely to obtain consultation for fear of exposing "inappropriate" feelings and feeling shamed (Celenza 2007). When the psychotherapist cannot use these means of safeguarding the treatment, he can become quite dangerous.

When loving and erotic feelings are stirred up in both patient and therapist, the therapist can lose his sense of stability and hurt his patient in ways from which neither will recover. This can discourage trainees from discussing difficulties before they get out of hand with their supervisors and creates a costly illusion of safety for other therapists who minimize the danger that this could happen to them. A paper in the *U.C.L.A. Law Review* stated:

[In] many states, sexual misconduct regulations categorically prohibit various healthcare professionals from having sexual contact with current patients and with former patients for years after the end of therapy. In many instances, these categorical bans reach conduct that gives no cause for concern: fewer harms are risked by sex between an optician and a former client, for instance, than are risked by sex between a psychologist and a former patient.

(Gorman 2008, p. 983)

This makes the psychotherapy patient and the psychotherapist uniquely vulnerable. Sexual boundary violations are subject to criminal charges and loss of one's professional license in many states. "The psychoanalyst knows that he is working with highly explosive forces and that he needs to proceed with as much caution and conscientiousness as a chemist" (Freud 1915, p. 170).

Patients who have been sexually exploited by their therapists have been compared to victims of incest and have similar symptoms: shame, guilt, and feelings of responsibility for their victimization, feelings of isolation and forced silence, poor self-esteem, suicide and self-harming behavior, and denial (Strean 1993; Sussman 1992).

Those who go into this work may want the feeling of deep connectedness with their patients that was lacking in their lives growing up or may be currently lacking. The inherent imbalance of power and loving feelings can intersect in psychotherapy and become sexualized. "Power is sexy because it always was" (Celenza 2007, p. 180), because we are born into a power relationship toward a person more powerful than we are, to whom we direct our loving feelings. Thus, women tend to be attracted to powerful men to whom they may submit masochistically (Bartky 1990).

The therapist may come to feel love for his patient, a special kind of psychoanalytic love

> heightened by obstacles, taboos, and impossibilities . . . That makes it all the more delectable. The therapist is like a knight who must prove his devotion by *not* lying down with his lady. That was, after all, the final and truest test of a knight's love, if he could steal into his lady's chamber and climb into bed beside her, while her naked body appealed to all his normal . . . appetites, without laying a hand on her. In therapy, the patient lies down—literally or figuratively—and is more naked than naked, more exposed than mere nudity could ever reveal. The therapist proves his devotion by not responding sexually. His quest is to restore what has been lost or stolen from the castle of her self-regard. It is a difficult task . . . a journey fraught with obstacles and danger and strife. There are dragons to slay. There are whirlwinds to tame. There are enemies without. There are monsters within.
>
> (Ackerman 1995, p. 326)

It is this special psychoanalytic love that patients want (Friedman 2005), even as they relentlessly seek erotic love. Because they tell therapists their deepest secrets and allow therapists to see them in their darkest moments, when the therapist yields to this temptation it can produce a syndrome of betrayal that includes ambivalence, guilt, feelings of emptiness, inability to trust, sexual confusion, and increased risk for suicide (Gorman 2008; Pope & Bouhoutsos 1986).

Young (2014) lost her training analyst due to his sexual boundary violation with another patient, and described the result as collateral damage, nuclear fallout:

The radioactivity of such events in psychoanalytic institutes has a very long half-life that extends well beyond the original ethical failure of one analyst. The transgressing analyst harms not only the patient . . . His ethical failure generates expanding circles of damage, as surely as a nuclear blast. While the initial patient is Ground Zero in the destruction, the shock wave rolls over the analyst's other patients fully particularly candidate analysands. The fallout descends further on the analyst's family, colleagues, friends and institute, ultimately irradiating the entire psychoanalytic community.

(Young 2014, pp. 122–123)

Kathy Sinsheimer (2014) described it as a tsunami:

A tsunami, churning deep and wide, can engulf an institute when it is revealed that an analyst is leaving because of committing ethical violations. Without an explanation from the analyst—often a significant, powerful figure in the community—members are left without adequate information to successfully navigate the raging waters. There are pressures to both speak and not speak of what one knows.

(Sinsheimer 2014, p. 147)

An unacceptably high incidence rate of erotic contact between therapists and patients—7–12 percent—has been found among U.S. mental health practitioners (Celenza 2007). Sexual boundary violations are considered the most egregious of all boundary violations in the mental health profession, due to the power imbalance inherent in the structure of the therapist–patient relationship. Several studies suggest that psychologists and psychiatrists have equal prevalence rates, while social workers have a significantly lower rate (Celenza 2007). I suggest that because social work from its origins has been relationship-based, with the moral and ethical quality of the relationship central to social work practice, it serves a protective function (Murphy et al. 2013). Similarly, Celenza attributes the lower incidence among social workers to her belief that they have less need for status and power (Celenza, private correspondence).

Interestingly, although psychodynamic psychotherapy seems to pose the greater risk because of the more intense and intimate nature of the work compared to other therapies, it has the lowest rate. This may derive from psychodynamic psychotherapy's having the greater awareness of the importance of clear, non-exploitive roles, boundaries, and responsibilities, and that the more loosely bounded maintenance of the therapeutic frame in cognitive and humanistic approaches may predispose therapists to boundary crossings such as excessive self-disclosure and non-erotic touch (Celenza 2007).

The problem of sexual boundary violations has a long history but has been studied a short time because there are many taboos against discussion, notably the incest taboo (Celenza 2007). "When a colleague transgresses, he or she brings shame upon the profession much like an incestuous father brings shame upon the family. Hence, the secret is kept even when many are aware of its existence" (op. cit., p. xxiii). Celenza found several very human facets to this problem: the therapist's disavowed aggression, his inability to tolerate the patient's negative transference, and a certain narcissistic fragility that accompanies the breakdown in an otherwise well-functioning therapist. She suggests that all of us who practice psychotherapy may be vulnerable at some point in our professional lives, making it crucial that we understand that the dangerous slide down the slippery slope is comprised of small, easy-to-take missteps, none of which can be taken out of context as a signal that that the therapeutic process is threatened. Many of these steps may be part of a therapist's natural style and may enhance the therapeutic relationship. It is not the behaviors themselves that are problematic but whether they are engaged in for narcissistically driven reasons.

The Boundary Violations Vulnerability Index (Celenza 2007) is a valuable tool for clinicians to use to determine if they are involved in seemingly harm-less boundary crossings, such as accepting a gift or hugging the patient, or more serious boundary violations. Celenza has identified eight risk factors that thera-pists can consider, including long-standing narcissistic vulnerability, grandiose but covert rescue fantasies, intolerance of negative transference due to poor self-esteem, a childhood history of emotional deprivation and sexualization, a fam-ily history of covert as well as sanctioned boundary violations, unresolved anger toward authority figures, a restricted awareness of their own fantasies, especially angry, aggressive ones, and a transformation of countertransference hate to coun-tertransference love. We can understand these scenarios as grandiose rescue and re-parenting enactments (Celenza 2007).

There has been an empirical study of 368 practicing psychologists, of whom 77 percent were married, in which 13 (3.5 percent) reported at least one sexual boundary violation with a supervisee or student (Lamb et al. 2003). Eighty-four percent were male psychologists. Fifty-five percent were clinical psychologists; 45 percent were counseling psychologists. Ninety-seven percent had doctoral degrees and 66 percent were in independent practice. Of those reporting mul-tiple sexual relationships, one reported two with clients, one reported two with students, one reported four with students and one reported one with a client and five with students. Fifty-nine percent of all these relationships occurred after the formal relationship had ended. Reflecting backward, 50 percent thought that the relationship was not worth having. When asked if they would engage in another sexual relationship if they had the opportunity, on a scale of 1–7 (1 = yes, definitely; 7 = no, definitely), 9 of 10 respondents indicated a rating of 6 or 7. In contrast to the high percentage of men reporting sexual boundary violations as professionals, women represented the great majority of those who reported such involvements as clients, supervisees, or students, most of them with teachers. The majority reported a significant impact on their professional work: "I learned how naive I was about power dynamics and how people are vulnerable . . . and I am now more aware of those dynamics." Another reported trusting himself less; some spoke of not getting so close with students, maintaining a greater distance.

One reported feeling cheap, sleazy; another felt quite guilty. They said that dissatisfaction in their personal lives was a contributing force. Some reported that interacting socially in group situations or continuing to see the client after treatment ended, or spending time together outside treatment were contributing factors. A shocking forty percent saw no harm in pursuing a sexual relationship, a clear indication of lack of training in how psychodynamics operate. Some wished that their graduate training had included more explicit discussions, mandated workshops, and/or written materials related to professional boundaries and graduate students' vulnerabilities. Most offenders (80 percent) sought out peer consultation, which they found valuable.

The more intensive and challenging the psychotherapy is to the therapist, the more the pressure on the therapist's equilibrium can stir up vulnerable parts of the self, activating the therapist's wounds (Celenza 2010). A therapist may become a wounding healer with only one of his patients while conducting good treatment with the rest of his patients. That one patient may not be responding to treatment, making the therapist feel impotent and disconnected. Having sex with the patient can become the "solution" to the problem, restoring the therapist's sense of potency and connectedness.

The typical transgressor is a middle-aged male in a solo private practice who becomes involved in a sexual relationship with a female patient while she is in treatment. The therapist's seduction of the patient has little to do with the patient's physical attractiveness: "It is most common to hear the transgressor say (in retrospect), 'I never thought I'd be sexual with any patient and certainly not this one'" (Celenza 2007, p. 13).

All who practice this "impossible profession" are susceptible, no matter how well-trained or analyzed. The more that difficult factors in our lives converge, such as illness, death, divorce, and loss, the more vulnerable we become. The violation seems to occur when treatment is at an impasse, shifting the process from an enormously frustrating and challenging one to a process of seduction and gratification, subverting the treatment so that the therapist's needs become the central focus (Celenza 2007). Celenza's findings confirm what Searles (1979) said, that so many cases of therapists' sexual acting out with patients are largely motivated by the patient's thwarting the therapist's omnipotent-healer strivings. The therapist "has succumbed to the illusion that a magically curative copulation will resolve the patient's illness which tenaciously has resisted all the more sophisticated psychotherapeutic techniques learned in his adult-life training and practice" (Searles 1979, p. 431).

Sexual contact between therapists and patients occur at an unacceptably high incidence rate (9 to 12 per cent) among mental health practitioners (Celenza 2007; Gabbard & Lester 2002). Studies show the typical transgressor to be a middle-aged male therapist in a private practice who engages in a sexual relationship with a female patient and is a one-time offender. Seven to nine percent of male therapists engage in sexual boundary violations, while female therapists account for a relatively low prevalence, yet engage in sexual boundary violations largely with female patients (Celenza 2007). Celenza found that they may not have identified themselves as homosexual prior to their transgression; preliminary data suggests they may use the relationship with a female patient to explore their own sexuality.

Those who have transgressed more than once may suffer from what Jones (1923) called "The God Complex," a pathological unconscious belief that one is God, accompanied by an extraordinary sense of entitlement. Probably the one with the most heinous God complex was Jules Masserman, a prominent psychiatrist and psychoanalyst. He was a former president of the American Psychiatric Association and a former co-chairman of the psychiatry department at Northwestern University School of Medicine. He had also been president of the American Society for Group Therapy, the American Association for Social Psychiatry, the American Society for Biological Psychiatry, and the American Academy of Psychoanalysis. He published twenty books and more than 400 articles. He also edited numerous books and journals and had a hand in the making of more than a dozen films. He wielded a great deal of power in the Chicago psychiatric community and could be a formidable adversary (Noel 1992).

As monstrous as Masserman's behavior toward his patients was, equally shocking was the response of the psychiatric community. Barbara Noel (1992), one of the women who sued him, wrote *You Must Be Dreaming*, which became a television film. She had been his patient for eighteen years, in thrall to Dr. Masserman. She awoke on the couch during a session in 1984 involving the intravenous use of sodium amytal, in the midst of being raped by him. Wanting to find a new therapist, when the first psychiatrist she called heard what the difficulty was and then heard Masserman's name, there was dead silence followed by telling her he was too busy to see her. She was stunned to find that the second psychiatrist she consulted did not believe her and offered to help her understand why she was thinking in this way. If she could do that, then she should go back into Dr. Masserman's care to work through her real problems with him.

> I was particularly angry that Jules Masserman was still a practicing, much acclaimed psychoanalyst and psychiatrist and that not a word about this scandal had been written by the press or by anyone in his community. Instead of being questioned or condemned, Jules Masserman was being lauded throughout the psychiatric community. There must have been whispers at the least. But although many of his colleagues must have heard about the charges against him, they were apparently able to dismiss or ignore them. Indeed, despite any private concerns some individuals may have had, the psychiatric community seemed to close ranks and go out of their way to pay homage to Jules Masserman.
>
> (Noel 1992, pp. 219–220)

Ms. Noel filed a complaint with the Illinois Psychiatric Society which found cause for sanctions, and voted to suspend, rather than expel, him. Expulsion would have created much unwanted publicity because the name of a member who has been expelled must be reported in *Psychiatric News*, the A.P.A.'s newspaper, to warn the public, while they have a choice to report suspension. A spokesman for the national group declined to discuss the specific grounds for the suspension, which received no publicity. Apparently the Illinois Psychiatric Society continued inviting Masserman to their meetings. Less than a month after the three settlements out of court, Dr. Masserman was honored by the Eleventh World Congress of Social Psychiatry. Dr. John Carlton, the president of the World Congress, called Masserman "the most prominent psychiatrist in the world" (Noel 1992, p. 220). Masserman settled out of court with Barbara Noel.

The psychotherapist who marries his patient

Celenza (2007) raised the provocative question of how we consider the case of a therapist who marries a patient, something about which there is no literature or systematic study. Because the therapist's power is contextualized in the structure of the therapeutic setting, this asymmetric aspect of the relationship stirs up the patient's longing to know the therapist in a sexual way. If a therapist marries his patient, can the structure of this contextualized relationship be dissolved? The pair that was formerly a therapist–patient pair will never be in the equivalent situation of a couple who did not meet under the auspices of a structured power imbalance. In the transgressor–victim couples Celenza has seen, there was often a marked power imbalance on a personal level, with the transgressor experiencing the patient/victim as the dominant of the two, ignoring the structured power imbalance inherent in the therapeutic relationship.

The damage inflicted by a wounding healer

I have treated a few patients who had been severely damaged by wounding healer psychotherapists, one of whom is a man I knew professionally, whom I'll call Richard. I never would have imagined him to have the God complex, to be the traumatizing narcissist (Shaw 2014) he was. I went to his website and there it was, clear as day, in the way he described the treatment he provided. He also had a seductive message for prospective patients on YouTube. Although he never had a physically sexual relationship with his patient, he created a most destructive seductive relationship with her, resulting in her starting to cut herself, followed by two psychiatric hospitalizations.

Richard was not someone who committed a serious boundary violation once during a most stressful time in his life. He was a psychopath, one of the minority of those who commit repeated violations (Gabbard & Lester 2002; Sussman 1992), a serial offender quite accustomed to committing serious boundary violations, with no remorse or intention of stopping. These offenses by this type of therapist reflect just one aspect of a personality style characterized by poor impulse control, a poor superego, and transparent exploitation of others. They are extremely narcissistic, having little or no empathy for their victims.

Melinda, age thirty-one, told me she began treatment with Richard because she was depressed and anxious, which was causing trouble in her relationship with the man she lived with. Nine years after beginning treatment with Richard, which lasted around three and a half years, and three years after ending that treatment, Melinda was referred to me by a psychiatrist she had seen at a private psychotherapy center. The referring psychiatrist knew that I had expertise in treating patients who harmed themselves physically, and Melinda was cutting herself.

In the initial consultation I asked to see her wounds and discovered that a recent one was different from the older, more faded scars; it was more jagged and vertical. Vertical cuts are more dangerous than horizontal ones, and associated with suicidality, which I questioned her about. She was uncertain whether she intended to kill herself, and thought perhaps she just wanted to see more blood. Self-mutilation is a predictor of suicidality (Farber 2000, 2012; Jenkins et al. 2002). She had never cut herself nor made a suicide attempt before beginning treatment with Richard, but after she began cutting herself, she began thinking about suicide. The intention may not be to die, but rather to end the psychic pain (Farber 1997, 2000, 2013; Farber et al. 2007). When attempts to end the pain that have worked no longer work so well, more life-threatening attempts come to the fore. When even these fail, then the only thing left to end the pain is death. Schneidman (1993) implored clinicians to abandon terms like "suicide attempt" or "gesture" and restrict themselves to evaluating the lethality of the act and the psychic pain of the individual contemplating death. Once starting treatment with me, the cutting, which had begun around two years after starting treatment with Richard, and continued after she ended that treatment, stopped.

In the initial consultation when I heard Richard's name I was shocked and had to struggle with my countertransference throughout the treatment. I knew him professionally, although not well, and would run into him occasionally.

He was approximately the same age as her father, who had taken little interest in her. Richard took a great interest in her, arousing a powerful "father hunger" (Maine 1991). The more dependent on him she felt, the more dependency he encouraged, shifting her twice-a-week psychotherapy to three times a week. Richard said he took the same interest Freud took in his daughter Anna, whom he analyzed. He told her that just as Freud really wanted to fuck Anna but analyzed her instead, he would really like to fuck her but would analyze her instead, presenting it, apparently, as a noble act of self-sacrifice. A sexual boundary violation need not involve physical behavior. Although Richard never had a physically sexual relationship with her, telling Melinda he wanted to immediately sexualized the relationship.

Richard told her that because his colleagues did not have the creativity that they both had, and had such ordinary minds, they could not appreciate what a creative treatment he had devised for her, so it was best that they not know about it. He compared himself to Freud, whose analysis of his own daughter was so creative. By the second year of treatment, she spoke with him daily by telephone. He brought her to a psychiatrist for medication management; the three went out to dinner afterward. I was dismayed to hear the psychiatrist's name; I knew him too. During the week they went running together, out to dinner, and to the races; occasionally on weekends Melinda spent time with him, his wife, and children. On weekends when she did not see him, she yearned for him terribly. After around two years of psychotherapy, Melinda began cutting herself. She called Richard, who drove her to the hospital, was treated in the Emergency Room for her physical wounds, and then hospitalized on the psychiatry ward. He warned her not to tell anyone about what happened. A patient who began cutting herself shortly after beginning treatment would certainly evoke serious questions about the treatment and the therapist. Because she did not have medical insurance, Richard paid the very large hospital bill.

As Melinda continued to cut herself, he advised her to call him instead when she got the urge. Apparently, what Richard could not allow himself to know was that cutting herself was a bodily expression of the rage she felt toward him that she could not verbalize because her feelings about him were such a confusing mix of love and hatred. Reminiscent of Ralph Greenson's "adoption therapy" for Marilyn Monroe (Farber & Green 1993), he told her that he was "adopting" her as his daughter and introduced her to others as his daughter. Although he had private relationships with others he was treating, she was the only one he had "adopted," which made her feel uniquely special. He took her to a holiday party hosted by the institute with which he and I were affiliated. He introduced her to his colleagues as his daughter, while they both enjoyed their secret, flaunting their transgression before his colleagues, conveying a hidden message of contempt for them and the profession. Richard became the Oedipal father to his adoring daughter.

> When he tells her she is an equal, he speaks to her adult self and cultivates a parentified daughter, likely repeating a way in which she was treated as a child. He also gives up the opportunity to help her resolve the oedipal dilemma that likely brought her to treatment in the first place.
>
> (Celenza 2007, p. 63)

During the time she saw him, she began having nightmares and flashbacks about experiences she had had with him, and began dissociating. After three and a half years, she ended the treatment but continued cutting herself and had to be hospitalized again. (The two hospitalizations cost more than $100,000.) Once again, Richard paid the bill after she signed an agreement that she would never tell anyone about the nature of their relationship.

Richard's arrogant grandiosity and perversity enraged me. When I saw him at professional meetings, it was all I could do not to shout out and expose him for what he had done, thus opening myself to legal charges, so I avoided meetings where I might run into him. I wanted to do something so that he could no longer practice. To this end, I consulted with Dr. Andrea Celenza, but my hands were tied.

Melinda had discovered a website called Therapist Exploitation Link Line (TELL) and through it found the lawyer she consulted. She wanted to take legal action and after beginning treatment with me, talked with her lawyer about what she could do so that Richard would lose his license to practice. He was a licensed psychoanalyst. She could have reported him to his professional licensing board but in the few months I saw her, she never did because she was too conflicted; she was enraged at him and, at the same time, also had many warm memories of him for making her feel so special and desirable. Although she stopped her treatment with me feeling unable to resolve her feelings about him, she has done well.

Years after I treated Melinda, Richard's infuriating website and YouTube video were still online. I found that no complaints have ever been filed against him. He remained in practice until his recent death. Anyone who has been abused or exploited by a psychotherapist can go to the TELL website for assistance; http://www.therapyabuse.org for much valuable information.

The self-wounding healer

There are wounded healers who hurt themselves, wounding themselves directly through cutting and burning themselves, or indirectly through the harm inflicted on themselves through eating disorders. When studying for my doctorate, I discovered there was a very strong comorbidity between eating disorders and self-mutilation, and further exploration revealed virtually nothing in the literature to explain it. At the same time, I was receiving training in treatment of those with eating disorders and so become intrigued and decided to do a study for my dissertation, exploring the factors I suspected might be involved (Farber 1995, 1997, 2000). The potentially life-threatening self-harm behavior the subjects presented was staggering, even more so when a surprising number of subjects identified themselves as professional social workers, psychologists, and psychiatric aides.

Fast forward to a number of years later, a candidate in a psychoanalytic training program consulted with me about her self-mutilating behavior getting worse. Those who interviewed her for the training program knew nothing about this or that she had been diagnosed with dissociative identity disorder and had been treated several times in an inpatient unit for trauma-related disorders. She cut herself the evening before seeing me. To assess the severity, I asked to see it. I was shocked to see a jagged network of moist, bloody cuts, very different from the "delicate self-cutting" (Pao 1969) seen in those who cut themselves less severely. I was appalled that someone so out of control had been admitted to a psychoanalytic training program undetected; I wondered how many others there were like her, wounded healers who wounded themselves. When I decided to collect chapters for this book, Annita Perez Sawyer (2015), who had inflicted terrible harm on herself, wrote about it in her memoir *Smoking Cigarettes, Eating Glass*. Her chapter is included in this book.

References

Ackerman, D. (1995). *A Natural History of Love*. New York: Vintage.

Bartky, S. (1990). *Femininity and Domination: Studies in the Phenomenology of Oppression*. New York and London: Routledge.

Celenza, A. (2007). *Sexual Boundary Violations: Therapeutic, Supervisory, and Academic Contexts*. Lanham, MD: Jason Aronson.

Celenza, A. (2010). The Analyst's Need and Desire. *Psychoanalytic Dialogues: The International Journal of Relational Perspectives, 20* (1): 60–69.

Celenza, A., & Gabbard, G. (2003). Analysts Who Commit Sexual Boundary Violations. A Lost Cause? *Journal of the American Psychoanalytic Association, 51* (2): 617–636.

Farber, S. (1995). A Psychoanalytically Informed Understanding of the Association between Binge-Purge Behavior and Self-Mutilating Behavior: A Study Comparing Binge-Purgers Who Self-Mutilate Severely with Binge-Purgers Who Self-Mutilate Less Severely or Not at All. Ph.D. dissertation in Clinical Social Work, New York University School of Social Work.

Farber, S. (1997). Self-Medication, Traumatic Reenactment, and Somatic Expression in Bulimic and Self-Mutilating Behavior. *Clinical Social Work Journal, 25* (1): 87–106.

Farber, S. (2000). *When the Body Is the Target: Self-Harm, Pain, and Traumatic Attachments*. Northvale, NJ: Jason Aronson.

Farber, S. (2012). *Hungry for Ecstasy: Trauma, the Brain, and the Influence of the Sixties*. Lanham, MD: Jason Aronson/Rowman & Littlefield.

Farber, S., & Green, M. (1993). *Hollywood on the Couch: A Candid Look at the Overheated Love Affair between Psychiatrists and Moviemakers*. New York: William Morrow.

Farber, S., Jackson, C., Tabin, J., & Bachar, E. (2007). Death and Annihilation Anxieties in Anorexia Nervosa, Bulimia, and Self-Mutilation. *Psychoanalytic Psychology, 24* (2): 289–305.

Freud, S. (1915). Instincts and Their Vicissitudes. In: *The Standard Edition of the Conplete Psychological Works of Sigmund Freud*, vol. 14 (pp. 117–140). London: Hogarth Press.

Friedman, L. (2005). Is There a Special Psychoanalytic Love? *Journal of the American Psychoanalytic Association, 53* (2): 349–375.

Gabbard, G., & Lester, E. (2002). *Boundaries and Boundary Violations in Psychoanalysis*. Washington, DC: American Psychiatric Publications.

Gorman, S. (2008). Sex outside of the Therapy Hour: Practical and Constitutional Limits on Therapist Sexual Misconduct Regulations. *U.C.L.A. Law Review*: 983–1039.

Jenkins, G., Hale, R., Papanastassiou, M., Crawford, M., & Tyrer, P. (2002). Suicide Rate 22 Years after Parasuicide: Cohort Study. *British Medical Journal, 325*: 1155.

Jones, E. (1923). The God Complex. In: *Essays in Applied Psycho-Analysis* (pp. 204–226). London: International Psychoanalytic Press.

Kidd, S. M. (2003). *The Secret Life of Bees*. New York: Penguin.

Lamb, D., Catanzaro, S., & Moorman, A. (2003). Psychologists Reflect on Their Sexual Relationships with Clients, Supervisees, and Students: Occurrence, Impact, Rationales and Collegial Intervention. *Professional Psychology: Research and Practice, 34*: 102–107.

Maine, M. (1991). *Father Hunger: Fathers, Daughters, and Food*. Carlsbad, CA: Gurze Designs & Books.

Murphy, D., Duggan, M., & Joseph, S. (2013). Relationship-Based Social Work and Its Compatibility with the Person-Centred Approach: Principled versus Instrumental Perspectives. *British Journal of Social Work, 43*: 703–719.

Noel, B. (1992). *You Must Be Dreaming.* New York: Simon & Schuster.

Pao, P. (1969). The Syndrome of Delicate Self-Cutting. *British Journal of Medical Psychology, 42*: 195–206.

Perez Sawyer, A. (2015). *Smoking Cigarettes, Eating Glass: A Psychologist's Memoir.* Santa Fe: Santa Fe Writer's Project.

Pope, K., & Bouhoutsos, J. (1986). *Sexual Intimacy between Therapists and Patients.* New York: Praeger.

Schneidman, E. (1993). *Suicide as Psychache: A Clinical Approach to Self-Destructive Behavior.* Northvale, NJ: Jason Aronson.

Searles, H. (1979). The Patient as Therapist to His Analyst. In: *Countertransference and Related Subjects: Selected Papers* (pp. 380–459). New York: International Universities Press.

Shaw, D. (2014). *Traumatic Narcissism: Relational Systems of Subjugation.* New York and London: Routledge.

Sinsheimer, K. (2014). Silencing: When a Community Loses an Analyst to Ethical Violations. In: R. Deutsch (ed.), *Traumatic Ruptures: Abandonment and Betrayal in the Analytic Relationship* (pp. 147–162). New York and London: Routledge.

Strean, H. (1993). *Therapists Who Have Sex with Their Patients: Treatment and Recovery.* New York and London: Routledge.

Sussman, M. (1992). *A Curious Calling.* Northvale, NJ: Jason Aronson.

Winnicott, D. (1958). Hate in the Countertransference. In: *Collected Papers: Through Paediatrics to Psychoanalysis* (pp. 194–203). New York: Basic Books.

Young, C. (2014). Collateral Damage: The Fallout from Analyst Loss due to Boundary Violations. In: R. Deutsch (ed.), *Traumatic Ruptures: Abandonment and Betrayal in the Analytic Relationship* (pp. 109–125). New York and London: Routledge.

Part II

The wounded healers speak

Chapter 7

This wounded healer says warp up the loom

Sharon K. Farber

When Hope Edelman (1994) became a parent, she found herself revisiting the loss of her mother in unanticipated ways. She asked what there is about becoming a mother that is so healing for a motherless daughter, mending something deep inside. I know what that is. My life has been formed around the loss of my mother from the time I was born and becoming a mother was healing for me.

I loved being pregnant with my son and didn't want it to end. It was the happiest time of my life; the physical discomfort was a small price to pay. I had a ten-month pregnancy. My husband Stuart, whose sense of humor attracted me to him, started calling me "Retento." Labor was slow and pitocin was used to speed it up. I thought I was looking forward to childbirth, but in retrospect my body was telling me something else. Perhaps it knew something the rest of me did not know.

The night after his birth, I had nightmares in the hospital about my mother's suicide attempt, something I had not thought about for a long time. It happened when I was eight or nine. I was not supposed to know about it and so I never spoke of it to anyone. I cried in school occasionally, not knowing why. It wasn't until my first session in psychoanalytic treatment, I surprised myself by speaking about it. The dam had finally broken.

For so long, I had harbored such unconscious anger at my mother who was so ready to abandon me, an anger that made me a depressed child. But over the years I was able to piece together some understanding of her life that helped me to appreciate all the more how she tried to help me have a better life than she ever had.

Having such nightmares immediately after childbirth was a terrible way to welcome my son into this world. I gave birth to him and a post-partum depression. It was not so severe as some I had heard of and I never had suicidal thoughts. I had terminated my lengthy and successful psychoanalytic treatment years before but this sent me back for another round. It all was tied up with the circumstances around my mother's pregnancy with me, her first child, and my birth.

While pregnant with me, my mother accidentally discovered the circumstances of her birth, a family secret. She came across her mother's death certificate and papers regarding her twin brother's death, and cemetery details. Her mother had delivered in barns and stables in Eastern Europe, running with her family from pogroms in Hungary, but in an American hospital, she and one of her two babies died. My mother found her way to the cemetery and visited her mother's grave, all alone. She told me about it when I was an adult; she had never talked about this before to anyone. The older I get the more I feel for her, imagining what it must have been like to make this traumatic discovery and harbor her secret knowledge. She must have had a post-partum depression, a terrible way to welcome me into this world. She must have been preoccupied with thoughts and feelings about the circumstances of her own birth as well as anxiety about her infant and/or herself dying in childbirth. Her behavior must have communicated to me how dissociated and frightened she was, and must have frightened me (Hesse & Main 1999; Hesse et al. 2003).

My mother's father remarried and she grew up cared for by a cold step-mother to whom she never really developed an attachment. She was never told that this woman was her step-mother or about the death of her mother and twin brother. When her step-mother died, I felt no loss: I had no attachment to her either. My mother grew up harboring the traumatic knowledge of her origins, then met and married my father, the handsome "Prince of Pelham Parkway." They did not live happily ever after.

After my son's birth I was a stay-at-home mother for the first three years, determined that my child would have a different experience than I had, the experience of having a mother who was there, physically and emotionally. My husband and I had moved to the suburbs early in my pregnancy and I knew no one. It was lonely and I missed the camaraderie and stimulation of my professional life. So much of being a stay-at-home mother was boring. I met some nice women but my new social life consisted of playgroups, which was really not so bad, but not much more. When my son was around three, I began training in psychoanalytic psycho-therapy, studying at a training institute in the evening with Gertrude and Ruben Blanck. I loved it and discovered that full-time motherhood had not completely destroyed my mind. I knew that when I started to work again, I did not want to work in a hospital and be treated once again as "the handmaiden to the physician," the way social workers, men included, were treated.

I attended a local community group and spoke to a group of parents about the transition to motherhood. To my surprise, one mother called me at home and said she had been thinking about going into psychotherapy and thought I might be a good therapist for her. I had no practice and no intention of starting one at the time, but after obsessing about whether seeing someone I might run into in my community would contaminate the transference, with my husband's encour-agement, I decided to do it. I sublet office space and started a private practice, discovering that I had a real knack for it. When I ran into difficulties, usually countertransference problems, I brought them into my own treatment.

I was fascinated with my son's growth and development and decided to get further training in child and adolescent psychotherapy. I gave talks to parents at his nursery school and when I started seeing child patients, hired a private supervisor. I loved the new concepts I was learning and here I was, back to the life of the mind. When my son was a teenager, I decided to get my doctorate in clinical social work, a very exciting time. He called it my Doctor Ed and came with me to Staples to help me select notebooks. On graduation day a faculty member at N.Y.U., Dr. Carol Tosone, introduced herself, saying she had heard such fascinating things about my dissertation. "Why don't you consider turning it into a book?" This was the shot in the arm that I needed. Within two months I had a contract for my first book, *When the Body Is the Target: Self-Harm, Pain, and Traumatic Attachments* (Farber 2000). Out of that came *Hungry for Ecstasy: Trauma, the Brain, and the Influence of the Sixties* (Farber 2013), and now this one.

Oddly enough, my post-partum depression and the disturbed and disturbing relationship I developed to my mother had much to do with my own ability to become so absorbed in thinking and writing (Farber 2013). I love to write and I write a lot, readily going into a state of deep absorption, a dissociated state of consciousness but not a pathological one (Hesse & Van IJzendoorn 1998). I am happiest when writing. I feel it as a need.

I start upon arising, before having breakfast or washing, often propelled by what I have been dreaming. The ability to become so absorbed began, I think, when I was an infant, after my mother discovered the shocking news about her origins. She must have been traumatized, unable to think and process her thoughts, dissociated, disturbed, and very disconnected from me. The mother's face is like the infant's mirror (Kernberg et al. 2006).

My mother, my first mirror, had undoubtedly been traumatized while pregnant with me and as long as I can remember, had always been quite anxious. I suspect that she was prone to dissociated states, in which she was physically there but otherwise not present, which must have been frightening to me. In her dissociated states, I must have been invisible to her, unseen, which is the origin, I suspect, of long-standing difficulties in looking at my face in the mirror and smiling in certain social situations.

When my mother discovered the loss of her own mother, it probably made it more likely that I would develop a disorganized attachment to her, a tendency toward dissociation. History repeats itself and for her and for me, childbirth was a time for dissociation, grief, and sadness. I can only reconstruct that I developed a tendency to retreat into myself, becoming increasingly more absorbed in what was going on in my own mind, a safer place to be than with her or my father, a tendency that persists today. My psychoanalytic treatment saved my life; the relationship to my analyst was a corrective emotional experience, the first really safe and secure attachment I had ever had. He saw and heard me.

At times my mother could be sensitive and responsive but I could not count on it. I can only wonder what it was like for her when she became a mother. When I was born, her mind must have gone back to the time when she was born, then abandoned. Her mother and twin brother died, yet she survived. I can only imagine that she felt guilt about surviving and wondered if that played a part in her suicide attempts, as well as the wish to be with her mother and twin brother. I know that her step-mother was a traumatizing, indifferent parent. I believe my mother cared for me as best she could, going in and out of dissociated states that were reflected in sudden shifts in behavior and facial expressions that had to have been confusing and frightening to me. Then later, she became ill with tuberculosis, at that time considered fatal. A real abandonment. I was afraid she would never come home from the sanitorium and that I would be left with my father, who for as long as I can remember, had been depressed and angry, and late in life was hospitalized for depression. He had obsessive-compulsive disorder as well, checking the gas jets on the stove compulsively and practicing the OCD version of Judaism. Orthodox Judaism has 613 *mitzvot* (commandments) and lends itself to OCD. My father put on *tfillin* (phylacteries) and a *tallis* (prayer shawl) every morning and prayed in Hebrew. Once, in adolescence, I asked what he was praying for. He did not know. He only knew that he had to do it. When I had trouble sleeping as a child, he warned me that if I did not go to sleep, Jack the policeman was going to climb in through the window and take me away. Not a good way to help a child fall asleep.

He owned a drugstore and managed to work but spent all day Sunday lying on his bed, looking up at the ceiling. When I was a teenager and cosmetics became part of my life, occasionally I asked him to bring home a particular lipstick or other product. He brought me products so old and deteriorated that they could not be sold. Garbage. Is that what I was to him? We never went out as a family except to attend a family function, such as a wedding. At those times my father was jolted into a manic state, becoming the life of the party, joking and singing to entertain everyone, then sinking back into his depression when it was over. At my wedding, he sang "Sonny Boy"; the lyrics about how much his son meant to him were far more appropriate for my brother's wedding than mine.

He made it clear that I should have been born a boy. He did not think college was necessary for a girl and refused to pay for it for me and certainly not graduate school. Some of this thinking was a result of his Orthodox background, in which girls were groomed to be married, stay home, and produce babies, one after the other. But I think he also was something of a misogynist. Fortunately I received a New York State and Barnard College scholarships, then a graduate school fellowship from the National Institute of Mental Health that helped me pay for my Master's degree in social work. Late in life, my father had hypomanic episodes, and probably was bipolar, but was never diagnosed and treated. I recall that many years before when I was studying with Gertrude and Ruben Blanck, a paper I wrote was selected to be read before their alumni association. I was excited and proud. Shortly after I began speaking, a woman from my class walked in late. Immediately I felt panic rise up in me. She worked in Mount Sinai's psychiatric inpatient service, where my father was hospitalized at that very moment. I had brought him there only a week before and was terrified she might make the connection that the patient Joseph Klayman was the father of Sharon Klayman Farber. I felt such shame, such exposure.

Dissociation has been called "the escape when there is no escape" (Putnam 1992, p. 104). Between my father and my mother, life in my own head was the best place to be. So many years of living in my own head had developed my imaginative and creative abilities. My absorption manifested as attentional difficulties, which made me think that I might have attention deficit disorder (Farber 2012). A psychiatric consultant doubted I had it. More recently, I came across some neuroscientific research on the relationship of creativity to psychosis, which found that highly creative, healthy people and people with schizophrenia have certain brain chemistry features in common. "In other words, thinking outside the box might be facilitated by having a somewhat less intact box" (de Manzano et al. 2010, p. 6; Farber 2013, p. 292). That is the up-side to having this disorder, just as it is in many with attention deficit disorder. I have to be careful to compensate for the problems it causes. There is a saying, "She can't walk and chew gum at the same time." That almost describes me. I cannot walk and have any kind of thoughtful conversation with someone; my feet slow down and bring me to a halt, as if they have a mind of their own. If I have an hour or two between patients, I might go upstairs to write and can become so absorbed that I do not realize that my next patient has arrived until they call on their cell phone. I've learned to keep a kitchen timer next to the computer. My husband and son often find me distracted when they are talking about something that does not interest me (Farber 2013). I believe my attentional difficulties, which manifested in my early thirties, grew out of my tendency to dissociate and become deeply absorbed in matters other than what was going on around me.

I tell you all this to try to explain something that puzzled me until writing this chapter. How does a mother whose post-partum depression hits immediately after delivery, who lives so much to in her own head, become attached to a baby she wanted to remain pregnant with forever? How does she start to love a baby whose birth is the occasion for horrendous nightmares and memories? The answer was breast-feeding.

I knew before he was born that I wanted to nurse him for the usual health reasons—protection from certain illnesses, allergies, ear infections. When I awoke after my nightmare and the nurse brought him to me and placed him on my chest, I asked anxiously "What do I do?" "Oh, I think you'll figure it out" she said and walked out of the room. I held him and drew him to my nipple. This little creature began making snorting noises like a little animal and latched onto my nipple as if he knew it was created especially for him. These breasts, which had only served to attract men, suddenly could do so much! Nursing was magic! I fed him with my own body and nothing else. I didn't have to try. He needed me so much. I felt whole. I looked forward to the let-down reflex, telling me that in a moment, my breast would be relieved of the pain of being engorged, and that I was releasing the milk that enabled him to live and thrive. He sucked and sucked, looked at me, smiled, and I smiled back. Then the rooting and snorting to get back to business and get that nipple back in his mouth. We fit together perfectly, like pieces of a puzzle. We were made for each other. We played. I loved it. So did he. I learned later that as he nursed and we snuggled and laughed, it stimulated to the secretion of oxytocin, the hormone of love and attachment, in his body and mine (Uvnas

Mosberg 2003). There was so much that I did not know about breast-feeding and did not have to know. My body just did it.

Breast-feeding ended when he was almost eight months old. I did not wean him; it would be more correct to say that he weaned me. I had already introduced solid food and he simply let me know he was done, finished. It was a sad day for me but did not last long. I took such pleasure in his growth and development.

Nature is so intelligent! It created breast-feeding and oxytocin and it makes babies so adorable that it makes you want to hold and snuggle and kiss them. So many new mothers will tell you that they expected to feel deep love immediately for their infant and when that did not happen, thought there was something wrong with them. They became mothers biologically when they gave birth but became mothers psychologically gradually (Stern & Bruschweiler-Stern 1998). The motherhood mindset starts in pregnancy. At the moment of birth, the new mother is not yet psychologically attached to her baby. That develops gradually to fill the center of her inner life, lasting throughout her life but not always occupying center stage.

So it seems to make absolute sense that when doctors, friends, and family recommend breast-feeding, in addition to doing it for the usual medical reasons, women should be told how it can help them to become attached to and love their newborn. Nursing is the prototypical attachment behavior and it helped me to love this child from the moment he rooted for my nipple. He is successful in his life beyond what I could have imagined. Today he and his wife have three children and live within walking distance. He is such a good father and husband, in addition to being most successful in his professional life. When I planted a belly kiss on my little granddaughter's belly and we laughed together, I told her that when her Daddy was little, I used to give him belly kisses too, and he laughed and laughed.

I started thinking of myself primarily as a mother rather than as a daughter. Between breast-feeding and returning to my analyst for round two of a very long-term treatment, I gradually emerged from my post-partum depression. Life was getting better. I'll never forget standing in the kitchen one hot August afternoon while my little guy was sitting on the potty chair in the bathroom and called out "Mommy, when I get to be a big man, I am going to marry you!" I was stunned. This was a sacred moment and I didn't want to blow it. Wanting to let him down gently, I thought for a moment, then told him that when he gets to be a big man, I will be an old lady. He did not care. So I told him I was already married to his Daddy. He didn't care about that either. So I told him that we are not allowed to marry more than one person but that when he gets to be a big man, he could find a nice lady that he could marry. He was very disappointed but a week or two later, it was clear that he'd been thinking about it. He asked me if, when he gets to be a big man, I can drive him around town, and slow the car down when we see a nice lady walking in the street so that he can get a good look at her hand to see if she is wearing a wedding ring.

Soon after, my husband and I left him with my parents on a Saturday. They usually enjoyed their time with him and he enjoyed it too, but this time when we came to pick him up, my mother was not there. My father said that she had run up to the roof of their building and seemed oddly unperturbed. I panicked because it had not occurred to me that she might still at times feel suicidal. We never allowed them to care for him after that. The specter of suicide never really left but I never expected a homicide attempt. Months later, I was serving lunch to him and a little friend when I got a call from the Emergency Room of North Central Bronx Hospital. My parents had been brought there after my mother slammed my father over the head with a candelabra. I used to work in the ER at Fordham Hospital and often had to make disturbing calls to family members. Never had it occurred to me that I would get one. My world had gotten better but my parents' hadn't.

I was enraged at both of them for doing this to me. I was just starting to emerge from my depression. And some of the time, my son was on the receiving end of my anger. I never hit him but at times became quite angry at him. I'll never forget once when this happened he just went to his room, climbed into bed and went to sleep. I was devastated that I had driven my child to the same depressed behavior that my father lived with. I feared that I had ruined him. And this made me even angrier at my parents.

At the end of his life, my father lay in the hospital going in and out of consciousness. Suddenly I heard him cry out, "Celia, stop beating me. Please, Celia." Celia was his older sister, who also suffered from major depression, as did her daughter. I wondered what other things happened in his life to harden him so. Shortly before he died, he told me that he knew he had not been a very good father to me. It was not even an apology. It was too little and too late.

Despite my parents' psychopathology making terrible intrusions into my life, I managed to become a good-enough mother. As an adolescent my son could not wait to get out of this little suburban town where "nothing was happening" but as an adult, he has chosen to live within walking distance and we have a grandparents' dream, three lovable grandchildren who love coming to our house and having us come to theirs.

What made it possible for me to become so resilient, to have a life in which, despite such rocky times, I was able to have friends, marry and love a man, develop a professional career? There was a time when my friends were dating and falling in love, and I was certain that I could never love anyone. I did not feel capable of that. After years of getting involved with men who treated me badly, I finally learned from my experience, got it right, and married a very smart, kind man with a wonderful sense of humor. We each brought baggage from our traumatic childhoods with us but despite some tough times, we stayed together and loved each other. And it keeps getting better and better. How had I become so capable of loving?

For starters, getting out of my parents' orbit was necessary. Although I grew up a depressed child, sometimes crying in school for no apparent reason, I had friends. I was fortunate that a woman who lived in the apartment next door took an interest in me. Miss Wilkinson lived with her sister and brother-in law and sometimes invited me in, allowing me to use their encyclopedia and other books. I loved books. There were few in my home, other than what I borrowed from the public library. Miss Wilkinson was not married but was maternal. One day she gave me a gift, a lock-and-key diary, the kind that was sold in the 5 and 10 cent store, telling me to write something in it every day—an observation of someone or something I saw, a thought or idea that came to me. Although I used the diary very erratically, that she thought that my thoughts and feelings were worth recording on paper meant a great deal to me and remained with me.

It was Hunter College High School that saved my life. In eighth grade I passed the entrance exam for Hunter, a publicly funded elite school in Manhattan for intellectually gifted girls, ranked by *The Wall Street Journal* as the top public high school in the U.S. My teacher, Joseph Imperial, convinced my mother that it was absolutely essential for me to go to Hunter, that she should do what she could to make it possible. When I published my first book, I acknowledged his caring in print. I hunted him down, met him for lunch, and was delighted when I could introduce him to friends, relatives, and colleagues at the book party at my house. My mother knew that I got good grades and was valedictorian of my class, and took what Joseph Imperial said very seriously. In retrospect, I realize she had made it her mission that I should have something better than she had.

My formidable father opposed my going to Hunter, saying "Who needs her to be smart? Just let her be normal." My mother, however, rose splendidly to the occasion, insisting on it and arranging for alternative transportation so that I would not have to spend well over an hour on the New York City bus and subways, not such safe places for a thirteen-year-old girl. This opportunity changed my life in so many ways and I will always be grateful to her. The life of the mind was valued there. Although many were very competitive at Hunter, I was oblivious to it. Being surrounded by other brainy girls was as if I'd died and gone to heaven. I discovered a sense of humor I never knew I had. Somehow the wonderful manic defense that humor can be had developed in me and I had a bunch of girls and teachers who appreciated it. I played to my audience, enjoying becoming quite outrageous at times. Classmates wrote in my high school yearbook that they will always remember my imitation of a tipped uterus. The crybaby had become the class clown. I was having fun, discovering who I was and could be, getting a second chance at life (Blos 1967). I still love being a ham. It serves me well in the public speaking I do.

In a creative writing class at Hunter I read James Joyce and learned to write in a stream of consciousness style, astonished at what my usually logical mind produced. Soon after I discovered that it was related to the free association of psychoanalysis, which got me interested in the psychoanalytic process itself. I worked as a camp counselor, first in a private camp and then at Camp Wel-Met, a social work agency camp. I was struck by the thoughtful attention paid to the well-being of the campers at Wel-Met. I wanted to return for a second summer but was told by my unit head that I had something of a problem with authority. He suggested psychotherapy and referred me to the man who became my analyst in my sophomore year of college. I had no hesitation; I knew on some level that there was a great deal of unburdening I had to do, a story I had to tell to someone who could listen and help me make sense of the mess. Then I stumbled upon Georg Groddeck's (1923) *The Book of the It*, so exciting to me because it linked free association with the mystery of the mind–body relationship. Groddeck, I soon discovered, was regarded by some as the father of psychosomatics, an eccentric angel, and a genius, and by others as a "wild analyst," a terrible embarrassment to psychoanalysis. Nevertheless I found his ideas exciting. Many years later I began incorporating expressive writing into the treatment of some patients, finding that it promoted free association (Farber 2005) and then started a *Psychology Today* blog called "The Mind-Body Connection." I ran a course at the Hudson Valley Writers' Center called "Writing for Physical and Emotional Well-Being."

Although Barnard was within commuting distance, I knew I could not bear to live at home and finagled an arrangement in which I lived off-campus, paying for it with a student loan. I majored in English, with a concentration in creative writing. I wanted to be a writer so after graduation looked for a job in the publishing field. I was told that once I improved my typing speed, there would be a job waiting for me. After endless hours of typing "The quick brown fox jumped over the lazy dog," I was ready to throw the typewriter out the window. An advertisement for a job working in the recreational therapy department of Gracie Square, a private psychiatric hospital in Manhattan, caught my eye and I worked there for a year, an unsettling experience that shook up my notions of normality and abnormality.

Many of the patients had a diagnosis of schizophrenia. I was told that they could not be treated with psychotherapy, only medication and electroshock therapy, and was advised not to bother paying much attention to what they were saying because it was meaningless. Although many spoke the language of primary process, I found that if I listened attentively, some of what was thought to be meaningless seemed to have meaning for them and had meaning for me when I could supply some of the linguistic links that were missing. I began to think that maybe schizophrenics could be treated with psychotherapy. Of course, I had no professional training at the time but I had the experience of being listened to in my own treatment and I know how powerful that was. It took no training for me to listen to these patients, and the more I did, I found that what had seemed so mysterious and remote was more understandable

I was stunned when I recognized one patient as the well-known author of a number of novels, most of which I had read. I sat down with him and discovered he had been admitted for treatment of major depression. While he wrote, he was in a wonderful state of mind—the words formed on the page and it was a feeling like no other. He felt so filled with the joy of it. It was finishing a book that was the problem. He felt such a terrible loss when it was time to stop. Usually he just had to drag himself through this time until the next book started to form in his mind and he could get started anew. But sometimes it did not work and his depression became so severe that he had to be hospitalized.

The patients liked to talk with me. Through becoming so attuned to my parents' moods, I seemed to have developed quite a capacity for empathy. My mother told me about traumatic experiences she had had growing up. I became the parental child in a real role reversal. This empathy became a gift I could use to help others as a psychotherapist. But first I had to develop some empathy for myself. In therapy sessions I became deeply absorbed in listening to my patients and following the process that was unfolding before me, just as I became so deeply absorbed in writing. When I become so attuned to my patient and the session flows beautifully, there is nothing like it. Although I never had it growing up, I could provide my patient with the experience of being deeply seen and heard, And when I can do this, especially with the most difficult challenging patients, it is very special. They know it and I know it. Although I grew up with little self-esteem, being able to do this makes me feel quite good about myself. It is no coincidence that I have become both a psychotherapist and a writer.

When I began writing and found so much pleasure in it that I did not want to stop, I thought of that author in the hospital. I have published two books before this one and with each, revised obsessively so that I did not have to end the writing. I wanted to remain pregnant with the book forever (Farber 2012). But revising and editing does not provide the same pleasure that writing does so I stopped, finally, and submitted the manuscript. But during that time I thought of that depressed author and feared that fate for myself. It never happened. It was easier to let go of the second book. Time goes by, I see my patients and want to sink into a new writing project, and then after some time with ideas percolating in my head, an idea starts to form. And there I go again. Another journal article, another book. I usually have a few writing projects going at the same time.

Before so much of my creativity went into writing and my clinical work, it went into weaving and other fiber arts. I bought a small frame loom and made several tapestries. My husband got into it too and found a book called *Working with The Wool: How to Weave a Navajo Rug* by Tiana Big Horse. He built and warped a frame loom in the basement. I laughed as I heard him doing his version of Native American chanting. In my eighth month of pregnancy, preparing to leave my job as a psychiatric social worker at Fordham Hospital, I ordered a four-harness floor loom, which arrived as a big box of wooden rods that I had to assemble, no easy task in the eighth month of pregnancy. I intuitively knew that once my body was finished creating a new life that I would still feel the need to create. When my son was a few months old, I was weaving, off and running. Just recently I gave my younger grandson, age eight, a small frame loom for Chanukah, warped it, and taught him how to use it.

The story about Penelope's loom has it that while her husband Odysseus was away, Penelope spent all day at her loom, staving off the advances of hopeful suitors by telling them that she would choose one to marry as soon as she finished weaving a burial shroud for her ailing father-in-law. She spent each day weaving. At night, she returned to undo what she had done during the day so that she never completed her project. Penelope's process of warping the loom, weaving, unraveling, and then re-creating is the essence of the creative process. "Keep the loom warped. When you finish weaving the rug, take it off the loom and immediately warp up again, ready for the next." Creative people are always creating, examining, and deconstructing our creations, and then creating more, a process that is always evolving and never complete.

At a time when around half of doctoral candidates never complete their dissertations, I loved writing mine. My husband had been diagnosed and treated for cancer with surgery and chemotherapy. I was able to be there for him and help him through this, continue my work with my patients, and become deeply absorbed in working on my doctoral dissertation. It had become a psychic retreat, in which I became deeply absorbed, keeping me from obsessing about whether the cancer cells were increasing or decreasing. I was able to help him get through this. Although my anxiety was sky-high, I was optimistic and my self-esteem was never greater. He is alive, well, and grateful. So am I.

Soon after completing my dissertation, I turned it into my first book (Farber 2000). Some years later, I realized that I had taken the meandering, indirect route to becoming a writer after all. After finishing one writing project, I kept the loom warped, percolating with what would become my next writing project. I never have writer's block.

It has been a long time since I was depressed. My own treatment did that for me, before I started writing so much. I published a number of journal articles and write a blog, "The Mind-Body Connection," for *Psychology Today* (Farber 2013). While writing I am in the best frame of mind. Its benefits have been so great that I have introduced writing into some patients' session, when it is easier for them to write than speak about certain thoughts and feelings (Farber 2005). I have also developed a course "Writing for Physical and Emotional Well-Being" as well as a course for clinicians who want to write in a lively, engaging way about their work and life. Although not a therapy group, it has certainly been therapeutic for some. I have introduced expressive writing into the treatment of a number of patients and use it a great deal with those with psychosomatic pain.

While writing this chapter, I got a call from a former patient, a brilliant scientist who had cut and burned herself since she was ten (Farber 2013). She had moved far away but was coming to my area with her husband and two daughters; she wanted to see me and wanted me to see her children because they were children she thought she would never have. She had been afraid that she would molest them sexually as her mother had done to her. While in treatment, she had several dreams in which we were in bed together and I molested her, clearly a wish for closeness and simultaneous fear that the closeness would end up with a repetition of the trauma. She had to work through her wish to trust me and her fear of it.

From the first time I met her, around sixteen years ago, the treatment felt like magic to her and she did remarkably well. She was able to become a loving, devoted mother. When she arrived with her husband and daughters, I could see the tears welling up as she introduced them in the waiting room. Her personal and professional life were going very well. She was happy, something she had never thought possible when we met. She cried as she told me how it felt as if she were born during her treatment. That made me cry too. When it was time to leave, she stood up and hugged me, something she had never done before. She trusted me.

It is moments like this that make this work such a joy. I love taking on very difficult, challenging patients. Yet I know not to have too many of them in treatment with me so that I am not overwhelmed by the demanding nature of the work. I grew up having to learn to take care of myself. I do it well.

I still live in my own head much of the time. I do not think that will ever change; it is just part of who I am. I love to be absorbed and have my mind stimulated at the same time, whether it is in writing or reading, or in conversation. But the need to escape through absorption is less than before and does not preclude my ability to enjoy relationships and smell the roses. Doing psychotherapy and writing are such isolating forms of work. When psychotherapy is done with the focus on the patient's needs, not the therapist's, it can feel lonely. So it is a pleasure to take a break and go meet a friend for lunch, someone who asks "How are you?" and really wants to know.

A few years ago I read Sue Monk Kidd's *The Secret Life of Bees* (2003) in which fourteen-year-old Lily spent so much of her life longing for her mother, who died under mysterious circumstances when Lily was four. Upon discovering that her mother had actually left her with her unloving father, she was very angry at her and felt that she had no parents, that she was a motherless child. She was told something that resonated deeply with me. "You have to find a mother inside yourself. We all do. Even if we already have a mother, we still have to find this part of ourselves inside" (p. 306). This resonated deeply with me, that you have to find a mother inside yourself. even if you already have a mother, you still have to find this part of yourself inside.

References

Blos, P. (1967). The Second Individuation Process of Adolescence. *Psychoanalytic Study of the Child, 22*: 162–186.

de Manzano, O., Cervenka, S., Karabanov, A., Farde, L., & Ullén, F. (2010). Thinking Outside a Less Intact Box: Thalamic Dopamine D2 Receptor Densities Are Negatively Related to Psychometric Creativity in Healthy Individuals. *PLoS ONE, 5* (5): 1–14.

Edelman, H. (1994). *Motherless Daughters: The Legacy of Loss*. New York: Delta.

Farber, S. (2000). *When the Body Is the Target: Self-Harm, Pain, and Traumatic Attachments*. Northvale, NJ: Jason Aronson.

Farber, S. (2005). Free Association Reconsidered: The Talking Cure, the Writing Cure. *Journal of the American Academy of Psychoanalysis and Dynamic Psychiatry, 23* (2): 249–273.

Farber, S. (2013). *Hungry for Ecstasy: Trauma, the Brain, and the Influence of the Sixties*. Lanham, MD: Jason Aronson/Rowman & Littlefield.

Farber, S. (2013). The Mind-Body Connection. https://www.psychologytoday.com/blog/the-mind-body-connection

Groddeck, G. (1923). *The Book of the It*. New York: New American Library.

Hesse, E., & Main, M. (1999). Second-Generation Effects of Unresolved Trauma in Non-Maltreating Parents: Dissociated, Frightened, and Threatening Parental Behavior. *Psychoanalytic Inquiry, 19* (4): 481–540.

Hesse, E., & Van IJzendoorn, M. (1998). Parental Loss of Close Family Members and Propensities towards Absorption in Offspring. *Developmental Science, 1* (2): 299–305.

Hesse, E., Main, M., Abrams, K. Y., & Rifkin, A. (2003). Unresolved States regarding Loss and Abuse Can Have "Second Generation" Effects: Disorganization, Role Inversion, and Frightening Ideation in Offspring of Traumatized Non-Maltreating Parents. In: D. Siegel & M. Solomon (eds.), *Healing Trauma: Attachment, Mind, Body and Brain* (pp. 57–106). New York: Norton.

Kernberg, P., Buhl-Nielsen, B., & Normandin, L. (2006). *Beyond the Reflection: The Role of the Mirror Paradigm in Clinical Practice.* New York: Other Press.

Kidd, S. (2003). *The Secret Life of Bees.* New York: Penguin.

Putnam, F. (1992). Discussion: Are Alter Personalities Fragments or Fiction? *Psychoanalytic Inquiry, 12*: 95–111.

Stern, D., & Bruschweiler-Stern, N. (1998). *The Birth of a Mother: How the Motherhood Experience Changes You Forever.* New York: Basic Books.

Uvnas Mosberg, K. (2003). *The Oxytocin Factor: Tapping the Hormone of Calm, Love, and Healing.* Cambridge, MA: Da Capo.

Chapter 8

Feet of clay

Psychoanalytic boundary violations and the wounded healer

Elisabeth Hanscombe

I found an eggshell on the nature strip in front of my analyst's house. I had walked down her path at the end of my last session before the Christmas break, my head down, and my eyes to the ground. The shell was white against the green of the freshly mowed grass and stood out against the yellow summer daisies that were sprouting there. I picked it up and cradled it in the flat of my hand. Its edges were torn and cracked in places. There was a small, creamy stain in the center. Otherwise, there was no sign of the bird that once lived inside.

In my fragile state on the eve of a Christmas break, I imagined the little thing, still in its shell, had fallen from the nest, and when the egg hit the earth, its shell broke open and the bird's life was aborted too soon, before it had ever had a chance to fly.

I took the shell with me into my car, wrapped it carefully in a tissue and then tucked it inside an empty corner of the glove box. I decided to keep it there as a souvenir. An accompaniment to my sorrow. Like a talisman, it helped me get through the long analytic break.

Each day during the holidays I measured my analyst's absence by counting the pills left in my contraceptive pill packet. I had only started back on a light dose after the birth of my third daughter. This baby's presence was a greater pleasure than any broken eggshell and yet the tiny piece in my car seemed to represent a part of me that felt equally broken. And having it there tucked away in the glove box of my car, safe and hidden, became a comfort even after the Christmas break was over and I had resumed my daily analytic visits.

In time I almost forgot about the shell. The months rolled by and my baby grew. I grew too, stronger as a person, and in my chosen career as a psychoanalytic psychotherapist, until one day the news broke—something was amiss within my professional family, within my psychoanalytic association—and my dream of joining this new and happy professional family was shattered.

This family was not so different from my own family of origin, it now seemed. It too was flawed. Before then I had believed by training to become a psychoanalytic psychotherapist I had come home at last. The Victorian Association of Psychotherapists was first formed in Melbourne, Australia, in the early 1970s to counter the absence of psychoanalytic ideas from mainstream therapeutic practice.

We were a small group then, a hardworking group of people who wanted to take on the work that Freud had begun in Europe all those years before. We were among the wounded healers, though we were not to speak of this. In those days, it was essential to give the impression of good health. However, my tendency towards secrecy and my wish to represent myself as invulnerable had begun years earlier within my actual family of origin.

Sunday night and my mother knocked at our front door as if we were visitors. Cars streaked by on Warrigal Road. There were only six of us left at home now and I was the tallest, even taller than my mother. She stood there hunched over in her green mohair coat, while the rest of us shivered in the cold. The liquidambar tree in the front yard, stripped of its autumn leaves, rose like a skeleton against the glare of headlights, while the house, an AV Jennings special in cream brick veneer, stood in darkness. My mother tried the door handle and sighed. "He's locked us out again."

The day before, my father had gone on a drinking binge, not for the first time. He threw the radiator at my mother because the porridge was lumpy and then fell asleep on the couch. My mother took her coat and purse, and waited with us on the nature strip for the blue Ventura bus, which took us to Ivanhoe. We spent the weekend there with my uncle, in his big double-story house until, with school the next day, we needed to come home, for books and uniforms and our ordinary lives.

My father, sober now but surly, let us back into the house, as I half-hid behind my mother, ready to run again. I had not wanted to go back home. I had not wanted to re-enter that place of unpredictability; that place where my father could one day let us look at small objects under his microscope to explore the wonders of the world and the next day be so crazy drunk that he sent us off to bed at three o'clock in the afternoon as if we were toddlers, even though I was already fourteen years old. And every night he roamed the house in search of the comfort of his daughters.

I did not know it then, but that night at the front door of my Cheltenham home, I had begun my journey as a wounded healer. That night in the shadow of that fear, I made up my mind to rescue people like me, from families like mine.

A year after I found the eggshell, my first psychoanalytic supervisor, who after my time in supervision had become my friend, visited on a Sunday afternoon. He wanted to talk to me about a complaint that had been lodged against him, he said. He came with his wife, also a therapist, and they sat at our kitchen table to chat over tea and biscuits.

"Can I have a word with you?" my friend asked. I led him up the hallway to my consulting room and closed the door behind us. He sat in the chair normally reserved for patients. "I've had to get legal advice," he said. He tried to smooth out the wrinkles on his forehead. "It was just an affair. When she told me she loved me, she'd been so distressed and Jenny was away all the time studying. I couldn't help it. I just fell in."

It hit me hard when I realized that—however much I might have wanted to believe otherwise—my respected and esteemed colleague and teacher had failed his patient by having sex with her, and this had been going on for months before his wife had found out and he called an end to the relationship and to the therapy. It was only then that my colleague's patient made the complaint.

That was nearly thirty years ago. My old supervisor, friend and colleague is now dead, but his death came long after he had been forced to resign.

The ethics committee met. As secretary at the time, I took the minutes. We sat around the room discussing the behavior of my friend, my former supervisor and this older respected member of my profession, and my heart began to crack open. I burst into tears. "We'll hold over this meeting till next time," the chairman said. 'We're all upset.

The next day, after I had pulled my car over to the curb in front of my analyst's house, I took the egg out of its hiding place and unwrapped it carefully. I carried it up the hill. My analyst stood at the door of her consulting room as usual and as I walked past I held out my hand to offer her its contents. Instinctively, she opened her hand and as the shell passed from me to her it cracked and fell into pieces.

Whenever things like this happen in psychoanalytic circles, when boundaries are seriously broken, there tends to be a lot of gossip and whispering behind the scenes, people presumed guilty before they have been found guilty. There's a fear of contagion and a wish to expel the offender, to rid our ranks of the sinner.

But we are all wounded healers and sometimes in our efforts to help, we can fall into the trap—if not of falling in love with our patients, like seeking comfort from the children, as did my father when I was a child—then of taking the moral high ground and wanting to expel all wrongdoers.

The cracked eggshell represented my sense of disillusion at a time when I had only just begun to realize that psychoanalysts were not the God-like folk I had once imagined. They too had feet of clay. Like many before me, I had come to idealize psychoanalysis and to imagine that it would turn me from the flawed individual of my troubled childhood into a superior being.

I was eleven years old when my mother first told me that my father was an alcoholic, as if that explained everything; as if that might help her and us to account for the man who pissed into empty wine bottles at night while everyone was asleep; as if that might make up for the man who at the height of summer sat in his chair in the lounge room and one by one removed every item of his clothing, until he sat naked in front of the television in the middle of the day. People walking along the street outside, alongside the roaring traffic of Warrigal Road, might peer in through the curtains, but my father showed no shame, as he sat there in his nakedness.

To my fourteen-year-old self this seemed all wrong. Other fathers did not take off their clothes in the middle of the day. Other fathers did not take out their camera and photograph themselves naked, seated on the edge of their beds, as mine did. My mother called it his hobby, my father's passion for photography. He bought all the necessary equipment and set up lights in the lounge room, bright lights on metal stalks that reflected back every stain in the carpet, every dust mote in the air. Not only did he photograph himself, we were his subjects, too, we children, and we lined up along the corridor outside the lounge room waiting for our turn.

"You," he said to me, "sit up straight. Tilt your chin to the right." I wanted to tilt it to the left. "Smile," he said. "Show us your teeth." I wanted to hide them. I did not want history to record the color of my teeth, of my two front incisors, which were turning grey from the holes behind them. My father did not see, or if he did, he did not care. "Smile wide now."

At the end of the day my father took the rolls of film into his dark room, which had once been the pantry in our old house and now served as a hidden place that smelled of chemicals and secrets. The first proofs he lined up in strips of negatives from pegs on the shower screen holder above the bath. From these he selected the best shots for further development. Shots that moved out of their tiny frames and into full-sized pictures, in black and white, my sisters, my brothers and me, spread-eagled along the sides of the bathtub as our images began to dry.

My curiosity about human nature as a fourteen-year-old along with my desire to help others led me into social work as a career. But after one year as a social worker at the Prince Henry's Hospital in St. Kilda Road, Melbourne, I discovered that my view of social work had been inflated. At least, the social workers employed in hospitals in the 1970s were considered little more than form-fillers and handmaidens to the doctors. So I shifted to work in a counselling agency and began my psychotherapy training along psychoanalytic lines. I wanted to work directly with people, to have an impact on their lives.

To this end, I trained for another four years and became a psychoanalytic psychologist, hoping again to help people from families like mine. People like me who struggle to make sense of themselves and their place in the world. Over the years my aspirations have developed just as psychoanalytic practice has evolved.

As a therapist, I prefer to work with words and non-spoken gestures, two people in separate chairs but deep in conversation in a quiet room. Touch frightens me. It bespeaks the possibility of invasion, of fingers poking around where they do not belong, and I am once again a little girl, fearful of my father's visits in the night, my father's visits when he climbs into bed with my older sister, a bed away from mine and I am fearful that my turn will be next.

"If he touches you, scream," my older sister said to me many years later when she had finally managed to escape the house, but she had never screamed herself, not until it was too late. Nor did I scream and nor did he touch me, only in my imagination, but still I avoided him.

Secrets, lies and silence are the daily nourishment of families. We speak on the surface, say words that feel safe and protect each other and ourselves from the explosive force of what we really think and feel. The secrets get under my skin while the memories hold fast beneath the surface.

Some people are too free with their hello/goodbye kisses, but not me. I think about them. I measure the moment. And here my childhood mantra applies. My sister's words ring in my head and I set my body rigid. I brace myself for contact, as if a knife is about to slice open my skin.

The days of leaning over my father to say goodnight, to receive the scraping of his rough thumb and finger on my forehead float across my memory. My father scraped a sign of the cross on the forehead of each of his children at bedtime. The sensation stays with me. My forehead bears the mark. The long frown down its center, worn away through the years like my mother's heels, a mark of his presence and a reminder to me to avoid touch.

My father's yellow, nicotine-stained fingers; the nails clipped short and clean, the smell of his brandy breath, the scrape of his accented words across my ears. "*Goedenacht*," he says in Dutch. "Goodnight,'" we say in English.

The thought then that as we all stand awake at this moment in one another's company, we are safe, but later in the darkness when each has scattered off to her own bed, when my father starts to wander the hallway and to check out the rooms in search of companionship, I freeze over and turn to face the wall. And so I became a therapist who uses talk to connect and to journey into a deeper understanding of what lies beneath.

When I write about the analytic world there is a tug of war in my mind similar to the struggle I experience when writing about my family. I must speak, I tell myself, tell it as I see it, but then another voice comes in and insists I stop. I will upset too many people.

All professions have their peculiarities. The analytic world is no exception and perhaps even more so because we are thought to be experts in dealing with what lies within the unconscious of others. As part of our training we are meant to explore our own unconscious minds. With the help of other therapists and analysts, we are meant to get to know ourselves, our faults and our strengths, and particularly our weaknesses so that we do not visit our difficulties on those who come to us for help. "Physician heal thyself," as the saying goes.

But most, if not all, people drawn into this profession are looking for some form of help for themselves. Most, if not all, of us, for reasons that go back to our childhoods, have not felt we have been recognized sufficiently by our first audience, our parents, and as a consequence we look to help others in order indirectly to help ourselves.

The night before I saw my first analyst, I dreamed I was visiting Freud in a quaint wooden cottage on the banks of a river. There were birds in a nearby tree. They twittered in their early morning revelry. I was in Europe, the land of my ancestors. It was Freud all right. I recognized him from pictures—the dark beard, neat and pointed, the dapper suit, the fob watch and chain across his breast coat pocket. He smiled, sat down in a wide leather chair and beckoned to me to sit across from him. "So, let us begin."

When I first considered becoming a therapist I did so with the paradoxical thought both of overcoming my difficulties and of joining the ranks of those who in my imagination had none.

In those days I lacked compassion for my vulnerable self. I considered her a nuisance who must be controlled. My analyst was the first to point out to me how much I had despised my own vulnerable infant self. I despised her until I found a compassionate analyst who did not herself despise her own vulnerability and thereby enabled me to enter into a different relationship with myself, one born of compassion and not of contempt.

Too often, as therapists, we despise our vulnerability. We want to stomp it out. We want to take a superior position in the face of our patients' vulnerabilities and not acknowledge our own neediness. This is dangerous. When we refuse to acknowledge and have compassion for our own vulnerability we project it out into those who come to see us. We overload them, those who are already troubled by their own vulnerabilities. This is the danger.

The joy is that with good and compassionate help for our own wounded selves we can help others to respect and value their own vulnerability too, and so our own vulnerability becomes our strength.

Chapter 9

Madame Johnson, witch doctor

Gretchen Heyer

If I speak of Africa today I say "I don't know." I explain how it's all a long time ago. I do not admit I've been claimed. Snared. I don't tell anyone that I call out to a faith healer, a witchdoctor, a charlatan. I call out to her in my dreams and wake with her name on my lips. Madame Johnson. I search for the trail of what prompted the call but it has gone. All I have is the movement of my lips. When I reach to touch them, it's as if I can feel the edges of a bottle cap with oil in it.

What happened? What did that woman do to me?

Here are the events in summary: for over a decade, my American Christian missionary family traveled through postcolonial Africa when countries were ruled by ancient faith and ritual as much as modern notions of power. And from Rhodesia to Sierra Leone to Liberia, mother fasted to be closer to God, as if God lived very far away from us. Being thin built a bridge all the way up to God. I struggled with growing awareness of oppressive authorities and our dysfunctional religion, finally dropping sixty pounds, half my body weight.

It was a time and place when those who starved were not doing so because they wanted to. The word "anorexia" was not part of anyone's vocabulary. There were no hospitals, no intravenous feedings. It took an African healer to thwart my starving, get in my way. And even now I hear her breath, that faint drip of water off the leaves outside the door to her hut as if it rained during the night. There is the cry of an owl. Footsteps pass back and forth. A single drop of water falls from the edge of thatch nearest to the door, the thatch that caves in slightly. The water vanishes into the red earth. It's not rain—dew. Another drop. Then the distant sound of voices. Even now I watch the way Madame Johnson turns her head to the figure blocking the square of light as I hear a scream, thin, high decibels I can almost recognize.

My voice surprises me. The lie of it surprises me as I lie on my bed hundreds of thousands of miles from her. And I tell myself she must have threatened me, the threat buried in layers of her flesh, in the warm odor of her skin. Because if Madame Johnson threatened me, I owe her nothing. Not one damn thing. I am loyal to no one.

This too is a lie.

But already I get ahead of myself. To be white in Africa is not the same for one person as it is for another, although it is a certain kind of separateness, an external mark of otherness and difference. It can be terrifying: the more terrifying when for some "white" is valued as "better." The lie of this betterness permeates the most simple acts, bringing with it an insecurity of falsehood. At least this is the way I remember it.

I was fourteen when I went to my second boarding school, this one in Jas, Nigeria, a secondary school for missionary kids from all over Africa. Long, slow days emerged out of the gauze of mosquito nets, a few crazy, determined bodies of mosquitoes caught in all that netting. Unless I misremember and there were no mosquito nets. The altitude was higher at that school and there was no need of mosquito nets. There was no need of me. No one knew I existed. I thought of this often. No one knew any of us in Africa existed.

In the afternoons I studied the movements of clouds and thought how across the ocean there were people who had eaten oatmeal for breakfast. Oatmeal had no fat to it, good fat or any other kind. I refused to eat fat. No eggs except for the whites. No meat or cheese or toast with butter, which was all the toast so I declined eating toast. No fried plantains or ground nuts or anything with palm oil even close to it. No oatmeal if it had milk in it. Or salt. I refused salt as well, which meant I refused mangos when they were fixed with salt, or apples shipped from America that were cut up for snacks. I declined crackers and soy flakes because they were filled with salt. The absence of hunger made colors brighter. Days longer. Sounds more pure. At long last, I was getting closer to God. My hair fell out. My ankles swelled so I could no longer walk. People stared, but who cared, I was almost next to God. I dropped sixty pounds, half my weight.

My father requested permission from the mission board to go back to America and bury a family member. The family member to be buried was me. My father left Liberia to find a job while mother packed. After he went, mother announced she was taking me to a witchdoctor—that unholy heathen medicine was all she had left.

I refused to allow my newfound holiness to be taken away from me. I ran. Mother tackled and we fell together, the weight of mother's body pinning me down. I hit her. Bit. She tied my arms and legs with ropes, shoving a rag in my mouth and lifting me to the floor of the van.

Metal roofs passed the windows, points of thatch, then empty sky dotted with specks of birds. Two chickens with their feet tied together lay on the tin floor beside me. One lifted its head. There was no white in its eyes, only dark pools rimmed in red. Ribbons of road rushed out behind and behind. One hour. Two. For a time the morning sun hung in front of the car, swallowing the road with everything on it. After a while grasslands became high bush with creepers tying the trees to lock something in, or lock me out.

The engine quieted. I shook my head to get the smell of petrol out. Mother's guide slid the van door open, untying the ropes on my hands and feet. He slung me over his shoulder. Stood. I felt like a sack of rice. But a sack of rice would be treated with more reverence. I felt like firewood—thatch—to be used and discarded. With my head upside down, the chickens in the guide's other hand dangled just below my eyes. They turned to look at me as if they knew; it was because of me we were to be sacrificed. The guide pushed through a wall of vines into a clearing filled with grass and a strange pink flower buzzing with bees. I felt myself lifted. Dropped.

In front of us, houses with mud walls and thatch roofs clustered around a grassless square. At the center of the square a small canopy of palm leaves had been built. Beneath it sat a mountain of woman, huge pendulous breasts swinging towards her stomach. A young man fanned the woman with a palm leaf, tiny leaves scuttling across the dirt with each wave of his fan. Thin, naked children playing together suddenly quieted and ran. Sounds of pestles beating and women talking stopped. The woman under the canopy leaned her head back. Laughed. The man fanning her called out. People swarmed the square, as if they had been hiding with the children, watching. Mother's guide bowed, and lifted the chickens.

"I beg you—I am Mister Fofana—I beg you, it is not fine for this girl—this tee-tee ready to die."

The young man with the palm leaf nodded, reaching for the chickens. Mister Fofana opened his billfold, pulling out a crumpled bill, then another. From one of the huts a child cried and shushed. The mammoth woman stood, wobbling towards us on tiny feet. The young man jumped to her side and she put one massive hand on his shoulder. Marbles of perspiration bubbled on his forehead as he held her up, speaking through his teeth.

"This is Madame Johnson, sah. If the tee-tee willing. Madame is fine, fine medicine."

Johnson was an American name. I thought about this. It was easier to think about than the fact there was no place to run. Anywhere I went, my white face and thin arms would give me away, send me back to the life I wanted to get away from. I wondered if Madame Johnson had descended from slaves once freed here or if she adopted the name to talk with us.

Mister Fofana pushed me forward. Madame Johnson bent, whispering to the man beside her. He listened for a moment, the furrows of his brow making a tic-tac-toe pattern with marbles of sweat. Then he shook his head.

"The medicine is for tee-tee and mama. Both of them."

Mother's elbow pressed in my side. A sea of faces loomed as people lifted us and set us down in front of a hut. A pink cloth hung over the door of the hut, dragging in the dirt at the bottom so it had a black edge to it. Mother reached for my hand, her fingers curling around mine as if she was frightened.

Other hands reached in front of me, pulling the pink cloth aside, pushing us forward into smells of earth and dried grass and sweat. No candles. I expected candles. It wasn't something I thought about until there were none. Candles didn't belong here. I didn't belong here, but here I was. From the other side of the mud wall a drumbeat. Hands on me, big warm hands. A woman chanted. Another joined her. Another. Hands touched my head, my neck. Hands pushed into my stomach and between my legs. Hands held my knees and my ankles. There was nothing to do but stay still for the hands. A small, cool object moved against my face and I felt the ridges of a bottle cap against my cheek. The cap tilted towards my mouth. A voice popped. A command was a command in any language. I opened my mouth. Swallowed. The liquid tasted oily, not bitter. It dribbled down the side of my mouth and into my shirt. The chant stopped. A groaning began, a long low groaning without variation or pause. The groans separated into voices, strange garbled voices in half-whispers, as if they had cried themselves hoarse, unheard for such a long time.

They could have been saying tomorrow would never come. We would journey forever in the dense blackness of the hut. They could have been saying there were things I would come to understand only by pushing straight into them and feeling the edges of their surfaces against my face. I pulled back the thin strands of what was left of my hair, leaning into the voices to find myself there. Drums beat louder. Giant women shapes swayed in the darkness. I felt my own body sway, as if I was going to get up and dance, but my body didn't move. My mind and body felt separate and had nothing to do with one another. I wanted to stay here forever. I wanted to shout. I put my fingers over my mouth to hold the shout in and felt moisture on my cheeks.

Someone pressed a stool against my thighs, as if knowing I would need it. Mother sat next to me. The hands lifted off. Where they had been my skin felt washed. The pink curtain opened and sun shone like a flash of pain. A familiar chicken walked through the open door and began to peck the dirt at my feet. One of the women shooed the chicken out, shooing mother and me out along with it. The sky shone blue. Odd. It should have been violet or black or even gray.

The young man who had stood with Madame Johnson waited for us in the middle of the square with his arms out. Mother bowed. She thanked Jesus. Then she thanked Madame Johnson, and Jesus again.

Night began to drop in the bush, not like a curtain but a heavy tarpaulin across the sky. Someone shrieked, and stopped. The air hung thick. I felt myself hungry, my appetite like something foreign, something that until that moment had been satiated by cardboard and now doubled its self. Tripled. Ahead, whiteness floated on the ground where a cloud had fallen. I watched the way Mister Fofana's feet rose and fell, one heel striking the ground, then the other. I watched his heels and tried to think—he was a man who knew where the ground was even when it was not visible. He turned to me.

"Are you tired?"

I shook my head. He did not ask if I was hungry and I did not know how to explain the growing appetite in me. Somewhere behind was mother. I watched his heels lift and fall. I wanted to ask him, what happens next? What happens after? I wanted to ask how it was that we were walking as if there was something ahead when I saw nothing. My feet disappeared into the fallen ground. My body dropped, hitting the earth that was warm from the day and held me firmly.

Mister Fofana stopped, waiting. He lifted the canteen that dangled against his thigh. Drank. He did not offer it to me. It occurred to me that he wanted me to be thirsty, to feel my thirst like a force of its own, to feel my hunger and the hard warmth of the earth. Overhead, starlight flitted down through the leaves.

Rationality has a certain force to it—a righteous, Darwinian sense. It explains so much: the loss of rainforests causing erosion causing poor crops causing starvation—nothing wrong with reason. It runs cars. Lights homes. Splints broken bones. It's just that we proponents of reason often claim a bit more territory than is our due, as if the unreasoned disappears, is a flaw. An anomaly.

And if all is reduced to reason, then we're in control, or at least almost in control. Although this does not explain how the rainforest is my second womb, or how the one I knew myself to be was now dead, which was not the same as the one I wanted dead—the one slipping out of her skin. The "me" Madame Johnson killed was that other one who organized it all. Made sense of things. The "me" Madame Johnson killed aimed for holiness, and almost achieved it.

In America I found a Jungian psychoanalyst to try and find my way. For eleven years I lay on the couch in his office twice a week. The relief—someone who didn't want me to agree but wouldn't back down either, who listened to what I had to say and picked it apart until I could put it together differently. I could hate, be hated. I could be unholy. And when I told him of Madame Johnson and how she once threatened me, I heard my own lie and finally knew—I owed her everything.

Madame Johnson understood that she needed to crush my self-oriented holiness before I could use myself, move myself this way or that. She understood this was just a way to keep my world so terribly small. And it seemed to me becoming a Jungian psychoanalyst myself could be a way to use all that Madame Johnson had given to me.

Although here I still want to lie, to explain how she must have moved away from her village to escape the killing and the war. This is a lie because Madame Johnson was not a person who ran from what frightened her, who avoided things. Madame Johnson belonged in the power structure of the country. In the 1990s the rebels destroyed that structure.

And if I put my head deep in my pillow and shut my eyes, I can almost picture the moving leaves that would have given her killers away—nothing as obscene as a waving branch. The leaves would have disappeared and reappeared in exactly the same place, like something covered them for a moment and moved on. In the stream a rock splashed as the killers glided closer. And Madame Johnson would have stared at the unpainted wall, given them room to do what they were there to do, what they were going to do anyway. She would have had compassion for her killers just as she had compassion for the shriveled white girl who once came to her, the shriveled little girl who has gone on to live half in another place.

It happens that way sometimes. We are not always where we appear to be. It can take a very long time to get close to that.

Chapter 10

Facing my demons

My journey of finding myself through mourning

Susan Kavaler-Adler

I became a psychologist and psychoanalyst with the image of a couch in my head. I began my own therapy as a doctoral student in clinical psychology and as a dancer. Being a dancer, as a well as a budding psychologist and psychoanalyst, my first choice of psychotherapy was dance therapy. But even back then, in my early twenties, the vision of the death of my father from cancer, when I was ten, was with me. One of my dance therapy demonstrations for a central New York dance therapy center emerged as a mournful circular dance with grief-stricken scream at the end. The cry of grief evolved out of my mournful dance. However, one day my mother came to one of these demonstrations and saw my dance of mourning. When she was in the room I could not be fully within myself with the feelings for my father, and my scream came out late, not organically from within. Of course this is what my mother noticed. The story of my life was right there, being left with the critical mother after my adoring father died, a father who cherished and celebrated me. But later I would learn there was much more to it. There was my father's punitive side and my guilt over my hatred towards my mother. There was also my constant need for recognition to counteract my mother's negative comparisons to my older sister.

All this would become part of my mourning process, which began when I entered a psychoanalytic therapy with a psychoanalyst, and my longings for my father, as well as my hatred for my mother, came out in the transference. It was lying on a couch, and then in a weekend marathon, that prompted the full explosion of grief from within me. After twenty-four hours of being awake at a weekend marathon with my first psychoanalyst, I erupted in response to another woman's proclaiming: "My mother came down hard on me, but my father always supported me!" I mean that I erupted with wails and cries of profound grief. I had never been more totally in the moment than in those moments when my longing for my dead father erupted from the very bruised, injured, and aching little girl part of me. I was so totally free of defensive control at that moment that I was able to stop all the release of anguished grief in an instant, when another woman in the group said to me: "I can feel your anguish as you sob out grief in your crying, Susan!" I was so centered in the core of myself where the grief pain came from that I had a deep organic control, which felt transcendent in those vivid moments of total psychophysical surrender. Also, all those in the large group, within that large room, seemed to be touched by my longings. Stopping to relate came as effortlessly as being in the longings within my own body and being.

That was just the beginning of dealing with at least thirty more years of facing the defenses against such surrender. I became an Argentine tango dancer as well as a psychoanalyst, and experienced the clinically alive moment, like the fully alive connection with myself, my partner, and the music in the dance moment. I created my theory of developmental mourning (Kavaler-Adler 1993, 1996, 2003, 2013, 2014a, 2014b), and my theories of the "demon lover complex" (Kavaler-Adler 1993, 1996, 2013, 2014b), of "love-creativity dialectic" (Kavaler-Adler 1996), and of "psychic regret" (Kavaler-Adler 2013). These theories built on my own full surrender to the grief for my father, and then for all those I lost in one way or another, going back to a primal emotional loss of my mother.

I also learned how much work with anger I had to do, to fully continue to mourn and develop. I began to understand that I experienced the greatest resistances to mourning when I internalized the hostility of the other, the hostility of any current person who symbolically represented my mother or father (or sister) in my unconscious images of others. When I internalized the other's hostility I would defensively turn the hostility against myself. I would then engage in self-persecution through contemptuous attitudes towards myself, rather than facing my anger towards other people in my life. This resulted in many forms of self-sabotage in dealing with others. Sometimes I would take out my rage on my husband, a repetition of my parents' scapegoating me for their anger at each other, when I was a child of seven, eight, or nine years old.

All these defensive operations blocked me in surrender to mourning, and thus blocked my surrender to living, and to living fully in the moment. Through all this I worked assiduously, sensitively, and deeply, with the mourning process as a developmental process with all my patients, in forty years of private practice. My wounding, my healing, and my struggles to face it all consciously allowed me to fully surrender to being in the moment and moments, and processes, of grief with my patients.

My demon lover experience: shame and rage converted into erotic excitement

The other side of my mourning was related to my attachment to my father, both as an angry and judgmental parent, and as a sadistic and romantic figure which interfered with my mourning process. This part of my attachment to my father actually interfered with my mourning and healing process. Although loving memories towards my father would induce a sense of grief and loss in me, I lived in a state of blocked mourning, rather than feeling the relief of my grief.

By the age of five I was beginning to become the scapegoat for all the displaced rage in my family. Did my romantic father ever stand up to my mother when he was hurt and angry? There is one incident I later learned of from my aunt, my mother's older sister, which distinctly says "no" to this question. Apparently, some time after their honeymoon vacation, my mother and father were supposed to go away together for another week's vacation. Unfortunately, my father's business as an attorney in a solo private practice, which prevented him from going away. My mother was angry and defiant in response. She said, "The hell with you! I'm going away with my girlfriend." As my mother's plane took off from the airport, and my aunt and my father were left behind, my father sat down and sobbed in an airport chair. He cried the anguish of a disappointed lover, and of a betrayed and abandoned lover. At least this is how my aunt reported it. My aunt also implied that my father never faced my mother with his hurt, nor with his angers.

So where would all my father's anger, as well as his lost romantic fantasies, go? Where else? I was "It." The same father who took ongoing streams of photos of me, luxuriating in my little-girl flirtation with him, was to turn against me. He was tall, strong-looking, and quite handsome—some said like a movie star. He sang romantic songs to me as he strolled with me in the park, or took me row-boating in Central Park, or rode on the Ferris wheel with me at Palisades Park. But then the other side of the romance erupted in some violence against me. I began to see my father's dark, angry, punitive side.

Once, when I was five, I wanted a slinky toy badly. My demands were decidedly unheard. My mother ignored me, turned cold, and said "no," the same coldness that she turned on my father. However, I was to gain no sympathy from my father when I took a dollar bill from my mother's wallet, and ran out of the apartment and down the stairs, heading to the toy store to buy my coveted toy. The incident turned the world around for me, as my father turned around with anger and rage towards me. In fact, I was apprehended by my haughty "good-girl" older sister. I was grabbed and pulled upstairs like a criminal. I was seen as the little thief.

The minute my sister got me into the apartment, I was picked up and thrown down on a couch in the living room, turned on my stomach, and my skirt was pulled up, and my underpants pulled down by my father, who spanked me viciously. The shame in this memory colored the whole room black, but I was aware of my mother and sister as a hostile audience jeering with contempt, as they witnessed my humiliation. Everyone in the room was filled with self-righteous wrath. Only I was terrified and screaming for my life. I remember still screaming out in blood curdling screams that I was sorry! But my father wouldn't stop! His bare hand kept coming down on me, sending agonizing pain through my entire body. I don't remember how many minutes this continued, but it seemed like an eternity. Only tears and darkness surrounded me. There was no comfort anywhere.

Certainly, my sexual view of myself had an underlying dark center of shame, even though I could still feel feminine and beautiful. The beautiful view of myself, originated with the romantic side of my father. The shame-ridden side originated with the punitive father, from my five-year-old spanking experience. However, the shame was only part of the picture. The shame had an instinctual intensity attached to it that was also profoundly exciting. The pain in my little-girl body had been replaced by intense body stimulation and excitement, which arose in me the minute the word "spanking" was said. But more addictively igniting, in my interior psychic life, are the sexual fantasies of being spanked or of doing the spanking. How I hate and feel cursed by this compulsive avenue to sexual arousal, and to intense, erotic, orgasmic arousal and release.

All the anger, sadism, and masochistic pain of a pointedly five-year-old drama stays with me forever, lodged in the unconscious, and now more conscious, depths of my female sexuality. All the pain is turned to erotic excitement, as I now control and conduct the fantasies that always re-create—in one way or another—the original experience of mortifying humiliation. My intense attachment to my father at five is sealed inside of me forever, as I struggle and fight him with desperate love and terrifying fear. We had this red bottom intensity linking us together forever. Later he would only punish me by depriving me of the privilege of watching T.V. for a night. I also think he converted to this form of punishment, in part, out of guilt. Still, this spanking had the self-righteous belief and rationalization that he was trying to save me from growing up to be a thief. Little did he know that he had screwed up my sexuality for life, or at least until I could learn to play with my internal life through psychoanalysis, rather than being stuck in a dark interior state of my psychic fantasy. For a good deal of my life, I would perpetually hate and despise the very nature of my own sexual fantasy life. Although pure love and romance could turn me on, the base of my sexuality seemed strangely primordial. For no matter what mood I was in, I could always count on the "spanking fantasies" to turn me on, when all else failed. Under the more surface feeling of beauty, which still remained attached to the memories of my father's romantic songs, holding, caressing, and cherishing photos of me, there would always lurk, deep down in the basement of my psyche, the vicious feeling of forced submission to my father's once sadistic passion. After the actual act of the spanking, my father actually followed up occasionally with sadistic teasing, provoking me with such lines as "You're not too old for a spanking!" My prince had turned into a demon lover. I was just five years old. No wonder I wrote so voluminously of women writers and artists and their demon lovers, as well as of my patients and their demon lovers (Kavaler-Adler 1993, 1996).

Maternal abandonment

I believe that the primal maternal emotional abandonment, without any actual physical abandonment, underlay the sadomasochistic fantasy attachment I formed with my father.

On the one hand, I have seen a picture many times in the family album, in a section entitled "Enter Susie," in which my mother was holding me in my first year of infancy with tremendous and effusive warmth, affection, and tenderness. On the other hand, I have pictures of me at two years old, where I am alone, with no mother, and I look slightly depressed. Then I come to vibrant life again when I am in photos flirting with my father at five years old. I primp and gesture with seductive movements in a little skirted bathing suit, or dance around, or do acrobatics for my father, all dressed up in little-girl dresses and hats. Somewhere in the two-year phase I seem to have lost an alive sense of self. So to feel whole again, after my primal mother loss, I had to merge with a man. And I was vociferous in my demands for the man to mirror and support me in all of my own self-growth— even though I could inspire myself. In this way I developed my distinct and vivid ambition as a creative person in my life.

I went through a powerful romance with an idealized muse/demon figure in between my marriages. In the first year, unconsciously in parallel with the first year with my mother, I was adored and cherished and treated as special, which reverberated also with the romantic side of my father and his special treatment of me. In that year we danced all over Europe together, and dreamed of an enchanted life together abroad. In the second year, all the ambivalence got played out, with the man oscillating from adoration to critical devaluation, adding some sadism, ultimately proving he couldn't sustain the connection. So the demon lover theme got played out: mutual idealization and adoration, followed by a sadomasochistic struggle that had its sexual overtones and enactments.

Then years later, after some work in psychoanalysis, I met my future husband (of three and half decades now). The adoration was there without idealization. Anger naturally developed, but although my husband and I had thoughts of leaving, neither of us did. As I had done a good deal of mourning my primal losses by then, we were eventually able to talk and communicate. Consequently, rifts in our relationship could be worked out. Our love deepened and deepened.

My experience of getting there, my healing and mourning in psychoanalysis

So the initial pain of longing for my father became complicated by my anger towards him remaining unconscious. For many years I had repressed my anger towards my father, and instead felt all that anger towards my mother and towards men in my life. Meanwhile, I continued to idealize my deceased father. I would always start off relationships with men who I felt physically and emotionally attracted to by falling in love, and wanting to spend all my time with them. I would want to become absorbed in their admiration and attention. I would also be fascinated with who they were, and would want to know everything about them. There would be a lot of love and tenderness, but at some point I would start to provoke them into anger. Suddenly I felt compelled to create disputes and defend my individual identity. I would not at first realize I was angry at them. I would just provoke the men into annoyance and anger with me. Suddenly we would be arguing a lot. I did not know where my anger was coming from.

Sometimes I would start to scream. I wrote a paper in my early twenties called "From Tenderness to Sadomasochism;" the title seemed to be the theme of my life. I didn't realize that I was wrapped up in a vicious cycle of early childhood repetition compulsion until I experienced the same vicious cycle in my sessions with my psychoanalyst; as with my male analyst too, I would feel enthralled, and in love. He would become my muse/god father figure—at least in my mind. Then I would find I was provoking him. I was unconsciously holding myself back, or actively fighting him. I would have dreams of trying to rescue my dying father, who was drowning, until I could later mourn his loss, bit by bit. However, I would have other dreams of being all alone with a possessive or abandoning mother. In this dream, my mother would want to prevent me from leaving her house. She threatened to kill me through suffocation if I stayed in the house. Just like the witch in Hansel and Gretel, she would put me in the oven if I stayed with her to avoid the terrors of being outside the house (womb). Outside the house were the "Chinese bulldogs" on a gate I had to get over, two bulldogs that seemed to represent my mother and my sister, as I associated to my dream in psychoanalytic sessions. In this dream there was no father to help me separate from my mother. I had been left without him after his death. I wanted to get away, which I did in reality by finding a great, warm, fatherly boyfriend.

However, the boyfriend would turn into a possessive mother too, and I would want to get away from him. And in between there would be the fights, and through associations to my provocations with my analyst, I learned that these "fights" were evidence of me re-creating the emotional rage and antagonism of the five-year-old spanking experience with my father. In fact, my analyst would even interpret to me, when he felt provoked, "You would like me to spank you now." It became much more erotic in the room between him and me. Suddenly, it was me and my father, and there was no mother. So I did not feel safe alone with my father on some deep level, even though I spent years after the spanking being held, comforted, and warmly hugged by him, and would be serenaded by his romantic songs to me. When he died, the loss of all that warmth and love and romance was devastating. I tried to hold on to him by turning him into a god.

My dreams revealed my dilemma. In one dream I was sinking under the water of the unconscious because I had lost my idealized god father through his death. When my father turned his rage against me and spanked me, all my love turned into hate, and turned into fantasies of sadomasochistic submission to a sadistic father.

In my long-term marriage I would start to scream. I could not stop screaming at men. I would repeat my mother's screaming at me by screaming at them, but I wasn't just doing to them what my mother had done to me. I was also re-creating the raging screams of the past, from the time of being a little girl who hated my father. Some part of me continued to hate her father, while also holding on more consciously to a much idealized view of my father—especially after I had totally lost him forever through his long-drawn-out death from cancer. Consciously, I experienced this hate as a vindictive and retaliatory rage towards my mother.

Anger at my analyst's countertransference

Increasingly, I would experience this rage in my psychoanalysis. My analyst could easily become my critical mother when he commented on my provocative behavior. He would also become the seductive and romantic father, who had praised me to the heights, and then would suddenly turn upon me with judgments—reinforcing my mother's criticisms, rather than supporting me in the face of my mother's overt hostility towards me. However, as my analyst began to become infatuated with me, and acted like he was in love with me, I was faced with a real current reason for my anger at him, as he became actively seductive. This became confusing. I then had very real reasons for my anger, and it became a frightening challenge to put this anger into words, rather than to scream and rage or actively leave the analysis.

One day, my male analyst expressed a profound attraction to me, which also involved a romantic infatuation. He not only talked about my legs being gorgeous, and implied that my husband couldn't appreciate my legs, or me, fully. He also told me that he was having a desire to kiss my feet, and he wondered if my husband would be willing to kiss my feet. The emotional power of how my analyst expressed this was so profound that I actually felt like he was down on the floor kissing my feet! I felt myself being drawn into a powerful fantasy of my own of being a radiant beauty that my analyst couldn't resist. However, underneath this magic spell of romantic infatuation, and behind the fantasy of being the special princess for my idealized prince analyst, I was very scared!

I was in a very vulnerable spot. I had been subject to believing my analyst's interpretations of what was going on between us, but this time he wasn't outside the scene between us. He was no longer observing with objectivity and psychoanalytic reverie and insight. He was all wrapped up in the scene with me. Also, his expressions of attraction to me made me feel good, and excited, so I couldn't yet get my bearings and comment on what was going on. And I was afraid to break the "spell." I always wanted to feel special like I had felt with my father. My father's adoration of me was my only escape from my mother's critical attitude towards me, and from my father's judgments, and from my family's (including my sister) scapegoating of me. So how could I walk away from this? But more urgently, how could I express my experience of it, when I feared my analyst would react with some kind of retaliatory rage, like I had felt so much from my mother, and from my father when he spanked me. I also did not want to hurt my analyst, who was a fantasy father for me. I was feeling myself freeze up a bit.

Then I breathed deeply, and decided I had to speak. I felt the terror in my body as I went from freezing up to shaking. I told my analyst that he seemed to be competing with my husband, just at a time when I was feeling disappointed in my husband, which was not helping me deal with my feelings for my husband at all. Now I had to stop this work and face my anger towards my analyst. I said: "You are confusing me. We have been speaking about me dealing with my anger towards my father, which sometimes comes out with you, so that I can re-find my love for my father and be able to grieve and mourn the loss of him. But how can I do this when you are getting in the way with your seductive adoration of me? You make me feel like I want to have a love affair with you, rather than to face the very difficult work of expressing my anger towards you.

My analyst was shocked, as if forced to awaken out of a dream or trance. He had a lot of problems admitting that he had been overly seductive with me. He had problems seeing that I was all alone now with this fear of him and this anger at him. Yet we began a conversation about what had just happened that went on for weeks. I was not sure I could stay with him, and eventually I did move on to another analyst. But meanwhile, my expression of articulate anger allowed me to have more courage to face the anger at others in my life. I continued the work of sorting out the anger at my mother and father from the past, and sorting out my anger at those in my current life—including my analyst. This could lead to surrender to grief, grief for my father in particular."

Carrying on working through

Gradually, I began to accept my anger at people in my life with a little less guilt, which helped me to communicate my current anger with more sensitivity, and with less rage. Only years later in analysis could I feel the sadness of grief consistently. In fact, earlier on in the analysis my rage would take over, as it had when I was a child who was fighting against submission to my father—which was also compounded by the lack of recognition of my mother—and was further greatly complicated by the profound loss of my father when I was ten.

At ten, I could cry when my father died. But then there was no ongoing grief and sadness. Instead I would provoke others into fights. Now, however, I felt the sobbing of grief and loss in my analysis, as I identified with the grief of my analyst losing his wife. I realized that that sadness had been there all along—way back to the marathon experience with my "father" analyst. Nevertheless, my anger at my father, and my fear of being left alone with my mother, had blocked the pure sadness of grief, I now hoped that my analysis would be a safe place to express it. I had become very sensitive to all my patients' defenses against grief: both the idealizing and the angry distancing defenses. So I lived through with them what I had lived through in myself. I was healing bit by bit in the wounded divide between myself and my father by grieving the loss of my father, and through the grief of re-finding my love for him. Eventually, I even found the love for my mother, which had been blocked by many layers by anger. So the complicated grief of mourning the love and loss of my father became a mourning process that lasted over many years.

I confronted my mother with her critical attacks on me, and she attempted to apologize. Then I could love her enough to feel the grief of loss in relation to the mother I never had. This helped me to respect the sister I had come to feel cold towards, even if not to love her deeply as I had loved my father, and early on my mother. The whole picture came together over time, as bit by bit I mourned the loss of my father. I also mourned the loss of a mother from the time of my two-year-old separation years. I even faced the anger at my sister as I mourned. I started to forgive my sister, began to appreciate her and feel grateful to her for caring for my mother when she was ill. I started to see the vulnerability behind my sister's somewhat cold and contrived exterior self. I was able to begin to feel my love for her son. Facing the coldness in myself, related to my repressed anger, helped me to mourn my losses, and to re-find the very early love in my life. Then I could develop compassion for others who might defend against their own feelings, and against their own unconscious memories and internal life, with coldness and contempt.

On "not getting stuck": creativity evolving from mourning

I became freer to use my talents to write, teach, and perform Argentine tango, and, of course, to practice psychoanalytic psychotherapy and psychoanalysis. I wrote many books, about sixty journal articles, and gave ongoing professional presentations. I also wrote some creative nonfiction, as well as essays and edited book chapters. I developed an institute that I founded to teach candidates in psychotherapy and psychoanalysis. I loved to teach and supervise, and lead writing groups, to help others with their personal and professional development. I became increasingly adept at doing long-term subtle and intricate clinical treatment, using dialectic of British and American object relations theorists, along with my own theories, to help others grow. I developed my artistic side, not only in writing, but in dance as well. I did dance performances as well as dancing socially many nights a week as an advanced Argentine tango dancer. I performed with a top professional Argentine tango teacher and performer at the International Emotionally Focused Therapy conference, in the Grand Ballroom of the Roosevelt Hotel. I had Argentine tango birthday parties every year, where I would perform with my husband, with other cherished partners, and where I would bring together the warmth of friends in both the psychoanalytic and Argentine tango communities. I also performed Argentine tango after lunches at my Institute's conferences, to help demonstrate how the dance is all about the connection, the mutuality of healthy relatedness, and the love-creativity dialectic.

My capacities for love and intimacy have evolved with the evolution of my long–term marriage, as my mourning process has flowered and come to fruition. The deepening of my relationship with my husband has been an ongoing journey.

References

Kavaler-Adler, S. (1993). *The Compulsion to Create: A Psychoanalytic Study of Women Artists*. London and New York: Routledge. (2nd and 3rd edns published as *The Compulsion to Create: Women Writers and Their Demon Lovers*. New York: Other Press, 2000; New York: O.R.I. Academic Press, 2013.)

Kavaler-Adler, S. (1996). *The Creative Mystique: From Red Shoes Frenzy to Love and Creativity*. London: Routledge. (2nd edn, New York: O.R.I. Academic Press, 2014.)

Kavaler-Adler, S. (2003). *Mourning, Spirituality and Psychic Change: A New Object Relations View of Psychoanalysis*. London: Brunner-Routledge.

Kavaler-Adler, S. (2013). *The Anatomy of Regret: From Death Instinct to Reparation and Symbolization through Vivid Clinical Cases*. London: Karnac.

Kavaler-Adler, S. (2014a). *The Klein-Winnicott Dialectic: Transformative New Metapsychology and Interactive Clinical Theory*. London: Karnac.

Kavaler-Adler, S. (2014b). Fear of Intimacy. In: S. Akhtar (ed.), *Fear* (pp. 85–121). London: Karnac.

Chapter 11

Silent broken memories

Ruth M. Lijtmaer

Sometimes the second generation of survivors of trauma is haunted by unspoken events and memories of the first generation. Being the daughter of a woman who escaped the Holocaust affected my personal and professional development and, later, my work with patients.

When I was growing up, my mother told me that she was born in a town called Bialystok, in Poland. She told me she left Poland in 1938 with "the last boat" before World War II started, and migrated to Argentina with her parents when she was fifteen years old. She spoke Polish at school and Yiddish at home. I had frequently asked her to tell me stories about her childhood or to teach me Polish. Her response always was "I do not remember." Her tone of voice told me I had done something wrong. I was conflicted about whether I should pursue asking her. It was strange that my mother would answer all my questions except for this one. I could not imagine what was wrong. I finally gave up. It was only as a young adult and after my own migration to the U.S. that I became aware and at times obsessed by not knowing her history and my history. I realized that I became an immigrant as she had been. Even though my migration was voluntary and hers was forced, the political events in Argentina made me feel and become an exile, just as she had been. It was during my training in the U.S. and seeing patients who had suffered political persecution that things started to fall into place for me. Well, some of them (Lijtmaer 2014, 2015).

From my adolescence I was involved in political movements against injustice. When I was at university I was drawn into the student movement against the military government. It was the military coup in 1966; not too many people talk about that period of Argentina's history. As students we met in the café before or after classes to discuss the topics of the classes and, of course, politics. More than once, policemen entered the café on horseback and threw tear gas to disperse us. Other times we marched peacefully with banners against the government; tear gas was our enemy. We organized underground study groups about Freud and other prohibited topics at the instructor's office. Those were dangerous times for the instructors and for us, the students. We could only enter the instructor's building one or two at a time and leave the same way. We did not know if somebody was watching the building.

I migrated to the U.S. in 1971. Five years later, a campaign was begun by the Argentine government against suspected dissidents and subversives (from 1976 to 1983). Many people, both opponents of the government as well as innocent people, disappeared. They were taken to secret government detention centers where they were tortured and eventually killed. These people are known as *los desaparecidos* or *the disappeared*. All that happened much later when I was already in the U.S. However, these historical events tie in with my history because, like an exile, I could not go back for many years, resembling my mother's exile from Poland.

I remembered that when I was a child, my mother used to write and receive letters written in Yiddish from a male cousin who lived in Israel. She told me that her cousin used to live in Bialystok with them for periods of time until the war broke. Then he migrated to Israel while she and her parents went to Argentina. It was much later, when she was already widowed, that she told me that her cousin had been in a concentration camp. When I asked further questions, she remained silent. Shortly after, she decided to visit him. She had not seen him for fifty years! When she came back she told me the following story: "I was in the plane, in a three-seater and the couple next to me started to talk in a language that seemed familiar to me. All of a sudden I found myself talking to them in that language. It was Polish that I had not spoken for so many years!" This story opened a door for me about what it was like for her as a child growing up in Poland. Remembering what it was like to learn Spanish, my first language, I knew that my mother's inability to remember her first language, Polish, was connected to very painful memories that she had repressed.

Here in the U.S., it took some years for me to be able to go back to Argentina to visit, due to the military dictatorship. In my first visit I realized that my mother had a stronger Polish accent in Spanish that I had remembered. This fact reminded me how my sister and I, as children, used to joke with my mother about some of her friends' strong accents in Spanish. Actually one of her friends had numbers printed on her forearm. When I saw it I asked her what it was; she told me it was a family "thing." I felt strangely confused by her answer. In hindsight, knowing that most of my mother's friends were Eastern Europeans who escaped the Holocaust, I wonder if she had a need to have some type of group identity, a sense of sameness and belonging so that she could identify with others that were exiles as she was. This may have helped her ease her pain.

After her early death, I had to clean her apartment in Argentina. I found a box with pictures and letters that I had never seen before. It was then that I started to learn about her past and, of course, mine. I was the daughter of a woman who had suffered prejudice and bigotry as a child. I found a note written in 1937 in Yiddish that I translated. It talked about the discrimination that Jewish children suffered at school and how they were treated differently, with disdain. I also found all those letters written to her cousin. And many pictures. One of them was of my mother and grandmother, elegantly dressed, on a cobblestone street. When I turned it over, it was inscribed "Bialystok, 1937." Another picture was indoors, my mother with an older woman, smiling, at the kitchen table. On the other side was written

"Bialystok 1938." I found her third-grade class picture and other pictures taken in Poland before 1938. I realized that I, as a young adult, did not fully believe my mother left Poland on "the last boat." With all this information I questioned whether she had been conflicted in telling me her story to protect me from those events, or if she was afraid to talk about them because they might become real for her. Did my mother feel rage, shame, or guilt? I will never know.

I also found my fifth-grade composition notebook. One of the assignments was to write what I wanted to be when I grew up. I wrote that I wanted to help people. This made me think of my choosing this helping profession. Was my choice connected to her silence and pain? Remembering all these, I wondered if, during my youth, my need for justice and human rights, my passionate involvement in politics against a repressive regime, were influenced by my mother's silence. I also wondered if my curiosity about the Holocaust manifested in my watching movies and reading books about it. Was my search for something that I wanted to know but did not know or did not know how to process?

After all those discoveries I realized that whenever I saw a patient who had suffered some kind of political repression or other human rights violations, I had to be watchful of my countertransference. I fear identifying with the patient in such a way that my own boundaries can be temporarily suspended as I absorb disgust, pain, and grief or other emotions associated with the patient's trauma. I also learned that, with these kinds of traumatized patients, we cannot take anything for granted.

With all this information, I decided to visit my mother's town. Before going I did research on the internet. I found that my real maiden name was different from the one I thought I had. It was obviously changed when my mother and my grandparents arrived in Argentina. I also learned that my grandfather had left alone before my mother and grandmother, who arrived later. I learned of the boat's name and port of departure. I also found the street name and number of their house. When I arrived in Bialystok I hired a guide to take me to the house she lived in. I needed a physical place to integrate my losses, and find a link to my past. I was shocked to find that the street did not exist anymore. Too many questions and secrets unanswered!

In some families the skeletons and ghosts are eventually revealed; when they can be articulated, processed, and known, they no longer haunt us as shadows. For me, this is not the case. My family secrets remain as ghosts in me. My search is over; it is the closing of a door that cannot be opened.

References

Lijtmaer, R. (2014). "The Ghosts of the Past Are Remaining with Me." Paper presented in the panel "Apparitions, Ghosts and Trauma: Lingering Untold Stories," at the International Federation for Psychoanalytic Education, San Francisco, California, November 6.

Lijtmaer, R. (2015). "Untold Stories and the Power of Silence in the Intergenerational Transmission of Social Trauma." Paper presented at the International Ferenczi Conference, Toronto, Canada, May 7.

Chapter 12

"Open the curtains and let in the light"

Colleen Russell

My thirty-six-year-old mother died a sudden death when I was fifteen years old and alone. Her death was a pivotal event in my life and a traumatic loss that, along with cumulative experiences in childhood, adolescence, and young adulthood, served as the impetus for my career choice as a psychotherapist. It changed my basic beliefs about self, other, and the world. Since 1992 I have maintained an active general psychotherapy practice in San Anselmo in the San Francisco area, Marin County, San Francisco Bay Area, working with individuals, couples, families, and groups. I provide support to a diverse population with many life challenges. My specialties are loss, trauma, motherless daughters, and high-demand group or cult education and recovery. "Motherless daughters" refer to women who have lost their mothers through death, illness, separation, or estrangement in childhood, adolescence, or adulthood. People who seek my help in the field of cult education and recovery are former members including those born and raised in such groups, family members of someone currently involved, and mental health professionals.

As I write, vivid sensed images of the day, decades ago, emerge. I awoke late on a hot July morning in the 1960s in the San Fernando Valley. There were farm-houses, orange groves, fields of green, signs of fresh corn and eggs for sale, horse ranches, and eucalyptus-lined boulevards that took one over the hills to Malibu for a day at the beach.

Like many psychotherapists, my specialties have developed from my personal and professional experience and training. I openly disclose to my mother-less daughters group and former cult members that I am one of them. I seem to have a natural propensity to help others, which grew out of my role as parentified child, often helping my mother at night when she stumbled and fell in a confused stupor from the barbiturates she had become addicted to. My grandmother, one of a handful of general physicians in the San Fernando Valley pre-World War II, prescribed Nembutal to my mother to help her sleep. At that time the effects of barbiturates on the central nervous system were unknown, and rehabilitation centers didn't exist.

One of my earliest memories at five years of age follows.

> Knowing something is wrong, I open the door of my parent's darkened bedroom. There is my mama, looking frail and lying on the bed. "Mama's

sick . . . don't come in," my father sternly tells me, but I go in anyway. I immediately *open the curtains to let in some light* before walking to the bed to give Mama a hug. I have a deeply felt sense of the love we share, and a perception of her vulnerability.

To my mother, I was "Twinkle" as in "Twinkle, Twinkle, Little Star," the nickname she gave me and which family, friends, and neighbors called me during my early childhood. The name and those memories partly define me and in retrospect were a harbinger of what was to come. I associate it with feelings of love, triumph, action, and courage, and alternately, discouragement, inadequacy, and helplessness. Through all these years the vivid image, usually with pleasant associations, frequently returns, as I literally open the curtains to let in some light in our home. I do this metaphorically for myself and collaboratively with clients who invite me into their darkness.

As I write, these perceptions of the day of my mother's death, decades ago, emerge. I told myself to never forget, and I haven't.

A fifteen-year-old, I awake with a sense of soreness from large curlers I have slept on all night. These remain until sometime after I hear the siren outside. I vaguely see my room, and the direction of my bed facing the door in the redwood-framed house my father and paternal grandfather built, with a strong foundation and dreams of a better life ahead. And on this last day of July, I am surprised that I awake with an intense feeling of hope, enthusiasm, even joy. A better life is possible.

My mother was stunningly beautiful, with alabaster skin, green eyes, titian-colored hair, and perfectly proportioned features. Highly creative, brilliant, and driven to perfection, she spent years training in ballet, jazz, ballroom, voice, and piano, performing with my father, whom she persuaded to be her dance partner when they met in high school. Writing and philosophy were interests that seemed to come naturally. She was a straight A student in high school while performing for war veterans. A child prodigy, she began playing classical piano by ear when she was four years old. There was so much more than the tortured side of life she lived, and I, at times, experienced, due to her prescription drug dependency.

And now I see my mother at my bedroom door in a white, oversized tee shirt she often sleeps in, black eyeshade on her forehead, stressed expression on her face. This is in stark contrast to my positive feelings and fantasies just moments earlier. Again, she demands her pills that I hid, at her request. Indescribable despair and darkness overcome me as she persists with her demands. A sudden fury arises. I jump up to get the overnight case, filled with multiple bottles of pills, and throw them in her direction, yelling "I can't take this anymore! I can't stand our life!" And then the words I will deeply regret until the end of my life, "Go ahead and kill yourself if you want to!" My mother takes the case and disappears down the hall, into the bathroom, closing the door behind her.

As I walk into the kitchen a few minutes later, my mother staggers toward me from the hallway, a stricken look on her face, silent, as though making an effort to walk and tell me something. I am alarmed . . . terrified . . . angry . . . what has she done? Could the pills take effect this quickly? She collapses on the floor, limp, and immediately I kneel down, calling, "Mom, Mom." No response. "Mom, don't leave me!" "Mom, don't leave me now!" I am terrified.

I call my grandmother, a physician, trying to be as calm as possible so she won't panic. With worn black medicine bag in hand, she arrives sometime later and briefly examines her daughter, before calling the ambulance. She maintains her professional composure, with no visible emotion I can discern. I've never seen her cry. I hear the siren outside and walk to open the door. A kid in the neighborhood yells, "Someone's been murdered!" The police arrive and I let two officers in. I'm suddenly ashamed and embarrassed, feeling protective of anyone seeing my mother in this condition, ashamed that we have anything like this happening in our family, and that others know. With my grandmother somewhere in the background, the medics feebly try to resuscitate my mother. Deep down I have the sense that she was already gone before the medics arrived. I watch the two men place my mother on the gurney to take her body away. I don't remember what they said. Before we all get up, I remember that the curlers are still in my hair.

In the midst of the terror and helplessness before my grandmother arrived, I had what I now would describe as a dissociative episode. It's possible that the meaning I assign to this experience relates to the ideology of the Christian high-demand group my mother and I joined months before her death.

For reasons unclear, I try to drag my mother's limp body to my bedroom, the nearest bedroom, where I want to place her on my bed, but I don't have the strength. And in a moment, an incredible, deep sense of calm, love, and warmth seems to surround and fill me which seems like a sacred moment. I feel my mother's soul leaving, upward, out of her body, For a moment, I sense that my mother or an unseen presence is giving me a message that I will be OK. Somehow in the midst of the terror, I feel consoled, empowered, loved, and reassured.

I've learned through personal experience and training as well as listening to others' narratives that navigating the consequences of trauma and profound loss involves cycles of grieving; gaining insight; changing self-identity and lifestyle; disconfirming deeply held, inaccurate, self-limiting, self-sabotaging beliefs, and having corrective emotional (or relational) experiences or better outcomes then in the past. Healing is a step-by-step process of creating a life of meaning and finding one's place in the world.

At my mother's memorial, I am feeling exhausted and numb . . . I don't shed a tear. The family has assigned the responsibilities of arranging the details of the memorial to me as my mother wished. Worse than the ordeal of greeting friends, family members, and associates is seeing my mother's body dressed in the matching blouse and skirt I have chosen for her. It's a soft, subtle, orange-flowered pattern that goes with her orange lipstick and naturally curly, thick red hair. I think about the color of the casket lining I've chosen, a beautiful pink fabric, the color of love, I've been told, and I suddenly realize it might not be a good choice with the orange. I think about touching my mother's cold, hard body, and I try to hold back because it scares me. But I fulfill my promise that if she died, I will ensure that she has her makeup, hair, and dress arranged the way she liked. Viewing her there in front of me, I feel numb and exhausted . . . all I want to do is to go back "home" to Aunt Ruthie's and go to bed.

I regard my maternal Great Aunt Ruthie as my second mother, and I am fortunate to have had her love and guidance throughout my childhood and adolescence. Our close relationship extended into adulthood, and for seven years before her death she lived in our home in Mill Valley, California with my husband and two sons. She generously helped us all, a valued member of the family. Ruthie was always there for me; and with her and my Uncle Fred, I felt completely loved, valued, accepted, and protected.

A few days after my mother's memorial, our singing teacher and her husband drove me to the home of the female founder of a mystical Christian retreat I now identify as a high-demand group. At the time, neither my family nor I knew the plan was for me to permanently move in with her two adopted Korean–American children. I was aware of the written and signed agreement between my mother and the founder, made less than a year before my mother's death, that stipulated if my mother died I could live with her at the retreat in San Diego County.

My separation at fifteen from my maternal relatives, including my Aunt Ruthie, was abrupt and painful. At a hearing for my custody, the judge let me choose with whom I wanted to live (Aunt Ruthie and Uncle Fred; my father; or the founder of the retreat). I convinced him that the retreat was in my best interest. Living apart from my family had some benefits by distancing me from the aftermath of my mother's death. The physical environment at the retreat was beautiful, with rolling hills, meadows, and trees. I loved the founder and her children. As an only child, I delighted in becoming part of a sibling sub-group. I sang in the choir, took silent nature walks, participated in weekly community breakfasts, and experienced a new lifestyle and role in the spiritual leader's family. Ultimately, however, it didn't work out well.

During the year and a half that I lived at the retreat, I became increasingly aware of the leader's narcissistic and authoritarian style, and the relational system of subjugation she created amongst her followers, whom she regarded as extensions of herself. Whatever she said was the Truth. Adults of all ages seemed to regress to childlike levels in their attitudes toward this omnipotent mother since, as she claimed, she had the direct spiritual connection with the Divine. I soon found that her self-professed clairvoyance was a fraud. When I didn't conform to her expectations, she rejected me, and when her children told me that "Mother" had told them she'd be financially rewarded by proceeds from my mother's estate, I further questioned her intentions and the safety and appropriateness of my new home.

Distressed with the growing awareness that the retreat was not a good fit, I received a telegram from the founder's attorney while visiting my Aunt Ruthie and Uncle Fred. In cold language with no explanation given, it stated that I was not to return to the retreat or contact the founder or her children. I was heart-broken.

With help from my Aunt Ruthie and others, I graduated from high school and began college, then lived in my own studio apartment, getting to and from with the car my mother left me.

At eighteen, I was in the process of launching out, thrilled to create a life of my own making, attending college, adding an adorable cockapoo and talking mynah bird to my family. But during this transition, just four years after my mother's death, and two years after leaving the retreat, I was vulnerable to cult recruitment. At nineteen, I met a man thirteen years my senior, who persuaded me to join an Eastern high-demand group. According to the ideology, if I was to become an honorable initiate, I had to "accept all" or leave the path and miss the opportunity of many lifetimes. Under pressure to not be controlled by my "negative" mind, I made the decision to "accept all" of the beliefs even though I thought some of them were absurd. I was encouraged to disregard my past and my personal goals (including pursuing an undergraduate degree in psychology) so I could focus on the primary task of helping to "connect Souls to the 'Master'" for their (and my) spiritual development.

In some ways, there was a match between the ideology and my internalized, inaccurate, self-limiting beliefs. As an example, feelings of anger, protestation, or rebellion, were "bad" and "lethal," while the love of and service for the Master was "good." I was drawn to the group for altruistic and idealistic reasons but I found that it was an authoritarian environment that ultimately obstructed my pursuit of developmental goals. A male narcissistic leader positioned himself as the intermediary between God and all the rest of us. Disagreements or even questions about the Master or ideology were not tolerated. Those who expressed such doubts were labeled as having something wrong with them.

To be fair, not all experiences were negative. For me, benefits included abstinence from drugs and alcohol, interacting with many people, teaching, writing, and working for the "common cause." But after seven years, I became disillusioned with what I observed: many higher initiates failed to maintain sustained, emotionally intimate relationships or careers. Certainly, as a 27-year-old "higher initiate," I didn't presume to be as "spiritually enlightened" as I was supposed to be.

I formulated my plan to withdraw, becoming inactive to learn if I could function in society-at-large without actually withdrawing totally. Intrigued with studying acting as I had been in high school, I was accepted into an intensive two-year acting school with an esteemed acting teacher and group far healthier than the one I had left behind. With highly motivated and bright people, I was encouraged to use my critical thinking skills, connect with myself and others, and study characters from acclaimed plays and short stories. I utilized my creativity and discovered my likes and dislikes, beginning to create a more autonomous life with healthy relationships.

At twenty-nine, I married my current husband in a relationship that has been extremely fulfilling. We remain best friends and share many common interests. With the success of marriage, attaining my Master's degree in clinical psychology, becoming a mother, beginning and sustaining my practice, I continued to develop myself and find ways to give to those I cared about.

I am deeply grateful for the continued support I've received from my individual therapist with whom I've been working for thirty-plus years, JoAnn. Our sessions are less frequent now. She has been a predictable, safe, supportive presence in my life—what I needed all along.

Chapter 13

Soaring above the ashes of the past

Emily Samuelson

On January 10, 1991, I had my first memory of sexual abuse. It took tremendous pressure to break me down so that any protection against remembering would lose its grip. Life had to pummel me until I surrendered.

Five years earlier, I had moved to a new city with my fiancé. It was the second move I had made for his medical career. I had to say goodbye to good friends and rewarding work. Again.

We married. Within a year, I was pregnant. He became more distant emotionally. Soon there were many late nights at work and trendy sunglasses that completed his stylish new wardrobe. Although we had weathered other rocky times, I couldn't find my way back to him. As the months marched toward my due date, there was more distance between us.

Thirty-six hours after the first twinge of labor, our daughter was born. It was mid-March 1989. Within the week, I packed up our apartment and we moved into our new house. I unpacked the boxes during the day between diaper changes and breast-feeding. At night my husband came home and contemptuously questioned me, "So what have *you* been doing all day?" Me? I was just unpacking stacks of boxes between breast-feedings, washing down cabinets, laundering baby puke from onesies, and trying to squeeze in a shower every few days when the baby actually took a nap for longer than a laundry cycle. Oh, and trying to finish my dissertation. And dealing with my demanding mother who lived near our new home.

My marriage was already on life-support and the prognosis was poor. I knew I had to turbocharge finishing my dissertation so I could find work to support my daughter and me. I pecked the keyboard with one arm while I nursed the baby in the other. Finally, the statistics were completed, I wrote the concluding chapters, and I dropped off the final copy in the mail to the chair of my dissertation committee. It was the beginning of May.

A few days later, I drove out of town to say goodbye to a close friend who was moving across the country. I brought my daughter with me. My husband stayed home, busy at work in the hospital. Returning home the next afternoon, I spotted a scuffed pair of shoes neatly lined up at the foot of the living room sofa—navy blue pumps, size 7½ B. I wear an 8½. When I asked my husband about them, he gave some tall tale about a colleague visiting and going out running and wasn't that crazy how she forgot her shoes? I tuned out the rest.

In June, I defended my dissertation. Somehow, my ability to compartmentalize allowed me to focus my attention, and I successfully defended my four years of research. My baby was three months old.

My marriage was miserable. I slogged through the summer in a daze. Finally, in August, I told my husband that we either worked on it in couples therapy or it was over. He refused. Now I had to jumpstart my job-hunting. The head psychologist of a large school for emotionally disturbed children had abruptly quit her job and it was offered to me. Two weeks after I started my new job as the head psychologist of a large school for emotionally disturbed children, my husband moved out of the house. My daughter was now all of seven months old.

I had always loved my work and my work loved me. I always had influence and respect every place I worked. But, now, all I heard was a chorus of: "Dr. A always used to help us with that, but you . . . ," "Dr. A told us . . . ," "That's not how Dr. A did it." Goodbye professional esteem. Hi there, humiliation and help-lessness. In the past, my professional life kept me going no matter what drama was unfolding in my personal life. Now I had nothing to hold on to.

I survived the holidays. In January 1990, my oldest sister was diagnosed with lymphoma. In February, my mother was diagnosed with melanoma. Drowning, I began therapy. "I know something's trying to come up in me," I told my therapist, "but I have to get through my licensing exam." I spent the year preparing whenever I had free time. In November, I took the exam and passed.

Then came January 10, 1991.

It was one more in a long line of terrible days at work. I was in the padded time-out room with a student. I did whatever I could to get him to tell me what was going on so I could help him. After I prodded and poked and teased and tested . . . success! We had something to work with. Later, one of the teachers who had been nearby accused me of being provocative with the student. I shrunk with shame.

In my therapist's office that evening, I struggled to silence the word echoing in my head. *Provocative. Provocative.* I couldn't convince myself to relax and let it go, and neither could my therapist. Finally, as I stretched out on the sofa, my therapist encouraged me to imagine a little girl coming to the door to tell me what she needed. Instead, I was back in my pink childhood bedroom. The door opened and a man walked in. He pulled back the sheets and lay down beside the little girl. Panic shook me. It was my father.

It was impossible and it was true.

From that day on, I stumbled through my very own horror movie. Nothing could stop frightening images from popping into my head. My body was tormented with knotted muscles. Emotions surfaced from deep inside, connected to nothing in the present. I found myself weeping and howling like an animal with its foot caught in a bear trap.

I tried desperately to convince myself that I must have worked with too many sexually abused children. Then I'd have a flashback with the feel of my father's hairy chest on me and I knew it was true. Afterward, my doubts roared back. *Maybe this is my overactive imagination. That has to be it.* Then I'd wander around the living room at night, hearing a little girl wailing in my head. A couple of hours later, I'd be dressed in my professional wardrobe and be a therapist—for sexually abused children.

When I could no longer dismiss the trembling, weeping girl I became during flashbacks, I had to admit that the impossible was true. I was a victim of incest.

When my therapist moved across the country, I began therapy with a long list of other therapists who helped me explore my pain. I was determined to heal. I did talk therapy, hypnotherapy, dance therapy, journal therapy, massage therapy, herbal treatments, acupuncture, medication, reflexology, tapping on acupuncture points, and Eye Movement Desensitization and Reprocessing (EMDR). I even worked with a shaman.

I was lucky that a dance therapist knew of a group of other therapists who were survivors and I was so glad to find them. We met weekly, shared our stories, cried and chuckled and shook our heads, marveling that we were doing such good work with our clients while we did such excruciating work on ourselves. Those women were my lifelines. When I felt deep compassion for them, it wasn't such a huge leap to start feeling it for myself.

At the beginning of my healing, I was only able to crawl through the wreckage of the past. Then I began to piece together the story of my abuse. Arranging the chronology tethered the abuse to the past. To heal, I had to unearth the feelings I buried in childhood. It took a lot of work to unlearn the lessons that were burned into my brain.

It took about three years to get through the flood of flashbacks. Each time I fought them with all my might. It felt as if I was fighting for my life, but I was fighting against the death of the idealized childhood I had clung to. I was never one to surrender to my memories until the pressure became unbearable. Then, after I learned another secret I had been keeping from myself, I felt more whole. Whenever I dove into the agony of my abuse, I thought I might die from the pain. Often I wanted to. But I didn't. I healed.

In my quest to understand, I read voraciously about dissociation. The father I remembered was a man of quiet integrity. He was the parent I ran to whenever I got hurt. One time when I fell off my bike, I walked home with a flap of skin dangling from my knee and blood dripping down my leg. I hobbled through the front door. "Dad!" I yelled. He came running down the hall. With his arm around me, I slowly edged down the hallway. He gently cleaned the wound with a fresh washcloth, then bandaged it. "I think you're going to be okay," he reassured me. He urged me to hop back onto my bike, and with his confidence behind me, I took off.

The small scar on that knee always reminded me of his gentle care. The man who kissed my boo-boos was the one who caused new ones.

The difference between my father in the day and my father in the night is like a giggling clown with a big red nose strutting through the door to strangle hordes of little children. One side of him was kind and the other sadistic. During a flashback, I once heard a little girl's voice in my head saying, "I want my real Daddy, the one who wears glasses, not you!"

I've come to the conclusion that my father had dissociative identity disorder. It is the only way I can understand how a gentle man could commit such horrific abuse. Now maybe I came up with this diagnosis so I could hold on to the love I felt from my father and ditch that Other Part as the one who abused me. The illusion of their separateness is somehow comforting. Everything I value about myself—my earnestness and integrity, my belief in social justice and compassion—are traits I modeled from him.

The greatest paradox in my life has been this: I could survive the father of the nighttime because of the Daddy I had during the day.

As I worked through my abuse, I reclaimed some power, anger, and righteous indignation. In transforming from victim to survivor, I moved from being acted upon to being active. No matter how much unbearable pain I felt, I was still standing. I began to see the strengths I developed that allowed me to live despite my suffering.

The journey from victim to survivor in a monumental feat, but it's not the end of the road. At first, the identity of Survivor was like a coat that provided warmth and comfort. Worn too long, it became binding. The term "survivor" can connote someone who has triumphed over adversity or someone still clinging to the lifeboat. Being a survivor is a constant link to victimhood. Just like a widow is defined by the loss of her spouse and an amputee by a missing limb, a survivor is defined by having been victimized. If I experienced life only as then and now, being victimized and surviving, there would be no room for a self-determined future. For me, becoming an empowered, authentic person is what thriving is all about.

I had to face my deepest fears, grieve my losses, and find the courage to confront what was done to me. Ultimately, I made the tumultuous trek from victimhood to empowerment. I summoned courage from somewhere deep inside. When I met other survivors who were further down the healing path than me, they struck me as heroes. I didn't feel like one. I was just *me*. It's taken me years to be able to say I became the hero in my own life. Now I don't need anyone to rescue me. I've done that already.

Healing is a hero's journey. There are stages of answering the call, meeting allies and enemies, descending into the labyrinth to face one's greatest challenges, emerging changed, and bringing gifts to share with the community.

Just like the hero in myth, I was called to explore the unknown deep inside of me. I became acquainted with pieces of myself I never knew, parts that were stuck in a nightmare for decades. They shaped my life from behind the scenes, poisoning me with doubt, anxiety, and self-loathing. During the descent, there was a time when I felt broken into hundreds of pieces. The life I thought I had led was an illusion. I had to develop new ways of seeing myself. I needed allies to do battle with the past. In my travels I discovered who my true allies were, and, unfortunately, my enemies too. That was devastating. My family denied my experience and turned its collective back on me. I felt as alone in the universe as I must have felt during my abuse, but my determination to heal gave me the impetus to keep moving forward.

By spiraling deep into my past to recover my power and my right to be, I began to heal. As I emerged from the abyss, the victim part of me died and I realized I had changed. I returned home from the journey with gifts to share. I had newborn wisdom and greater compassion, which helped me deepen my work with clients. I started out silenced, but emerged with a powerful voice. I faced the wrath of my family, but, in choosing to speak the truth anyway, I felt grounded, courageous, and more integrated. I discovered joy.

As I look back on the many years I've been trying to heal, I can see how much territory I've traveled. My history had pulled me away from new adventures that would place me in a position of exposure or vulnerability. Thrown in front of a group with all eyes on me, I used to tremble inside and lose touch with the bold part of me. Now I feel more comfortable shining in front of others. Without a heavy burden of shame, I can embrace my flawed self with compassion.

I am a wounded healer. I use the discoveries from my own healing process to guide others on their paths. Having lived through my own suffering, I am not afraid of the suffering of others. I am able to hold a safe space for them to experience all of their feelings, and none of it scares me. I can hold out the promise that it is possible to move beyond the pain.

I know I'll cycle through many more journeys as I move even further in my healing and edge closer to wholeness. There will always be new challenges to meet and aspects of my self that yearn to be healed. But each time I hit the path again, I can travel with greater conviction and confidence. Sometimes that shortens the distance I have to cross.

I felt cursed for so many years and, to be honest, there are still rough moments when I feel that way. But, in the big scheme of things, I can see the ways my abuse gave me many gifts. It widened my heart and deepened my compassion. Its reverberations nudged me to recognize my strength, make deep and lasting friendships, and develop the wisdom and empathy to help others who are suffering. I marvel that, despite everything that was done to me, I am still capable of love. To me, that is the ultimate proof of surviving the darkness of abuse.

There is no endpoint to healing. I can't become all healed and whole forever, because I am human, not a perfect being. My moments of feeling whole are the promise of the joys the journey can bring. Together all of my experiences help me explore what it is to be human.

Chapter 14

My hand on her shoulder

Annita Perez Sawyer

The exhortations began a year in advance: "50th Reunion: White Plains High School, 1961; May 14–15, 2011. Save the Date!" I ignored them. I remembered so little. I'd been so disturbed. Why would I ever want to go near the place again? (Sawyer 2015).

"Healing from trauma means returning to that painful scene," my therapist, Jacky, insisted. I needed to redefine my relationship with my past—take control and stand tall where I'd wanted only to disappear. *Easy for you to say*, I thought, envious of her poise and self-confidence.

But I knew she was right. With shame and a global sense of fear hovering over my few vague memories of high school, it made sense for me to return and see what I could learn. Nevertheless, the sullen teenager with haunted eyes I recognized in the hospital records photograph still frightened me.

"Let's keep it on the agenda," I told Jacky. "I can't decide now."

Months passed. Encouraging mailings increased. My resistance softened.

My husband and I were clearing the table after dinner when I told him I was thinking I'd attend the reunion. "Sounds right," he said. "When do we go?"

"Would you mind terribly if I went alone?" I said, loading dishes into the sink. As he handed me another plate, I turned to scan his face, alert to signs of anger or disappointment—*eyebrows raised? Jaw set hard?* "I need to prove to myself I can do it."

His whole body relaxed into a smile. "Oh, good," he said. "I'd much rather support you from here."

You can do this, I reassured myself, scraping off the last of the food. My thoughts drifted back to when I'd first revealed my past in public, an address to the personality disorders research group six years earlier at New York Presbyterian Hospital in Westchester, the psychiatric hospital where I'd initially been admitted.

I stopped rinsing the dish in my hand and slipped into the scene.

April 2004. I'd arrived early, making my way from the parking lot with the help of a map scribbled on the back of an envelope by the psychiatrist who had invited me to present. Walking in, I'd scrutinized the faded carpets on the old wooden floors, the juxtaposition of windows and walls, the ceiling's odd angles, wondering if I'd ever been in this building before, one of many in the well-known psychiatric complex known locally as Bloomingdales. (The address is 21 Bloomingdale Road.) I struggled to remember myself as a teenager locked in there decades earlier—beyond all the shock treatments that erased most of my memory, beyond the doctors who gave up on me before I was twenty.

I glanced around the conference room. Are they expecting a doctor or a patient? Anger sparkled like dust on a sunbeam. For a moment I was seventeen, shivering, naked, wet sheets wrapped tight against my skin, lying on a gurney in the hall, the smell of sour sweat hovering in a cloud around my head.

I forced myself to look again at the men and women who had come to hear me, young clinicians and interns sprinkled among renowned analysts and researchers crowded around the table and lining the edges of the room.

"My message of transcendence is myself," I began, working to keep my voice full. "Me. Alive. Here. I speak as a seasoned psychologist, and I speak as a woman who was a teenager admitted to this institution more than forty years ago.

"As a young patient here I suffered through years of terrifying treatment for the wrong diagnosis, treatment that made me worse. After that, I was transferred out for lack of improvement." A surge of energy—rage? fear? joy?—swept through me, catching me off guard. Under the table, I clasped my hands together as tightly as I could, so as not to fly apart into pieces.

I set the last of the dinner dishes in the rack and dried my hands, still considering that conference. I'd longed to impress the group of researchers with the power of my story; at the same time I'd worried that they wouldn't believe me, that they might consider me crazy or a self-important twit. I'd been clinically trained by the best; I knew a great deal about psychoanalytic principles. Yet my own battle, my disdain for the mistreated child I had been, was far from over.

I tried for a reasonable perspective on my talk. Yes, I'd been anxious and dissociated at a few points. I lost my place several times. Afterward I'd answered some questions directly; with others, I froze. Yet they called me brave. Their thanks felt sincere. I returned to speak at grand rounds the next year.

Exposing myself to my classmates at the reunion felt riskier than addressing professionals I hadn't known. I'd only had contact with Sara and Sue, my two closest high school friends.

Sara wouldn't be at the reunion. I'd recognize Sue. But what if I didn't recognize other people? Worse, what if someone asked me directly about events I'd participated in but couldn't remember? Okay, at our age many people complain of memory lapses. I could probably get away with that.

For a biography, the reunion committee had wanted a half-page statement from every participant. What if I told the truth? Why go at all if I didn't? I was sick of pretending, weary of the loneliness imposed by secrets. I began my statement with accomplishments—the Yale diplomas, my psychology practice—so they'd assume I was now more or less normal. I spent hours honing the rest. I didn't want to frighten or alienate anyone. The statement began,

> I left our class toward the end of junior year (May 1960) when I was admitted to a psychiatric hospital. A year later I returned to school, but in the middle of my senior year I was hospitalized again.

I'd have explained more if I dared. Barely seventeen, I'd been suicidal and paralyzed with fear. Frustrated doctors diagnosed me with schizophrenia, a popular diagnosis at the time. I was given ECT, which terrified me and erased my memory. I'd received a total of 89 shock treatments before they transferred me, "unimproved," to a teaching hospital in N.Y.C. When I arrived at the new hospital, I was twenty years old and I didn't know how many weeks were in a year. The statement continued,

> I spent more than five years in two hospitals. Eventually, with skilled psychotherapy, I recovered.

I was treated by a number of psychiatry residents, but I began to recover only after I was assigned to one who captured my attention by actually seeing me as an individual, not just another case in his file. He "got" me. When I spoke in disturbed metaphor he answered in kind.

"Garbage is vile; it stinks," I confided early on. "Everyone will be glad when it's thrown off the bridge." "I'll call a police boat and have them catch it with their net," my therapist replied. "Some people look for treasures in garbage." We both loved puns. "What a pain in the neck!" he exclaimed, after I'd smashed my head against the wall again. I had to laugh. One summer day, overcome with shame, I sought refuge under a batch of winter coats stuffed into a far closet. I needed to disappear. When he found me, he crawled into the closet and sat on the floor across from me until I was ready to talk. Over time these actions translated into profound acceptance: I knew he wanted to help me be my self.

> I met my husband at the School of General Studies at Columbia. After we married I joined him in New Haven. We have two adult children and two grandchildren.

With good luck and persistence I graduated in Yale's first undergraduate class to include women. This in turn added weight to my applications for a clinical psychology internship and a Yale Ph.D. I wanted to become a psychologist so that I could pass on the healing psychotherapy that had saved my life.

> Except for close family and a few friends I kept my psychiatric history a secret. Shock treatment administered early in the hospitalization had left

me without most memory of my first twenty years. I avoided everyone from my earlier life, ashamed of being unable to remember them. A decade ago I read my old hospital records, and this triggered memories I had assumed were lost.

When I read the records, the magnitude of my reaction caught me off guard. Freezing terror took over my nights and much of each day. Anxiety choked my breath. As a clinician I understood that I was caught in flashbacks: all of my early experiences, including my father's sexual advances and my expecting to die before every shock treatment, were stored as physically based memories, even though dissociation and ECT had disrupted ordinary recall. Other distressing, long-discarded symptoms detailed in the doctors' notes reappeared.

The many years of slow recovery proved a far cry from the months I'd imagined when I made my original plan. "I figure I'll have the summer to process whatever I discover in the records," I'd explained to my husband when we met with Jacky, my therapist and our marriage counselor, before the hospitals' packages arrived. Now, a decade later, at least I could chuckle at how naive my time-line had been.

Most of the revived old symptoms had receded, although not all had disappeared. Headaches, nightmares, intrusive images, and destructive impulses rarely bothered me. I no longer ground myself down with self-loathing. The disabling anxiety was mostly gone. Although dissociation remained a factor in my everyday life—perhaps embedded in my personality—I lived in the present more than ever before. I might always be disorganized and a bit obsessive, but my self-confidence had grown as I made peace with those quirks. I'd made progress with shyness. I awoke optimistic more often than not.

Yet at times I succumbed to an ancient grief: the seasoned professional, on a mission to change the world, could be swept away by a terrified woman who was sure she had wrecked her career and possibly all her adult relationships by exposing her vulnerability. My shame, the legacy of incest and psychiatric hospitals, blindsided me and brought a fear that felt ineradicable. It stuck to my bones; it took root in my cells; it lay so deeply ingrained that sometimes I questioned whether I would recognize myself without it.

On the day of the reunion, I arrived at the White Plains Crowne Plaza just before noon, distracted and anxious. Days earlier, I'd looked forward to the challenge, but that morning, when it was time to leave the house, I wanted to cancel the whole trip. Why had I agreed to lunch? Standing outside the hotel door, I wished I could flee. *You're okay. You can do this*, I incanted. Taking a deep breath, I walked in.

On the far side of a crowded lobby I found a dozen or so well-dressed older men and women talking in a group. Not one looked familiar. I didn't intend to stare, but I must have.

A bearded man in a green linen sports jacket noticed me. "Annita!" he said, extending his arms to give me a warm hug I returned with relief: I'd found the right place. Others near him smiled and greeted me. "Shall we eat?" The welcoming stranger led us a few steps into a small, spare dining room. At the long, narrow table, he motioned to a seat beside him, and, grateful, I sat.

Later, I met Sue in the lobby, as planned. Now at least one person knew how I felt. To my surprise, Sue felt equally anxious.

In my hotel room before dinner, I fluffed my insistently flat gray-brown hair and checked my outfit one more time: black jacket and slacks, a turquoise linen blouse, my favorite silk scarf. I slipped on the silver ring my son had made for me when he was six. His sister's silver basket brooch graced my lapel, while the pendant they'd given me for my sixty-fifth birthday shone on a chain at my neck. Armed with my precious talismans, I headed out.

A mass of people had gathered in the spacious lobby, greeting one another, calling out names, expressing surprise, hugging and laughing. I stared at the badge in my hands, at the girl with dark bangs and big eyes who smiled at me from the enlarged yearbook photo above my old name. I wanted to feel kindly toward her. If I looked at her as a stranger would, I could sense her appeal. Still, I fought contempt. I had always thought of her as a wimp, a compliant goody-goody who had acted out of fear. *She did her best to be the person she thought she was supposed to be: she smiled because it was expected.* Was that so terrible? She had also smiled because she had believed, as I did still, that life was lonely, and a smile, for a moment, could transcend any boundaries and connect two hearts. After all those years, why did I have so much trouble bringing us together? My last healing step would be to embrace *her* as *me*.

I heard my name and turned. A small, dark-eyed woman dressed in black beckoned to me. "We were just talking about you," she said, nodding at a tall man beside her. "We were so glad to read your bio. You were with us in English senior year. Then you disappeared." She took my hand in hers, her eyes searching mine. Her friend reached for my other hand. "No one told us where you had gone," he said. "We worried that you had died." I stood, taking in their concerned, sad faces, squeezing both hands. I wanted never to let go.

In a whirlwind, mostly listening, I moved from one group to another. I discovered that many classmates had kept in touch with each other. Good friends had stayed close. There were a number of couples now married who had been dating fifty years earlier. I pushed back grief, along with envy at what I had missed. *Don't think it. Don't you dare . . . .*

Along with dizzying accomplishments and genius offspring, I heard about hip replacement surgeries, skiing accidents, elderly parents, and departed spouses. In companionable openness we shared tales of grandchildren and gardens, interesting hobbies, long-deferred dreams finally fulfilled. There were wry references to aching joints and failing memories, abandoned retirements, unemployed adult children who'd returned to live at home. I wasn't the only one seeking perspective on a tumultuous and humbling life.

Perhaps this was more my wish than fact, but as a group we seemed to be no longer in thrall to pride. After fifty years, what bound us together was knowing firsthand that life was messy and unfair. Friends shared their teenage fantasies and laughed about behavior they would have died before admitting then.

"I'm Roger. I'd like you to meet my better half." A soft-spoken man put his hand on my arm, reminding me who he was as he introduced his wife. They lived in the same midwest town as John, who had traveled to the reunion with them. Roger, John, and I had been in junior high together.

"John's too embarrassed to say this himself," Roger began with a smirk, "but he said I could tell you that he saw you in a play in fifth grade and was smitten. You were his first love." Roger paused to scratch his head. "Of course, I'm not innocent here," he said, laughing. "My first crush began with you, too. In our homeroom in junior high. I joined the stage crew so I could watch you rehearse. It was your smile that got me."

I laughed. "Talk about flattered!" I moved closer to the wall, sipping from a glass of white wine, to ponder my friends' early crushes. I wanted so badly to remember at least something. They were boys I knew I'd admired. John had been the smartest person in our school. I wished I'd enjoyed their attention. Despite my introverted preoccupations, they had seen me as intelligent and kind. My deep inner fear that I was a filthy outcast wasn't holding up.

A little while later Roger approached me where I was standing alone. He looked serious. "I read your bio," he said, his eyes on my face. "I wanted to tell you that for several years I had a summer job at the psychiatric hospital here," he continued in a confidential tone. "I began the summer after my sophomore year, and I returned for the next three summers, including during college."

"I was in that hospital then," I blurted out, almost interrupting. "What did you do there?"

Roger spoke carefully. "I never saw you; I didn't know you were a patient. I worked as an aide on the male floors. As part of that, I escorted patients to all sorts of appointments, including to shock treatment."

My brain felt on fire. I ran a hand through my hair, then fiddled with my scarf. "At some point, could we talk in detail about the shock treatment?" I asked after a pause, aiming for a detached, professional air. "I have my own picture of what happened, but there's no telling if I'm right."

We agreed to meet for breakfast the next morning.

The prospect of learning the truth about my shock treatment momentarily preempted all my attention. I smiled at classmates and said hello, but my mind was back fifty years earlier in Bloomingdales, searching old buildings and bleak halls again, struggling to remember. In time, however, the cheerful chatter, welcome smiles, and enticing dinner smells broke through with good effect. I joined Sue in the dining room.

After dinner, I half-listened to speeches about events I didn't recall and watched a slide show made from old photographs. A band began to play. Several people approached and warmly shook my hand. I recognized some names, but talk was difficult in the clamor. Much as I might have wished otherwise, I remembered far fewer people than seemed to know me. At around eleven, I left.

Upstairs, I wandered about my room, exhausted, but too restless to consider sleep. A million bits of information bounced around my head. I wanted to gather them and hold them close—sort them, organize them—to piece together a coherent sense of who I was.

"In order to forget you were abused, you had to forget the self you were," Jacky had explained to me. "Blanking out trauma means blanking out everything; one doesn't get to pick and choose." With Jacky's help, I'd recovered a consistent sense of what I'd experienced as a child, the shame and self-loathing that I'd directed at myself, especially during adolescence. Now I longed for a more balanced understanding of who that young person had been out in the world, of how others had seen me.

Here were people who remembered the girl Jacky and I had come to call Anni. They had liked her. Some had even loved her. I'd seen it in their faces. They'd respected her; they missed her—in contrast with my own hands-off way of keeping me and Anni separate.

Summoning the generous spirit that energized the gathering below, I sought to conjure up the person my classmates knew without turning on her, to approach my young self with compassion. As I borrowed their eyes to assess the present woman they called brave, I felt a window open. For a time, I understood: yes, it takes courage to be honest, because everyone knows that a psychiatric history and diagnosis carry stigma. The threat of diminished respect and loss of standing is real. Yet the self can endure.

They welcomed you. They're glad to see you now. I struggled to fit the disparate pieces into one emotional box.

Early Sunday morning Roger and I met for breakfast as we'd planned. We talked briefly about shock treatment, but others soon joined us, and we had to stop. A few weeks later, after he had returned home, Roger expanded on his reflections and sent them to me in an email message.

Roger had helped to prepare patients for ECT, wrapping them in the cold wet packs he called mummy wrap. He assisted patients in the treatment room. He witnessed administering the shock and observed the convulsion that followed. Every detail matched what I recalled.

Reading Roger's report on my computer for the first time, I garbled sentences and stumbled over words, desperate to take in everything at once. After that, I reviewed each step, every detail multiple times. *It fits! It's true!* Roger's recollections matched mine down to details of mummy wrap and waiting in line. At last, I could counter the spiteful, doubting voices that had dogged me for years. I wasn't a liar. My memories were reliable, and my impressions had integrity. I would need time to absorb the full magnitude of what this meant.

By late Sunday morning rain was descending in sheets. Our reunion picnic had been moved into the high school cafeteria. After chatting a few minutes in an interminable food line, I took off to explore the rest of the building. I wanted to see if being in that physical space, especially the hallways, might jog my memory. Maybe I could even verify my impression of lockers that stretched toward infinity!

Student art and brightly-colored posters dotted the industrial walls, but that didn't lessen the cold factory feeling I carried from decades before. As I walked the long, empty corridors, hearing the echo of my footsteps, I tried to imagine myself as an adolescent there. My mental picture of the lockers hadn't been too far off. Although I failed to conjure up a specific historical event, I did sense my reality as an overwhelmed teenager, struggling to perform, sinking, even as I tried so hard to swim against the tide. Tears welled in my eyes, but they disappeared as soon as I noticed them.

Back in the cafeteria, I found others revisiting their own high school days. One elegant, popular girl I'd remembered envying but knowing only from a distance, took my hand, thanking me for my honesty. Audrey, another classmate whose name I recognized, described the fragile Annita she had known in 1960, when her own mother was dying.

Audrey, too, had struggled, working to hold her family together while she continued to shine in class. During our high school years her traumatic situation had remained secret, as had mine. In those days vulnerability equaled moral weakness. Cancer, mental illness, divorce, all were treated as shameful. We hid them. Audrey was one of the few friends who had perceived my distress. I grieved for young Audrey, while, even in retrospect, her story lessened my loneliness: someone had understood my precarious grip.

Anger, grief, regret, and gratitude interspersed with occasional bursts of joy swirled within me. Again I searched my heart for generosity to accept the girl I had been and to feel warmly toward the woman who stood in the cafeteria smiling and accepting compliments.

The adolescent fear of my classmates' hostile reactions had been a projection of my own contempt for my condition. Some of my classmates had been puzzled by my withdrawal. A few had worried. One friend, and perhaps others, had interpreted my dissociated state as aloofness or snobbery, as my rejecting her. But most had respected and liked me. While I'd focused on hiding my vulnerability, they were busy doing the same. We gathered evidence to support our worst ideas about ourselves. We were adolescents!

Windshield wipers swished and rain pounded on the roof as I drove home. I dodged puddles along a parkway I'd traveled most of my life—to Sunday dinners with aunts and grandparents as a child, to see my parents in White Plains, and to events in New York City as an adult. Snug inside my rain-lashed car I traveled up and down the steep hills, over and under old bridges, past drenched blossoms pouring off trees in the center divide. I was thinking about my life, especially high school and now the reunion. I felt disappointed that I'd wasted so much energy feeling alienated and ashamed, when most likely I'd never been shunned or feared. I wondered how many years I'd lost to living dissociated, not fully in this world, and how often I'd deprived those I loved of my genuine presence. I also felt closer to forgiving myself.

Imagining a teenaged Anni in the passenger seat beside me, I stretched out my arm and set my hand on her shoulder.

Reference

Perez Sawyer, A. (2015). *Smoking Cigarettes, Eating Glass: A Psychologist's Memoir.* Santa Fe, NM: Santa Fe Writer's Project.

Chapter 15

The monsters inside

Eric Sherman

I was four years old when my father went crazy.

He had taken himself off the lithium that controlled his mood swings, convinced he could conquer his demons through sheer act of will. He began his decline late one night, as I slept in the bedroom adjacent to my parents'. As I look back, I am amazed that my infant sister and I were able to sleep through it all, unaware of the storm brewing in the bedroom next door.

In a matter of hours, my father went from a state of agitation to despair. Pacing the bedroom, he railed against his boss for denying him a promotion. It was not the first time my father had been held back professionally, the victim of an unfortunate tendency toward belligerence I would see many times as I grew older. My beleaguered mother tried to calm him, alternately speaking soothingly and begging him to keep his voice down. Sometime before midnight, he collapsed on the bed and fell into her arms. My mother, a nervous woman with striking hazel eyes, cradled my father as he burrowed his head into her shoulder and wept. When he finally calmed down, she called my father's psychiatrist, who set up an appointment for the next morning.

In the grips of his mania, my father would never have agreed to see the psychiatrist; it would have meant admitting a weakness. Manic dad was Superman. But now, depressed and defeated, he relented. I can imagine his face in the same expression I came to know in later years—hollow eyes heavy with resignation, looking both distant and pleading. Perhaps he also felt some sense of relief about seeing the psychiatrist the next day, because ultimately he fell asleep. My mother, exhausted and frightened, spent a fitful night dreading what the next day might bring.

The next morning, my father awoke early in a full psychotic state. As he turned on the bedside lamp and leapt out of bed, he roused my mother, who followed his motion to the nearby closet. Rummaging through his work clothes, he pulled out a dark suit, white shirt, and conservative tie, draping them haphazardly over the wooden valet stand next to the closet. In happier times, I enjoyed pretending that the stand, which looked to me like an actual person, was a special playmate with whom I had detailed conversations. I am alone in these memories. Even as a four-year-old, I was precocious and self-reliant.

As my father kicked off his slippers and began to get ready for a shower, my mother should have known that something was wrong. Something about my father's motions seemed jerky, uneven. But it was early in the morning after a harrowing night, and it has always been my mother's habit to seek comfort in denial, hoping that everything would work out if she didn't think about it too much. Likely she assumed my father was preparing for work as usual, and wondered if it would be necessary to keep the emergency psychiatrist appointment she had made the night before. If she insisted my father stay home and see the psychiatrist, what if he refused? My mother was already a master at squirming around my father's stubbornness without further instigating him. Would this be worth the fight?

Then my father said something that made my mother sit up on the bed in terror. "I want to take Eric with me. I want him to see what kind of man his grandfather was."

My mother jumped out of bed and rushed to my father's side. She put her hand gently on his arm and looked up into his eyes. "Ben, what are you talking about?" she asked.

My father stared down at her like she was the crazy one. His voice was pressured, my mother noticed, and a little too loud. "I want to take Eric to the funeral this morning. It's important that he see how great a man his grandfather was."

My mother's jaw tightened. My grandfather had died two years earlier; there was no funeral that day. Clearly my father was in the midst of a full-blown psychotic episode, and if that wasn't frightening enough, he was intent on taking me with him.

"Ben, please, *please* listen to me!" my mother cried, tightening her grip on his arm. My father acted as if he hadn't heard her. Slipping out of her grip, he quickly walked into the bathroom and locked the door behind him. As he started to shower for a funeral that was happening only in his mind, my mother ran to the rotary phone by the side of the bed and made two desperate calls. The first was to her mother, who lived nearby and promised to be over within minutes to help take care of my sister and me. The second was to the psychiatrist. He suggested getting my father to the emergency room. My mother knew how difficult this would be. How could she possibly get her agitated husband, in the throes of a delusion, to acknowledge that there was something wrong with him and agree to go to the hospital? How could she protect her two young children?

My mother is sketchy about what happened next. When exactly did I wake up? Did I cry? I find it telling that the one part of the day's horror my mother cannot remember is what happened to *me*.

She does remember this: at some point while my father shaved, my grandmother arrived. After conferring with my mother, she slipped into my bedroom to distract my sister and me. Clearly, by now I was awake. But the sight of my grandmother further agitated my father. He had never warmed to her and she had never trusted him. My father dressed quickly, not even bothering to fasten his tie. "I am taking Eric with me," he insisted, as he stepped into the small hallway outside his bedroom and started walking toward mine.

I am taking Eric with me. Into his delusion. Into imminent danger. I cannot imagine what would have happened had my mother not summoned the strength to do what happened next. With me clearly in danger, she tried to tackle my father, a deranged man who outweighed her by fifty pounds. Crying hysterically, she punched him several times and flung her arms around him in an attempt to restrain him. Now my father was angry, and with his face twisted with fury, he shoved her away and stormed out of the apartment toward the subway station three blocks away, leaving me, my sister, and my grandmother behind. My mother, still in her robe and slippers, ran onto the street, pleading with him to come back to the apartment. Did anyone try to help her? My mother can't recall. At the subway, she begged the token booth clerk to call the police. My father had left without money or tokens, and was by now in a confused, agitated state. As he rummaged through his pockets, the police arrived; the precinct was only a few blocks away. I can imagine the look of confusion and defeat on my father's face as they led him into the squad car that took him to the hospital.

He remained in the psychiatric unit for several weeks. Neither my sister nor I were deemed old enough to visit him. Daddy was tired and needed some rest, I was told. It was best not to burden me with details, my mother felt. One of my grandmothers watched me and my sister on the days I was not at nursery school.

In the weeks following my father's breakdown, my mother was a wreck, overwhelmed by guilt that she had not intervened earlier to protect him. Exhausted, she shuttled between trips to the hospital, trying to pretend—for herself and her children—that things were normal, that everything would be fine. When my father returned home, she held vigil every night, refusing to go to bed until long after he turned in. She was petrified he would have another breakdown while she slept, and so she deprived herself of slumber.

And me? I was, as always, a good boy, well behaved, and seemingly untouched by what was going on around me. But how can that be? How could I not have been affected by the events of that morning, the crying and raised voices I had to have heard, the terror my mother must have carried in the weeks that followed? I was four, old enough to have some sense of the chaos that went on around me, to have memories of a period so stark and traumatic. And yet, despite the turmoil—or more likely because of it—I remember very little of this period. Not the terrifying morning my father went crazy and tried to take me into his psychotic world. Not the months following, when life returned to an uneasy normal that would never be the same. The events I have described were told to me as an adult, mostly by my mother. It is a topic my father never would have broached, one of the many experiences of shame and defeat in what would increasingly become a rather sad life.

One of the things I do remember about that time is that, like my mother, I became terrified of going to bed. I would cry and beg to stay up as long as possible. It was the only way I behaved poorly. My father's breakdown began while I slept; my survival instincts would not let that happen again, even if it meant tormenting myself with insomnia. Strangely, my mother never connected my night terrors to my father's breakdown, or to her own difficulty sleeping. She told herself I was simply a finicky sleeper, that some children were just like that. But I was more than just a finicky sleeper, because this I do remember as if it happened yesterday: many nights, after my mother would tuck me in and leave my bedroom, I would become terrified by the sight of giant monsters, their arms outstretched to grab me. They stalked the wall adjacent to my bed—the wall between my bedroom and my parents'.

"Mommy, mommy, monsters are coming to get me!" I would cry out, until my mother came back into the room and pretended to wipe the monsters off the wall. She would kiss me and reassure me, just as she had done my manic father that night, and for a few moments I, too, would calm down. But not for long.

"Mommy, mommy, the monsters are on my eyelids," I screamed, kicking and blinking my eyes furiously. Now a little impatient, my mother returned to my room to reassure me that there were no monsters. Would I please just go to sleep? *Please*!

Oh mom, of course there were monsters. I was no doubt reliving the terror of that period that I could not otherwise give voice to. The monster was my deranged father, his arms outstretched to take me with him into his insanity. The fact that the fear I experienced was projected onto the wall that separated my bedroom from my parents—the bedroom where my father had his breakdown—and then was back inside of me should have been a clue to my mother that my fears needed to be taken more seriously. But since she and my father were each still battling their own internal monsters—their own guilt and fear of another imminent breakdown—and since I seemed to need so little attention when my father and sister needed so much, my mother assumed I was coping well. She had to, since she had little more energy to give.

Amidst so much chaos, I became the forgotten good child. I excelled in school, hungry to earn the love and acceptance I craved at home. Ironically, this brought me the scorn of other children, but that was a risk I was willing to take. It was the praise of attentive parent substitutes I was hungry for, not siblings. And yet I was terrified of the failure I was sure would engulf me; that I, too, would fall apart like my father. Before every test, I would dissolve in tears, petrified that I had not studied enough, that I was not good enough, smart enough, and that I was sure to be found out as deficient. I almost always got the highest grade in the class, but it did little to reassure me. No matter how much I excelled, I felt like a fraud.

Adolescence brought another terrible secret. Not only did I have to hide the fact that surely I was crazy like my father, now I was aware of being different from the other teenagers in a way that only caused me further shame. I was attracted to other males (Sherman 2014). It was all too much to bear. How could I be the perfect boy—the son who would finally please and reach his father—if there was something else about me that seemed wrong, damaged, sick. Something else to be kept down at any cost. And so I utilized the coping skill I learned from my mother: denial. I became a master of dissociation, of keeping a secret from myself. As I have written elsewhere (Sherman 2014), I became a master of knowing and not knowing, of looking at other boys and young men, becoming momentarily aroused, and then—filled with shame—instantaneously unaware that it had ever happened. Unfortunately, this defense mechanism only made me feel more crazy, the exact feeling I was trying to avoid.

And so, by the time I became a teenager, I slipped into depression. I lost weight and looked gaunt and unhappy, yet I felt heavy and burdened, and did not know why. My mother was concerned, but didn't know what to do. To admit that I needed therapy might recognize she needed it as well, and she could not fathom this. I became angry—very angry—at my mother, my father, even my sister for getting the attention I never did. At times I acted like a monster to them myself. I became my angry, critical father *and* my depressed mother, all in one package.

I would express my anger at my father by belittling him, hoping to provoke him, feeling it was better to get an angry response than no response at all. What I really wanted was not his fury but his love. But like my mother, he was deep in his own depression, as well as blinded by his own narcissism and sense of failure. He was in no position to recognize me as anything but a threat or disappointment. And so provoking his wrath by pointing out his obesity (a side effect of the lithium) was a way to avoid being forgotten altogether. And so I yelled and cajoled at home and redoubled my efforts to be the perfect student at school. I was a hellion in my apartment and an angel in the world.

Always be perfect. In college, I had not one but two majors, worked long hours on the school newspaper, and was still elected to Phi Beta Kappa. Yet inside I seethed and wailed in pain. I was filled with self-loathing. Once again, this only proved my fear that I was unstable, damaged, just like my father.

As soon as I graduated college, I entered therapy. I could no longer keep my misery and shame at bay. And yet, entering therapy only provoked my shame, since it served as a proof of my weakness. And so I fought my therapist, tried to convince her that I was hopeless and would never change, tried to make her feel the despondency I felt within me. I dared her to abandon me, as my mother and father had. After all, I was convinced it was only a matter of time before she would. Psychologically, I was trying to project my self-loathing into her so that she could contain it for me, could understand the pain I was in without being repulsed by it.

Somehow, she did. Despite all my attempts to make her hate me, she refused to give up. With the help of therapy, I learned that my anger and despair were not signs of defectiveness but rather unhealed wounds going back at least to age four and my father's breakdown. I came to understand that part of my need to be perfect was to try to save my father from the insanity that had engulfed him that morning, and continued to bedevil him throughout his life. He died of a pulmonary embolism at the age of fifty-seven, while a patient at a psychiatric hospital after yet another breakdown. I was twenty-four, already successful as a journalist but psychologically unable to mourn the loss of the figure who loomed so large in my unconscious. It would take many more years of therapy before that process could begin, before I could begin to have compassion for both him and myself.

Despite my accomplishments as a journalist—by then I was interviewing celebrities for one of the country's largest-circulation magazines—I was still unhappy. I wanted to find another profession in which I could use my creativity and sharp mind and actually help people, not just pampered celebrities. (With the help of therapy I had come to realize that my intelligence was a genuine gift, not some fluke.) The need to heal—my father, my mother, and especially myself—propelled me to return to school to learn to cure others. The therapeutic journey, though difficult, was so rewarding and life-altering that I ended up choosing it for my profession. With the help of my treatment, I had come out of the closet. Although I was not yet ready for a loving relationship, I had begun at last to like myself. Slowly, I stopped being haunted by the specter of my father's mental illness, stopped being terrified that I, too, would suddenly fall apart.

Then, finally, I was ready to love and be loved. In 1995, while in my last year of psychoanalytic training, I met the one person who has remained a constant support, a vital instrument in my healing: my husband, Dennis. He has put up with my anger, my moodiness, my testing. His ability to love me unconditionally has given me something I always craved growing up—a feeling that I am worthy of love and attention.

While Dennis has been my greatest support, others along the way helped give me a sense that I was valued for my unique personality and talents. Though my mother was often overwhelmed, she still gave me the message that I was loved for who I was. Her reassurance, while not enough to keep my self-doubts at bay, at least made me feel that there was someone whose appreciation I did not have to earn. Also, while being the teacher's pet had its downsides, the attention and affirmation afforded to me by nearly all my instructors growing up helped bolster my self-confidence. My sixth-grade teacher in particular made me feel like I could do no wrong, helped me feel special at a time otherwise most awkward.

That feeling of worthiness—of unconditional support—is something I try to give my patients. My experience of shame, hiding, and feeling like there was something wrong and rotten inside of me makes me especially attuned to those who suffer in a similar fashion. I understand what it's like to hate yourself in a way that someone who has never gone through that process could not. My experience has also left me with a greater willingness than some analysts to self-disclose, to share some of my life experience with my patients, and not to hide behind some myth of analytic anonymity.

Yet my experience also poses challenges as a therapist. I can sometimes over-identify with self-defeating patients, imposing my experience on theirs or unconsciously distancing myself when I see aspects of myself I still do not like in them. I can also feel ashamed or frustrated not being able to reach a heavily defended person in pain, just as I was not able to reach my father. Such experiences, I believe, are inevitable. I try to be alert to them, to, in essence, "wake up" to them, to wonder what they are telling me about the patient and about myself.

Being swept up in an enactment in which I take on the role of critical, unstable parent or victimized child—with both the patient and me taking on either role—is how I get to know the client on a deep level and work through trauma from their own pasts. If I can inadvertently slip into being the unrecognizing parent who then catches himself, becomes attuned to the patient, and finds a way to reach her when she feels lost, I can go a long way to healing the patient's own wounds.

As I think about myself as a four-year-old, asleep through much of my father's breakdown, I am impressed by the remarkable ability of the human mind to protect and prevail. We all have our inner demons, our acts of courage and perseverance. Each day that we find a sense of purpose and meaning, we triumph over the monsters that populate our dreams.

Reference

Sherman, E. (2014). Sweet Dreams Are Made of These. (Or: How I Came Out and Came into My Own). In S. Kuchuck (ed.), *Clinical Implications of the Psychoanalyst's Life Experience* (pp. 112–121). New York, NY: Routledge.

Chapter 16

Wounded healer, healing wounder

A personal story

John A. Sloane

When I received the invitation from Sharon Farber to tell my own story as part of a book that would celebrate the wounded healer, a part of me said, "Yes! I'm one of those. Let's tell the world!" Another part of me was not so sure that I felt ready to celebrate or be celebrated, given what I was doing to one patient at the time, and how bad I felt about it. One way or another, we wind up repeatedly wounding and being wounded on the way toward healing our selves and others.

As I near my seventy-fifth birthday, I find myself tired of revisiting places of trauma where I am faced and filled with the anguish of wounds I play a part in causing or uncovering. I am often unable to understand or alleviate the pain, torn by conflicts I cannot resolve, ashamed of my temporary but timeless ignorance and impotence, and saddened by grief that does not go away. Strangely, though, I have learned that by bearing such pain, powerlessness, shame, rage, and despair without taking refuge in premature knowing and doing, healing happens often enough to make it all worthwhile—even worth celebrating! In fact, when asked when I plan to retire, I find myself saying, "I don't know who I'd be if I weren't doing what I do."

The single most traumatic and formative event of my life was the death of my father when I was a boy of ten, under circumstances that left me quite unsure whether I was "doer or done-to." Until then, my childhood was not overly traumatic, as childhoods go, in a white, middle-class, nominally Protestant family in a safe neighborhood in Toronto. World War II was just beginning on the other side of the globe, while burning Hitler in effigy at the end of our street was the only glimpse I got of what gripped the attention of adults far more than I knew. Unbeknownst to me at the time, my father chose to stay home to take care of his family, rather than join the armed forces as several of his friends did—and felt considerable shame as a result. He was a hard worker, though, a responsible chartered accountant who was often away seeing clients until a mysterious illness brought him home and brought out the worst in him in relation to me, his only son.

As a young teenager in Ireland, he had slept with a gun under his pillow to protect his family from the Sinn Fein, while his older brothers fought in World War I. When that war was over and the war between Catholics and Protestants was heating up in Ireland, he took refuge from "the Troubles" in Canada, where he met my mother, an artist, who later let go of her career in order to be there for my older sister and myself. She, too, had suffered great losses—her Methodist mother dying of cancer when she was a young teenager, and her much-loved and admired father sending her and her siblings away to live with distant relatives.

As my father grew sicker with the undiagnosed brain cancer that was consuming him, he was treated with new glasses at first, then with electroshock for depression. In his anguish and anger at what was happening to him, his Irish authority took center stage for me, judging and rejecting me for not being the young man he expected—and for resisting his efforts to teach me a lesson by corporal punishment. "Who do you think you are?" he would dismissively ask if I dared to open my mouth at the dinner table, let alone "talk back"—ironically asking the same question that Sharon is asking now, although in a very different tone. I was not allowed to question or protest the shaming effects of the old rule, "Children are to be seen but not heard."

I certainly felt alone with the guilty fallout from my long-overdue explosion of rage at him while he was standing below me at the bottom of our basement stairs. Whatever set the stage and what exactly I said are long gone in the fog of that brief but shattering all-out war. I had suddenly risen to a position of angry authority over him in a way that extinguished the light in his eyes. That memory became indelibly etched on my body and brain as the "cause" of his death that happened soon afterwards. Fortunately, no one else blamed me, as sometimes happens when a grief-stricken parent takes her anger out on her children. Instead, my mother did her best to cheer us up on a long road trip across the country to visit her widely dispersed brothers and sisters. Our own nuclear family and my world, however, were never the same. During my teens, my mother would wake up screaming in the night—while I was completely powerless to defend her against whatever ghosts were haunting her. I, too, had nightmares of being swept over waterfalls, tidal waves, and nuclear holocaust. In those dreams, I felt both terrified of and responsible for the "end of the world." Catastrophic relational trauma is not only what is done *to* us, but what we do to others we love, and what we witness, ignorant and impotent to prevent or repair it, leaving us with wordless dread.

Fortunately, I was able to dissociate well enough to be good in school and make friends who survived my occasional outbursts of temper, put up with my depression, and included me in their fun. I was able to find solace not only in the pages of *Playboy*, but also in the comforting arms of my mother as I went to sleep at night. She eased my fear of snakes under the bed, arousing other desires that went nowhere, thanks to her—except, much later, into my appreciation of Freud's understanding of the conflicted sexual longings that he termed the "Oedipus complex." Before my father became ill, I had also been comforted at night by his exciting, male-bonding tales of fear and courage, and his mournful but beautiful songs about Ireland—especially "A little bit of Heaven fell from out the sky one day."

Much later, while being interviewed for a residency program at the Menninger Clinic in Topeka, a psychoanalyst proudly declared, "Oh, so you won, eh?" I was dumbfounded. I did not have the words to tell him it did not feel like a victory to me! Although I had no idea where he was coming from, at the time, and was turned cold by his all-knowing authority and utter lack of empathy, I was, by then, sufficiently initiated into the mysteries of mental illness to keep my interest alive—partly by having spent the previous summer at a state hospital in New Hampshire. For reasons I could not explain, I enjoyed listening to seriously disturbed patients, and felt a powerful sense of compassion for the suffering I saw all around me there, even though it all felt so hopeless. It was, in fact, for that reason that I did an externship at the Menninger Clinic the following summer. Despite my encounter with absolute Freudian authority, I was not disappointed—although I was not so sure about one young man who had actually murdered his father! I kept my distance from him, but never forgot him.

When I finished medical school, I considered obstetrics, having so much enjoyed assisting at the miracle of birth, but decided, instead, to cover another doctor's general practice and marry a nurse who, *after* she said "Yes," was horrified to learn that I had my heart set on psychiatry! (Her own experiences in "the snake pit," as a student, had put her off that specialty completely.) Then, we took time off to travel through Europe, visiting the concentration camp at Dachau, among other things. There, we were brought face-to-face with the ultimate, catastrophic relational trauma, trans-generationally transmitted by excessive authority and "superior" force. On our return, I gave her time to get used to the idea of my going over to "the dark side," while I consolidated my identity as a physician in my own general practice. What I enjoyed most was listening to people tell me their troubles and trying to figure out what had made them who they were—often enough helping them feel a bit better.

After two years, I found a psychiatry training program that placed a high value on psychotherapy, even with the most difficult patients; the Institute of Living in Hartford, Connecticut. There, we began to raise our own family and enjoyed being part of a community founded on Eli Todd's principles of "Moral Treatment," committed to understanding and respecting the humanity of all people, whatever their diagnostic category. It was there that I first heard Harry Stack Sullivan's comment that "We are all more simply human than otherwise." It was not easy, though, being immersed in their mind-boggling loss of ego-boundaries, thought-fragmentation, intense feelings and lack of feelings (emotional deadness). So, when I found myself erupting in rage at no one in particular and taking it out on a plaster wall in our apartment, I got into therapy with a psychoanalyst who helped me keep my head above water and understand what it was like to be a patient.

My wife and I would have been happy to stay there, had we not both been afraid of my being drafted and sent to Vietnam. Inner conflict is one thing, armed conflict on the other side of the world, another. So after my residency, we returned to Toronto where I studied psychoanalysis at the Toronto Institute of

Psychoanalysis. There were conflicts between different schools, of course, but also a sense that the various "streams" were all heading in the same direction of healing our broken humanity. I was also fortunate to find a good enough analyst/father and a receptive, responsive supervisor. Both were courageous enough to write about their empathic failures, modeling ways of working and writing that led me into some very dark places—and back again to tell the tale in a paper entitled "Sleep, Death and Re-Birth: A Relational Perspective on Sleep in the Countertransference" (Sloane 2013).

In that paper, I describe a particular way in which I am prone to wounding my patients, one that has its roots in my own woundedness. Although I am not alone in my experience of sleepiness, I came to see it as an enactment that could be turned to therapeutic benefit—if I were able to own and acknowledge its destructiveness. It occurs in moments when I am unable to follow and be with the Other, emotionally. He or she is dying on me, in ways I feel unable to understand, powerless to prevent, and fearful of interrupting what I sense is essential to them. While there are times when I can find words to draw attention to what I experience as a disconnection, usually they have been experiencing me as "with them," and my interruption as disconnecting. If, on the other hand, I fail to intervene, I reach an "event horizon," beyond which I experience annihilation. They then protest my absence from a deep place of betrayal and abandonment. At that moment, the vitality of the relationship resumes and healing can begin, sometimes by working together, and sometimes, sadly, by the patient deciding to get rid of me by leaving!

Unfortunately, the ideal of openness about the less-than-ideal, wounded, or wounding aspects of the analyst led me down the garden path to being judged and rejected as a training analyst by the Institute that had, until then, been my professional home. That was a traumatic enactment for me, one I wrote about in another paper "Reflections on the Failure to Become a Training Analyst" (Sloane 2014b). I came to the conclusion that we *all* err in one direction or another, toward knowing or not-knowing, doing or not-doing; aggressively rooted authority over or receptive-responsive surrender/accommodation to a needed, trusted Other. Both poles can contribute to re-traumatization *and* to healing. Hopefully, we learn from our mistakes, becoming better healers through understanding such enactments well enough to acknowledge our part in them and then to offer/assert something of value to our patients, our colleagues, and our students.

Some of us need all the help we can get to heal ourselves, and I have been helped by many over the years. My patients, who have taken me to my own places of core vulnerability and madness (blurring of boundaries between self and other, reality and fantasy) that forced or enabled this physician to heal himself, are first and foremost among them. There were healing conversations with supervisors and colleagues, especially around the evolving relational literature. But some of us never outgrow our need for someone to talk to about where we are coming from, personally. Spouses, especially if they are not part of the analytic world, tire of such talk. So I found it necessary to write a self-analytic journal of day-to-day events, moods, dreams, and the like, which proved enormously useful in wording what would otherwise remain "unformulated." I knew, as I was writing, that some of it was related to a particular patient. But what I found, much to my surprise, was that what I thought was merely "my own" experience in the morning was echoed by *other* patients that day. Not only was *I* not alone, but I was better able to empathize with and find words for what was emerging in *them*. Not only that, but there were spooky reflections in the world around me in the news, music, poetry, films, and plays that felt like clusters of uncanny coincidence, or synchronicity.

Then, I began to do something I always thought I should do, but never quite felt up to: read the Bible. I did not have the time or attention span to read it systematically, but I could manage bite-sized bits selected by a guide ("Forward, Day by Day"), right after writing in my journal. There, too, I experienced synchronistic responses; relevant metaphorical elaborations or counterpoints to what I was putting into words from the inter-subjective field in which I lived and breathed and "had my being." In that peculiar dialogue, I felt free, as I had in my analysis, to be playfully expressive and creative with my take on what I found in the Bible: rich, warts-and-all human experiences of others who, like me, were trying to make sense of the world around them and of what lay beyond, above, or below it. I had no inclination to "take it literally," nor was I intimidated by the voice of an authority that was "willing" to enter into a kind of "squiggle game" with me! Instead, I was free to think for myself, passionately agree and disagree, and speak up (so to speak) at "our Father's" table! In other words, meaningful connections had the healing effect of "recognizing" my right to be who I am—enabling me to be there for others.

I would be less than honest if I did not acknowledge, here, the archetypal wounded healer, Jesus Christ. I was drawn to him, as I'm sure the reader will understand, because he represented the capacity to survive my all-out destructiveness and still be there in my imagination, at least, loving enough to hear, hold, and heal me. For me, though, that does not mean he is to be idealized beyond question, criticism, or rejection of the absolute authority in some of his recorded words. In my opinion, his words, like all words in the Bible are *human words*. As such, they are fallible and sometimes harmful. It all depends on how they are used, how they are heard, by whom, and under what circumstances. Timing, tone, and context matter! I have written in more detail about that experience in a paper on "The Loneliness of the Analyst and Its Alleviation through Faith in 'O'" (Sloane 2012).

My own longing to heal the world (*tikkun olam* in Hebrew) has taken me further afield. During the Cold War, alarmed by the immanence of "mutually assured destruction," I had been involved with the International Physicians for the Prevention of Nuclear War—until that madness came to an end. Since then, of course, the threat to global security has undergone even more widespread paranoid regression; an alarming spread of malignancy within and without, centered in and revolving around the Middle East. It has drawn on disaffected youth from many lands, determined to destroy the evil they see in our global village, becoming evil themselves. So, when Canada refused to recognize the legitimacy of Palestinian aspirations to statehood in the fall of 2012, I felt ashamed, even though I was also glad that we were standing by Israel, whose Jewish inhabitants we had failed during World War II. I wrote a paper, "In the Light of Eternity: A Personal Point of View on War in the Middle East" (Sloane 2014a), which I presented at the I.A.R.P.P. conference in Chile where it was well received and respectfully discussed. Since then, however, it has evoked passionate protest and interpretation as dangerously misguided and "blaming" of Israel. Trying to put what we see and sense into words in our offices is risky enough, but doing so in public is another matter. But I agree with Freud who openly expressed the idea in a letter to Einstein in 1932 that the only antidote he could imagine to the destructiveness of war was Eros, i.e. "ties of sentiment" between men. Anything that brings out "significant resemblances" between them, he suggested, allows them to identify with one another, thereby calling into play "a feeling of community . . . whereon is founded, in large measure, the whole edifice of human society" (Einstein, Freud, & Gilbert 1939).

What, then, do wounded healers have to contribute to that process of mutual recognition and identification with one another as vulnerable, fallible human beings who impinge—and are impinged upon—in ways that wound the "Other"? How can we learn to accept responsibility for the part we play in the repetition of trauma, and the embodiment of bad objects, so that the buck can stop here?

Although it is sometimes necessary to wound and be wounded, kill and be killed, we cannot destroy the Destroyer without destroying our selves. We are not only wounded healers, but healing wounders. Both are *parts* of us. We *can* cease our disavowal of those dissociated parts of ourselves, and make spaces in which to stand our ground—while relationships, thank God, sometimes heal themselves.

That is definitely something to celebrate! It is important, I think, to recognize that the prototype for all that is not only Christ, the archetypal male wounded healer, but ordinary good-enough mothers who have always been able to recognize and accept when they are *not* good enough in the eyes of their child—and willing to bear being rejected and wounded in the service of those they love. Sooner or later, they must also stand up for themselves as persons in their own right, and are doing so, increasingly, around the world. The time has come to recognize, respect, support, and celebrate that wherever we find it. Where—and who—would we be without it?

References

Einstein, A., Freud, S., & Gilbert, S. (1989). *Why War? An Exchange of Letters between Albert Einstein and Sigmund Freud.* (p.46). Ottawa, Canada: Shalom Press International.
Sloane, J. A. (2012). The Loneliness of the Analyst and Its Alleviation through Faith in "O." In: B. Willock, L. C. Bohm, and R. C. Curtis (eds.), *Loneliness and Longing: Conscious and Unconscious Aspects* (pp. 197–209). New York: Routledge.

Sloane, J. A. (2013). Sleep, Death and Rebirth: A Relational Perspective on Sleep in the Countertransference. *Contemporary Psychoanalysis*, *49* (4): 509–535.

Sloane, J. A. (2014a). "In the Light of Eternity: A Personal Point of View on War in the Middle East." Paper presented at the 2013 I.A.R.P.P. conference, Santiago, Chile. New York: I.A.R.P.P.

Sloane, J. A. (2014b). Reflections on the Failure to Become a Training Analyst. In: B. Willock, L. C. Bohm, and R. C. Curtis (eds.), *Understanding and Coping with Failure: Psychoanalytic Perspectives*. New York: Routledge.

Chapter 17

Wounded healer/wounded earth

The wound is in me/I am in the wound

Anthony Rankin Wilson

> The environmental crisis is an outward manifestation of a crisis of mind and
> spirit. There could be no greater misconception of its meaning than to believe
> it is concerned only with endangered wildlife . . . and pollution. These are part
> of it, but more importantly, the crisis is concerned with the kind of creatures we
> are and what we must become in order to survive.
>
> (Caldwell 2004)

Our human woundedness has spilled over extravagantly into the body of Earth.
In these times of ocean and climate change, of the sixth major extinction event,
and of the accumulating scientific and on-the-ground evidence of human-caused
ecocide, I am preoccupied by the intersection of human woundedness and the
woundedness of our planet's web of life. We who are psychotherapists and analysts will be increasingly called upon to relate to our patient's anxieties about
environmental destruction and loss of ways of life, and to our own.

What wounds of "mind and spirit" are made visible through our assaults upon
ecosystems? In 1972, analyst Harold Searles wrote that "Mankind is collectively
reacting to the real and urgent danger from environmental pollution much as does
the psychotically depressed patient bent upon suicide by self-neglect" (Searles
1972, p. 234). What is the relationship between my story of a family ghost and his
suicide and my haunted sensitivity to the environmental crisis?

Vincent's story

My paternal grandfather is a phantom. I know little more than what was told,
years ago now, by his youngest brother, my great-uncle Vincent. These are his
written words:

> In 1927, Rankin was found dead in bed one morning, having committed
> suicide. And alongside him there was a note which read, "Do not touch this
> cup, poison." . . . the coroner brought in a verdict of suicide . . . And this
> was printed in the newspapers of the day. Sometime later I remember seeing

Teresa, his wife, and two of her children, Jack, and his younger sister Teresa, sail from Liverpool on the *Empress of Canada.*

Jack's story

Jack was my father. As far as I know, he never spoke of his father's suicide to anyone, including my mother, until Vincent wrote a family history and opened Pandora's box in my mid-twenties. I didn't hear him speak of Rankin after Vincent's revelation. Jack was nineteen when, in Vincent's words, the "terrible blow" happened, and he emigrated to Canada with his mother and sister shortly after. In subsequent years my father rebuffed, with utter silence and passive withdrawal, any attempts I made to get to know Rankin through him, and to salvage something of an ancestral connection to my grandfather and his tragic end. Frustrated and angry, I didn't speak to my father for several years. I was thirty-six when Jack died at seventy-eight years of age. On good speaking terms before his death, we were, however, never able to break the secret's spell. The unsayable became darkly enshrined.

My story

> The wound . . . brutally brings awareness to the fact of limitation.
>
> (Hillman 1989, p. 116)

No, we never broke the spell. But the invisible narrative limited and saturated everything. The silence, deafening. Through the subsequent years of aged hindsight, following Vincent's shattering words, I see more how the secret powerfully permeated the emotional atmosphere of my home and family. The thin air of Jack's aloofness was most pronounced with his sons. His cool physical restraint placed a chill upon any body contact between father and son. Shame seemed to draw a shadow across his gaze. Beyond a glance I have no visual memory of him looking into my eyes, nor me his.

It seems bizarre, and somehow a cry from the grave, that my middle name is Rankin. As was my father's. Until my mid-twenties I had no idea where this unusual moniker had come from. I don't remember asking. Such was the force of this sequestered and repressive trauma zone. I was inevitably struck with inexplicable shame when, in primary school roll call, I had to stand and declare that I was "Anthony Rankin Wilson." I remember walking along 123rd Street, grade two lunch time, and a classmate taunting me with the strangeness of my middle name. I didn't speak about these experiences. I have been haunted ever since by Vincent's opening of Pandora's box, by this "enduring presence of an absence," in the clinically poetic words of Samuel Gerson (2009, p. 1345).

Like Hephaestus, the archetype of the wounded craftsman or healer who was credited with creating Pandora, I have tried to make meaning out of this void. I've written songs and recorded them so that I could listen back to a voice that too often sounds like someone other to myself (Gerson 2009).

Don't cast your shadow from the grave.
It's not what namesakes are for,
A target for the light you never gave,
I've been living in your shadow for so long.
I've been singing what you left unsung.

(Anthony Rankin Wilson, unpublished)

I have come to understand that we who are wounded healers must repeatedly circumnavigate our wounds, penetrate the scars of unfeeling, and find redemptive meaning in order to serve those who come to us for help with theirs. Our therapeutic conversations then can unfold through an atmosphere of shared embodied woundedness, sometimes in unusual ways.

A patient speaks of crushing an endangered species of snake in a terrified rage, much like the childhood experience of his father's stunting emotional abuse. I was, at first, most identified with the snake. I internally cringed and was enraged at the mindless violence. This reptile silenced forever. Its kin, one member closer to being extinguished. My grandfather's self-silencing suicide. My father's cruel, crushing silences. My patient knew well of my environmental sensibilities and was surprised that I did not crush him with judgment. It was through this embodied identification with the snake that I could first connect more deeply with his terrifying experiences of his father's rage. My patient then went on to feel the memories of several unremembered emotionally abusive encounters with his volatile father.

Such deepening identifications, as with the bludgeoned Massassauga Rattler, arouse my desire to also serve the wounded other-than-human. Better known as "Nature," a flawed concept whose most common meaning, that Nature is separate and "out there" and we are skin-encapsulated and "in here," has come to perpetuate dissociation and denial of our psychological, emotional, biological, and spiritual interdependence and kinship with the Others of Earth. Air. Robin and Dragonfly. Water. Plankton and Blue Whale. Soil. Earthworm and Oak.

The wound

My father was lost in his shame. I became lost in his. Traumatized, my father was frozen in time, and I fell under the muting, timeless spell of the unspeakable. I don't remember my father's touch. I can't imagine it now. He was committed to the secret, and once exposed, to its disavowal. The tragedy was real and at the same time unreal by virtue of unrecognition. This madness created a liminal divide where he was neither here nor there. There was no tender hand on my back, nor mutual father and adolescent chest-thumping bellows of challenge that serves to build masculine muscle. He hid behind my mother and sacrificed me to her needs for him.

I grew familiar with the feminine, too familiar, with little magnetic masculine to draw me into the mysterious phallic world of men who can penetrate the world with heart. With courage. The inexplicable shame handicapped the aggression I required to gather my gifts and make my unapologetic mark. I became too relational and nice. This masked a dissociated rage and cruelty. A low-grade depression kept the beasts mostly under control. Ancestral continuity had been truncated and fed my taste for unbelonging. This is a wound of interminable longing. A phantom limb. Rankin. And myself. Adrift in a universe of absented generational lineage. The wound says, "If there's no past, then how can there truly be a present, or a future?"

The wounded healer

> [T]he parent is the wound can metaphorically mean that our wounds can also parent us. Our wounds can become the fathers and mothers of our destinies.
>
> (Bolen 1990, p. 224)

A function of the wound is to enable embodiment, to open the emotional body to feeling, and disable inflated images of a self that is whole and has it all together. This is particularly important for the analyst and psychotherapist. It became vital to me. I emerged from my family of origin armed with pride to defend against the shame, and an image of myself as special. This inflation also protected me from its opposite—the feeling that I was nothing to my father except a bother and a threat— to his Oedipal status and to his secret. I imagine that I was also a threat to his fragile and defended self that teetered over the abyss of exposure and mortification.

After forty-one years of practice, having been kept in the dark by my father's traumatized and traumatizing refusal, I more deeply understand my original draw to the profession and the plethora of secrets it provides. I repeatedly discover my emotional arousal and attraction to the scent of the unspoken. I resonate with analyst Susie Orbach's (2012, p. 21) reflections: "It took me a long time not to be interested in the secret(s) per se . . . the thirst has gone. My interest has turned to curiosity: Why and in what way is something held to be a secret?" (Ohrbach 2001, p. 21).

And why and in what way has the slowly unfolding environmental crisis been held as a secret by our governments, and by my profession? From the beginnings of my curiosity and concern about such symptoms of the crisis as climate change and species loss, I have wondered about the nature of this compelling personal and clinical preoccupation.

What is its relationship to secrets and the unspoken? What connection exists between my bewilderment at political and professional silences and my archaic structures that cry out into a parental vacuum, "Something is wrong, but what is it?" In largely ignoring the environmental crisis, I wonder about how evolving clinical models continue to make the crisis, as analyst Donna Orange (2010, p. 5) writes, "invisible . . . or [relegated] to the background because it [does] not fit the theory." Does this trigger an earlier outrage at being kept in the dark and feeling invisible to my father?

What of my states of apocalyptic anxiety and doom? Does this forward-falling shadow of inevitable destruction and tragic loss arise from the vicarious trauma of my father's shame infused secret? Are these dark moods of mine more representative of a pathological accommodation that expects, in analyst Bernard Brandchaft's (Brandschaft et al. 2010, p. 152) words, a "scenario of catastrophic predestination"? Or might these states also be conjured by my wounded sensitivities to the experience and perception of a culture—and profession's—denial or disavowal of lost species, of lost connections to familiar and loved habitats, of impending losses of ways of life? And further, loss of the future's imagined certainties?

Jack failed to provide a witnessing function for me that would have substantiated my claim to the benefits of continuity, to a grandfather enfleshed through story. I have come to believe that this partially underlies a passionate desire to provide that for others, and in these times, for the other-than-human. For the past three years, unbidden and certainly odd to myself, I have been compelled to keep my own ongoing list of threatened and endangered species, 183 and counting. The eastern sand darter. The cobblestone tiger beetle. The piping plover. The bowhead whale. The pacific pond turtle. The woodland caribou. The slender popcornflower. I often wonder why I took this up and why I bother. Is the impetus, in part, a witnessing rising from the soil of Rankin's hidden grave? "I will say your name. I won't let you disappear into silence, unacknowledged."

Silence

It is questions such as these that I ask in this second decade of the twenty-first century. In my sixty-fifth year I am no longer able to separate the personal and the environmental. The wound is in me. And I am in the wound. Rankin, my grandfather, tragically silenced himself. My father, Jack, used silence to hide his shame. I experienced the silence of my grandfather and father as an incomprehensible void. I have tried to undo this silence through providing others with a safe place to break the intimidations and vulnerabilities of secrets.

What do my wounds mean, and yours, to collapsing ecosystems and species disappearing without felt human grief? Perhaps, through experiencing and relating to our human woundedness, we are called upon in these unprecedented times to make the other-than-human our witness, as earlier peoples have done, and to serve as a witness for the other-than-human as well. Perhaps, then, our wounds may indeed prove to be the "fathers and mothers of our destinies," personal and planetary.

Bibliography

Bolen, J. S. (1990). *Gods in Everyman*. New York: Harper & Row.
Brandchaft, B., Doctors, S., & Sorter, D. (2010). *Toward an Emancipatory Psychoanalysis: Brandchaft's Intersubjective Vision*. New York: Routledge.

Caldwell, L. K., quoted in D. D. N. Winter & S. M. Koger (2004). *The Psychology of Environmental Problems* (p. 1). Mahwah, NJ: Lawrence Erlbaum Associates.

Gerson, S. (2009) When The Third Is Dead: Memory, Mourning, and Witnessing in the Aftermath of the Holocaust. *International Journal of Psychoanalysis, 90*, 1341–1357.

Hillman, J. (ed.) (1989). *Puer Papers*. Dallas, TX: Spring Publications.

Orange, D. M. (2010). *Thinking for Clinicians: Philosophical Resources for Contemporary Psychoanalysis and the Humanistic Psychotherapies*. New York: Routledge.

Orbach, S. (2012). I Wanted the Stuff of Secrets to Be in the Light. In: S. Kuchuck (ed.) (2014), *Clinical Implications of the Psychoanalyst's Life Experience: When the Personal Becomes Professional* (pp. 17–25). New York: Routledge.

Searles, H. F. (1972). Unconscious Processes in Relation to the Environmental Crisis. *Psychoanalytic Review, 59* (3): 361.

Searles, H. F. (1979). *Countertransference and Related Subjects: Selected Papers*. New York: International Universities Press.

Epilogue

Now that this book is getting closer to publication, I am anticipating what it will be like when people whom I know and people I do not know, as well as some current and former patients, read my very personal self-disclosures. I feel vulnerable but also excited. Will they join in celebrating the wounded healer psychotherapist? Writing this material for publication requires a huge leap of faith. The psychotherapists who contributed chapters have taken that leap too. Their courage in doing so has helped me so much. I know I am not alone.

Just about a month after submitting the manuscript, I was with a long-term patient who knows that I write a lot. I've gotten her to write herself about her difficult times and her thoughts and feelings about them (Farber 2005). In the process she discovered that sometimes words that could not come out of her mouth could more readily glide from her pen. She had also discovered how unleashing her creativity made her feel much better (Farber 2013). I told her that when in the midst of writing, I often awaken with ideas and immediately go to sit at my computer and write, before washing, dressing, and having breakfast. When I do not awaken in a writing passion, I will get ready for the day and go out for a walk and have the pleasure of walking in a beautiful natural setting, with views of the Hudson River or the forest, enjoying the sunshine. When I do not do that and sit too long at the computer, depriving myself of the sunlight we all need to feel good, I feel the effect later. My patient asked what I was writing about and I told her that this book is about psychotherapists as wounded healers. I ended up telling her that I felt a little uneasy, anticipating the responses of readers.

The chapters written by psychotherapists may not be memoirs but they are memoir-ish. As Steven Kuchuck (2009) said, psychotherapists and psychoanalysts are finding themselves in exciting but often frightening and strange new territory. Serendipitously, it was two days later that I came across Mary Karr's *The Art of Memoir* (2015) in the library and borrowed it. I had read her powerful memoirs *The Liars' Club* (1995), *Cherry* (2001), and *Lit: A Memoir* (2009), in which she wrote about her apocalyptic childhood in the east Texas oil town, a town her hard-drinking father called "a town too ugly not to love." She had a drinking mother with several marriages and psychiatric hospitalizations behind her, whose secrets threatened to destroy them all. Her mother studied art and disappeared from time to time, and encouraged Mary to be sexually active. She was, and took LSD in her adolescence in the 1970s, and played with ideas. Mary longed for a solid family and thought she finally had one when she married a handsome, wealthy, Shakespeare-quoting poet and had a son they adore. But she could not escape her past, and drank herself deeper into depression and a suicide attempt, ending up in a psychiatric hospital she called "The Mental Marriott." With the help of Alcoholics Anonymous and several psychotherapists, she recovered from alcoholism and mental illness.

Having read her memoirs, I knew I wanted to read what she had written about the process of writing such a memoir. Would she write about the pain, the blood, sweat, and tears, and the sense of freedom I am feeling? Yes, she did.

> In some ways, writing a memoir is knocking yourself out with your own fist, if it's done right. Sure, there's the pleasure of doing work guaranteed to engage you emotionally—who's indifferent to their own history? The form always has profound psychological consequences on its author. I can't not. What project can match it for that? . . . But nobody I know who's written a great one described it as anything less than a major shit-eating contest. Any time you try to collapse the distance between your delusions about the past and what really happened, there's suffering involved . . . No matter how self-aware you are, memoir wrenches at your insides precisely because it makes you battle with your very self—your neat analyses and tidy excuses . . . Your small pieties and impenetrable, mostly unconscious poses invariably trip you up . . . In terms of cathartic effect, memoir is like therapy, the difference being that in therapy, *you* pay *them*.
>
> (Karr 2015, p. xx)

Karr speaks of the personal liberation that comes from the examined life:

> Liberation how? you might say. Why isn't it just as good to make up a version of events you can live with and stick to that? If your goal is to polish up a fake person you can sell to a public you perceive as dumb, the unexamined life will do perfectly well, thank you.
>
> But whether you're a memoirist or not, there's a psychic cost for lopping yourself from the past: it may continue to tug on you without your being aware of it. And lying about it can—for all but the most hardened sociopath—carve a lonely gap between your disguise and who you really are. The practiced liar also projects her own manipulative, double-dealing facade onto everyone she meets, which makes moving through the world a wary, anxious enterprise. It's hard enough to see what's going on without forcing yourself to look through the wool you've pulled over your own eyes.
>
> To watch someone scrutinize a painful history in depth . . . is to witness not inconsiderable pain. You have to lance a boil and suffer its stench as infection drains off. Yet all the scrupulous self-examinations over time I've

been witness to—whether on the page or off—always ended with acceptance and relief. For the more haunted among us, only looking back at the past can permit it finally to become past.

(op. cit., p. 12)

Reading *The Art of Memoir* brought back the memory of being terrified that a colleague who worked on Mount Sinai's locked psychiatric ward would make the connection that a patient named Joseph Klayman was the father of Sharon Klayman Farber. She also said that:

We each nurture a private terror that some core aspect(s) of either our selves or our story must be hidden or disowned. With every manuscript I've ever edited . . . the traits an author often fights hardest to hide may serve as undeniable facets of both self and story. You bumble onto scenes that blow up fond notions of the past, or whole shifts in attitude practically rewrite you where you stand.

(op. cit., p. 154)

In writing about our journeys from woundedness to healing, Karr wrote:

Just picking up a pen makes you part of a tradition of writers that dates thousands of years back . . . I still feel awe for us—yes, for the masters who wrought lasting beauty from their hard lives, but for the rest of us too, for the great courage all of us show in trying to wring some truth from the godawful mess of a single life. To bring oneself to others makes the whole planet less lonely.

(op. cit., p. 218)

I think Mary Karr would join us in celebrating the wounded healer psychotherapist.

References

Farber, S. (2005). Free Association Reconsidered: The Talking Cure, the Writing Cure. *Journal of the American Academy of Psychoanalysis and Dynamic Psychiatry*, *33* (2): 249–273.

Farber, S. (2013). *Hungry for Ecstasy: Trauma, the Brain, and the Influence of the Sixties*. Lanham, MD: Jason Aronson/Rowman & Littlefield.

Karr, M. (1995). *The Liars' Club: A Memoir*. New York: Penguin.

Karr, M. (2001). *Cherry*. New York: Penguin.

Karr, M. (2009). *Lit: A Memoir*. New York: Harper.

Kuchuck, S. (2009). Do Ask, Do Tell? Narcissistic Need as a Determinant of Analyst Self-Disclosure. *Psychoanalytic Review*, *96*: 1007–1024.

Index

 Taylor & Francis eBooks

Helping you to choose the right eBooks for your Library

Add Routledge titles to your library's digital collection today. Taylor and Francis ebooks contains over 50,000 titles in the Humanities, Social Sciences, Behavioural Sciences, Built Environment and Law.

Choose from a range of subject packages or create your own!

Benefits for you

>> Free MARC records
>> COUNTER-compliant usage statistics
>> Flexible purchase and pricing options
>> All titles DRM-free.

Benefits for your user

>> Off-site, anytime access via Athens or referring URL
>> Print or copy pages or chapters
>> Full content search
>> Bookmark, highlight and annotate text
>> Access to thousands of pages of quality research at the click of a button.

 Free Trials Available
We offer free trials to qualifying academic, corporate and government customers.

eCollections – Choose from over 30 subject eCollections, including:

Archaeology	Language Learning
Architecture	Law
Asian Studies	Literature
Business & Management	Media & Communication
Classical Studies	Middle East Studies
Construction	Music
Creative & Media Arts	Philosophy
Criminology & Criminal Justice	Planning
Economics	Politics
Education	Psychology & Mental Health
Energy	Religion
Engineering	Security
English Language & Linguistics	Social Work
Environment & Sustainability	Sociology
Geography	Sport
Health Studies	Theatre & Performance
History	Tourism, Hospitality & Events

For more information, pricing enquiries or to order a free trial, please contact your local sales team:
www.tandfebooks.com/page/sales

 Routledge
Taylor & Francis Group
The home of
Routledge books

www.tandfebooks.com

Made in the USA
Coppell, TX
01 December 2020